The Author

Born in Lancashire in 1947, ANTHONY HOLDEN has enjoyed a distinguished career in journalism as an award-winning *Saturday Times* columnist, Chief American Correspondent of the *Observer*, Assistant Editor of *The Times* and a founder-editor of Eddy Shah's *Today*. Now he devotes his time to writing and broadcasting. Author of eleven books, including the definitive best-seller *Charles, Prince of Wales*, and a widely praised collection of his journalism, *Of Presidents, Prime Ministers and Princes*, he has also published a number of translations from Ancient Greek and co-translated several operas, including *Don Giovanni* and *The Barber of Seville* for Jonathan Miller at English National Opera. Anthony Holden's most recent book, a major biography of Laurence Olivier, has recently been hailed as "definitive" *(The Times)*.

ANTHONY HOLDEN

CHARLES

A Biography

An M&S Paperback from
McClelland & Stewart Inc.
The Canadian Publishers

An M&S Paperback from McClelland & Stewart Inc.

First printing November 1989

Copyright © 1988 Anthony Holden Limited

First published in Great Britain by George Weidenfeld & Nicolson
Limited, 91 Clapham High Street, London SW47TA

Published by Weidenfeld & Nicolson, New York
A Division of Wheatland Corporation
841 Broadway
New York, New York 10003-4793

Canadian Cataloguing in Publication Data

Holden, Anthony, 1947–
Charles

(M&S paperback)
Bibliography: p.
Includes index.
ISBN 0-7710-4194-2

1. Charles, Prince of Wales, 1948 –   – Biography.
2. Great Britain – Princes and princesses –
Biography. I. Title.

DA591.A33H65 1989   941.085′092′4   C89-094040-1

Cover design by Andrew Smith
Cover photo by Tim Graham/Sygma

Typesetting by Trigraph Inc.
Printed and bound in Canada

McClelland & Stewart Inc.
The Canadian Publishers
481 University Avenue
Toronto, Ontario
M5G 2E9

This one's for you,
coach

Contents

"All the world and the glory of it, whatever is most attractive, whatever is most seductive, has always been offered to the Prince of Wales of the day, and always will be. It is not rational to expect the best virtue where temptation is applied in the most trying form at the frailest time of human life."

Walter Bagehot,
The English Constitution

Foreword

I T IS now nearly a decade since the publication of my biography *Charles, Prince of Wales*, by any standards a lengthy tome about a thirty-year-old man. Although much of it has long been woefully out of date, I am naturally pleased to find the book still in wide use as a work of reference (not least by other writers on the subject), and gratified to see it to this day beside certain desks in Buckingham Palace itself.

Before the book was even published I had fled the country, to take up a post in the United States, in the forlorn hope of avoiding becoming typecast as a royal specialist. When another job brought me back to England, just as the Prince announced his engagement, I was still waging the same struggle – though it was now more uphill than ever. My subject remained a source of such universal fascination, and the demand for my opinions on him so apparently insatiable, that I soon found myself returning ineluctably to the fray. Another book appeared to mark his wedding in 1981, and many an article and broadcast since.

So I have kept in close touch with the royal progress all these years. Though I meanwhile have managed to write on other subjects, it was indeed a rash hostage I granted to fortune in the 1981 preface, with an optimistic promise to disappear from the shadow of the Prince and Princess of Wales "forthwith, forever." As this book loomed, my colleagues in the royal retinue around Australia, the United States and the United Kingdom these last twelve months have not been slow, in their inimitable way, to remind me of it.

But the past decade has seen Prince Charles's personal landscape alter so much that some sort of update, even if only another interim report, had long become overdue. When I was first asked to produce a new book to mark the Prince's fortieth birthday in November 1988, the natural course seemed to be merely to amplify my earlier volume, much of which stands in no need of revision. The deeper I re-delved, however, the clearer it became that a wholly new approach was needed.

Prince Charles's marriage to the former Lady Diana Spencer, and the arrival of their first two children, have radically altered not only his entrenched bachelor habits, but his entire outlook on life. While the Prince's basic character has not of course much changed, the ways in which it finds expression – in both his private and public life – certainly have. In the last five years or so, moreover, the Prince of Wales has at last managed, with imagination and courage, to carve out for himself the role in public life which the British constitution so uncomfortably fails to define for him. After a long, rather tortuous voyage of self-discovery, he has launched himself upon a bold and complex personal crusade which merits detailed examination.

In the late twentieth century the British constitutional monarchy is less of an anachronism than it sometimes seems. Though no longer central to the political process, it performs a variety of symbolic, spiritual and religious roles in the life of the nation which far outweigh its commercial value as a mere tourist attraction. Though some of its younger members appear slow to understand this, and content to be cast as the rising stars of an over-crowded soap opera, the Prince of Wales's sense of history has combined with his natural *gravitas* to help him emerge as a substantial public figure. No one would have been too surprised, on the evidence of his genes, if he had turned out to be the supreme example of Monty Python's famous Upper Class Twits of the Year; in fact, as self-conscious custodian of a sacred trust, he has devoted himself and his time to his own perception of the public good far more than might have been expected.

Towards the end of this book, I argue that Charles is redefining the office of Prince of Wales. Even more remarkably, perhaps, despite a series of tactical errors, he is also giving the monarchy a contemporary relevance of which it had grown sorely in need. With his interest in architecture and conservation, employment and the inner cities, race relations and other urgent social concerns of the day, he is single-handedly lending the Crown a respectability among the thinking classes which it had lacked for several generations. To a large extent this is undermined by the popular press's continuing infatuation with his wife, and indeed by his wife's own infatuation with herself via the popular press. It does not help the Prince's pursuit of his goals, let alone his self-esteem, when one wilful flutter of his Princess's eyebrow can drown out a speech which has been months in the making. It is little wonder, therefore, that he now chooses to make most such excursions without her – though this in turn can mean that few journalists, alas, are on hand to carry his message to the world. Most of them will be elsewhere, reporting on Diana's latest hairstyle. One of my aims in this book has been to help to redress that balance.

On being told that I had been commissioned to write a new, up-to-date biography of him to mark his fortieth birthday, the Prince protested poignantly: "But I haven't achieved anything since the first one!" Quite apart from the fact that he has married and bred two children, thus ensuring the succession, the full irony of his alarming sense of failure has increasingly come home to me as I have ventured into many unwonted new areas of research. This time around it has not been enough to know something about the royal family and the British constitution. I have had to mug up on housing and agri-

cultural reform, "alternative" methods of growing vegetables and treating cancer, not to mention the inner cities
and modern architecture, while holding my own in conversation with urban planners, politicians of all hues, Jungian philosophers and sundry Presidents of the Royal
Institute of British Architects.

The present volume, therefore, draws on the previous
one only in the chapters dealing with the Prince's childhood and education (and Appendix B, detailing his
descent). Readers seeking a more comprehensive, narra-
tive account of his life up to thirty, and thence to his
wedding in 1981, are respectfully referred to my earlier
books. They also contain much more comparative detail
about the lives of previous Princes of Wales, and those of
the Prince's parents and grandparents.

The character sketch I drew of the Prince ten years ago
seems to me to have weathered the test of time fairly well.
The impression left by the book on most of its readers was
that they had met – most of them for the first time – a
figure both lonely and confused, by turns bored and frustrated, always conscientious and well-meaning, above all
desperate to make the most of his very difficult birthright.
It is a portrait which has since become familiar, perhaps
too much so. At the time a part of him resented it, protesting everywhere he went that he was *not* bored and lonely
all the time. "I'm *not*, am I?" Charles would say to his
then press secretary, John Dauth, or his private secretary,
Edward Adeane. "What has Holden saddled me with?"

Nor, I should hastily add, did the Prince to any extent
endorse the opinions and judgements I offered in that
book – or, as has often been suggested, approve its contents before publication. At my request he read the first
draft and came up with many factual corrections and
additions, which I was only too happy to implement. As a
result of this – and a speech he gave to the assembled
editors, proprietors and award-winners of Fleet Street, in
which he was kind enough to single me out for some light-

hearted approval – the myth grew that it was in some way an "official" biography. It was not, and nor is the present book. There will be no such volume until after his and no doubt my death, when the future King's handwritten annotations to my rather scruffy manuscript will be available to his official biographer in the Royal Archives at Windsor.

During my two years of research, interviews and travels at his side, however, the Prince did tell me at the time how pleased he was, and indeed relieved, that someone was at last explaining to an astonished world that the life of the Prince of Wales was not all wine and roses. It made a pleasant change, he said, to be chronicled for the first time by someone much his own age, with a similar education, from a sympathetically middle-class background. In many ways we were very different thirty-year-olds. Where he played polo, I played poker. I was married, with children; he, famously, was not. But a rapport of sorts was established and maintained on subsequent, more occasional travels all over the world – despite a certain, understandable resentment on the Prince's part that I seemed to be credited with knowing more about him than he did. His sense of humour, however, would usually pre-empt any embarrassment. "When were you last in Brazil?" he was asked at a reception in that country. "I'm not sure," he replied, gesturing over his shoulder in my direction. "Ask him. He'll know."

It was also on that ten-day swing through South America that another conversation took place which has always lingered very powerfully in my mind as a graphic example of the Prince's plight, then as now. At a formal reception in Brasilia for the British community, crammed with diplomatic high society, and graced by the then President of Brazil himself, Prince Charles offended protocol by approaching me with a question. In a wary whisper he asked: "Do you know anything about human rights in this country? No one will tell me a thing."

Like any inquisitive first-time visitor to a distant land, I had taken the trouble before leaving England to inform myself about the current political situation in Brazil. A visit to my friend David Simpson, then British director of Amnesty International, had brought me right up to date with the very subject on the Prince's mind. As concisely and discreetly as I could, bearing in mind that the President was standing not far away, I filled him in on the not altogether pleasant details. The Prince was sufficiently interested to ask for more, although his staff were pressing him to return to his duties with other, more significant guests. When he finally had to break away, still reluctant to do so, it was strikingly clear how much he would have preferred more of my little amateur briefing to yet another round of polite (and now sanitized) small-talk.

It was a revealing moment. Rarely had I had such a stark glimpse into the gilded cage the Prince of Wales must inhabit. On further inquiry among British diplomats present, I discovered that Foreign Office representatives abroad regard royal visits as something of a chore, more about the protocol of place settings and which-medals-to-wear-when than the political red meat of visits by, say, Cabinet ministers. As the Prince was due to give a press conference the next day in a bid to promote British exports to Brazil, Her Britannic Majesty's employees were in fact deliberately withholding the briefing papers on human rights in case he made some sort of gaffe. To a man of shrewd political instincts, even at that comparatively young age – intimately familiar, moreover, with the small print of British Cabinet papers – it seemed to me that the FO attitude to the Prince was both demeaning and insulting.

But his then staff, it appeared, were no more prepared to help him. Here was a busy professional man, with a job more complex than most, who was surrounded by believers in the status quo – yes-men, in fact, rarely prepared to challenge him, or willingly to escort him towards deep political waters. It was partly his own fault, as he had himself chosen and appointed them. But the young Prince Charles, I surmised, uncertain of himself and his purpose in life, could have done with more forceful men around him. I said as much in the subsequent book, even having the temerity to suggest that Edward Adeane's appointment as private secretary might prove too cautious, that the advice he would offer the Prince might be too conservative. Adeane later told me he thought he had "got off lightly"; but when he subsequently left the Prince's service, for reasons examined in these pages, I suspected that I had been proved right.

The same point struck me even more forcibly three years later, shortly before the Prince's marriage in 1981, when I was one of the guests at a small private lunch for him in the British Embassy in Washington. We had both just returned from Australia, where the vexed topic of his becoming Governor-General had again surfaced. At the end of this, my first visit to Australia, I had written a long and impassioned article in the *Observer* arguing why such an appointment – enjoyable though it might be for HRH himself, who much desired it – was illogical and wrong for Australia, a young, forward-looking nation of immigrants which needed to cut itself loose from the apron-strings of the revered "mother-country." Sydney, for instance, had become the third largest Greek city in the world, after Athens and New York; it would be as logical for King Constantine to become Governor-General. Charles was intrigued; we argued long and hard, and in the end he accepted the various points I was making – that, for instance, the kind of protest demonstration which I had seen greet him the previous week at Monash University, Melbourne, would follow him wherever he went as a patrician, pommy Governor-General, thus risking permanent damage both to traditional Anglo-Australian ties and perhaps to the monarchy itself. Again, he had not to my knowledge been presented with any such arguments by his own staff or political advisers, who worried only about the party political risks involved.

It is encounters such as these which have prolonged my sympathetic interest in the Prince, and informed my writing about him, for a decade. For ten years I have abided by the royal rules and kept them to myself. I choose to make some elderly anecdotes public now because I believe that the passage of time has turned them into items of passing historical interest, rather than topical indiscretions. All but the Washington conversation were present in spirit, if not in substance, in my earlier biography, for the purposes of which I was granted certain other privileges. Apart from reading the manuscript and giving me his comments, the Prince gave certain of his friends and acquaintances, who would not otherwise have done so, permission to talk to me; I was given access to certain files within Buckingham Palace; and I was accorded an insider's seat on various royal excursions – notably the terrifying experience of landing on black ice in a tiny twin-engined deHavilland Otter, with the Prince of Wales in macho mood at the controls.

There was no formal interview for that book, nor has there been for this. While thanking me recently for my "good intentions," Prince Charles decided this time around to let his public utterances speak for themselves, leaving other members of his circle to elaborate. He has been let down so badly by so many journalists and writers over the years that this is an understandable position for him to take. His participation in any aspect of this book, moreover, would be wrongly taken to imply his endorsement of *all* its contents, as seems to have happened the last time. For my part, I am glad of the consequent freedom to be objective. I suspect, however, that he has now retreated so far into his shell that his own silence is responsible for many of the tabloid misunderstandings which so irritate him.

There is an urgent case for reforming the entire public

relations system which liaises between the monarchy and its people. This is not the place to rehearse the arguments in detail; suffice it to say that I believe more openness would benefit both "sides" enormously. If it is the Prince's proclaimed mission to rid Britain of "the cat's cradle of red tape in which this country chokes from end to end," he might do well to start with Buckingham Palace. As long as reporters have to crawl through the undergrowth of the royal residences, literally as well as metaphorically, snuffling for stories like pigs for truffles, the tidal wave of invention will continue. Or, on a higher plane: were the Prince, for instance, to meet political editors on lobby terms to explain the background to his major speeches – as is normal practice for senior politicians – his public work would be better understood; and he would, as he devoutly wishes, be taken more seriously.

Here is one example of what can go wrong. On 21 February 1988, a profile of Prince Charles in the Sunday magazine of the *New York Times*, written by its London bureau chief, Howell Raines, caused quite a stir. There were two main spurs for newspaper excitement. The first was a leak from a lunch at which Charles had entertained three upmarket newspaper editors, revealing that he went "incandescent" with rage after misunderstanding one of his guest's remarks and wailed yet again about the miseries of his lot. The second was the revelation, elsewhere in the article, that Charles had once said "I wish I had been Bob Geldof." Yet again, on both fronts, the columnists went into overdrive. Whole feature pages were devoted to fantasies about Prince Bob, Charles Geldof and other such tantalizing spectres. In the absence of any response from the Palace, beyond leaks that the Prince was infuriated by the leaks, speculation again ran riot.

There were two separate questions: (a) the source of the leak – a whodunnit only too easily solved, and (b) whether or not it was understandable or healthy for Charles to go around wishing he were Bob Geldof. Inevitably the two

got confused. Four months later Alan Hamilton, the esti-
mable court correspondent of *The Times*, was still to be
found discussing the rights and wrongs of the matter in the
opinion pages of the glossy magazine *Royalty Monthly*.
After pointing the finger for leaks at Peregrine
Worsthorne, editor of the *Sunday Telegraph*, Hamilton
quoted his own editor, Charles Wilson, another guest at
the lunch, to the effect that he had never heard the Prince
say that he wished he was Bob Geldof.

Of course he hadn't – because the remark had not been
made at that lunch. Nor had Howell Raines ever suggested
that it was. Overexcited hastiness had got reporters" wires
crossed, casting doubt on what seemed a remarkable
quote. I, however, happen to know that neither
Worsthorne nor anyone else was Raines's source for the
Geldof remark, for the simple reason that I was myself. In
conversation with Raines, I asked him not to attribute it
to me – a request this highly professional journalist duly
respected – as I was merely the vessel through which it had
passed. The Prince had made the remark to a personal
acquaintance of mine not long after Geldof's Live Aid
concert in 1985. But its purport was not quite as simple as
just wishing he could turn into Bob Geldof. The remark
came in a context which gives it much more sense and
potency, and makes it an entirely understandable one for
the Prince to make. The answer to the riddle lies buried in
this book.

Charles-watching, therefore, is a complex business,
which has grown much more so since I first entered the
lists ten years ago. Since the arrival on the scene of the
Princess of Wales, the roadshow which follows the couple
around has grown to absurd and unmanageable proportions. On that swing through South America in 1977, I was
the only writer on the trip, accompanied by just three
photographers (four when we bumped into Lord
Snowdon in Manaus), often staying in the same hotel as
the Prince and his handful of staff; in Australia for the

bicentennial celebrations of 1988, I was one of 200 writers and photographers, as many as seventy of whom had flown out from Britain, permitted only to observe the couple from behind ropes, at a safe distance.

Traditionally, on all foreign visits by all members of the royal family, there would be a cocktail party early in the trip for members of the travelling press, of whatever nationality. It was a cunning piece of royal public relations, much appreciated by all concerned. Journalistic egos swelled at the chance to swap a few civilized words, strictly off the record, with their quarries; the royals, in turn, had a welcome opportunity to tease or complain, even to indulge in some discreet steering of their own coverage. Writers felt disarmed; the next day's reporting would always be positive. But the leaks from these occasions, begun by locals who simply did not understand the rules, gradually got out of hand – reaching the point in Germany last year when a local television reporter asked the Prince a question, then walked straight over to a waiting camera to repeat his answer. The Waleses have now distanced themselves even more from those who write about them – thus no doubt doubling the quota of speculation to fact – by abandoning these useful occasions, which amounted to a vital umbilical cord between them and the real world. They are, at the time of writing, the only members of the royal family to have done so.

One final aspect of this book's antecedents is worth a brief mention: the awkward fact that discretion is, of course, the price of membership of the royal circle. Lists of acknowledgements in books about royalty tend, therefore, to be rather scanty – usually leading the reader to wonder, often with good reason, about the provenance and reliability of the author's information. This author is, alas, no exception, in that he has over ten years of reasonably good behaviour built up a relationship of trust with many people in and around royal circles, who would not thank him for naming them here. To those in that category who have helped his research for this volume, he offers his necessarily discreet thanks.

In the interests of authenticity, therefore, it is worth recording here the names of some who contributed to the accuracy of my first volume – for the facts of the Prince's first thirty years remain unaltered and depend upon their witness. The section on the Prince's days at Hill House School was checked for accuracy by Colonel Henry Townend, its headmaster then as now; the section on Cheam by Peter Beck, its joint headmaster while the Prince was there; the section on Gordonstoun by Robert Waddell, the only master still there today who was during the Prince's time; the section on his university years by Dr Denis Marrian, Senior Tutor of Trinity College; by Lord Butler, then its Master; and by Edward Millward, the Prince's tutor in Welsh language and literature at the University College of Wales, Aberystwyth. Others whose help with that volume is reflected in this include: Ronald Allison, David Frost, John Grigg, Hywel Jones, Sir Tom McCaffrey, John Maclean, Sir Philip Magnus, Sir Ian Moncreiffe of that Ilk, Paul Officer, George Pratt, Dr Anil Seal, Lord Snowdon, Nicholas Soames MP, Viscount Tonypandy, Lord Wilson of Rievaulx and the Rt Rev. Dr Robert Woods. Many of the above have again helped me with my recent researches.

My remaining acknowledgements are for debts accumulated not only during the twelve months of research for the present volume, but the ten years of Charles-watching which have led up to it. Among the Prince's professional colleagues, most of whom know or have known him better than anyone, I have reason to be grateful to: Edward Adeane, his private secretary, 1979 – 85; the late Stephen Barry, his personal valet, 1970 – 82; Canon Sebastian Charles, secretary of Inner City Aid; Squadron-Leader Sir David Checketts, private secretary to the Prince of Wales, 1970 – 79; Lieutenant-Colonel David Cox, director of the Prince of Wales" Committee; Sir Ian Gourlay, Director-

General of the United World Colleges; Rod Hackney, President of the Royal Institute of British Architects; Sir Harold Haywood, immediate ex-director of the Prince's Trust and the Royal Jubilee Trusts, and his successor, Tom Shebbeare; Charles Knevitt, secretary of *The Times*/RIBA Community Enterprise Scheme, formerly secretary of Inner City Aid; Stephen O'Brien, chief executive of Business in the Community; John Pervin, chief executive of the Prince's Youth Business Trust; Michael Shea, press secretary to the Queen, 1978 – 87.

My request for an interview with the Prime Minister, to discuss the Prince of Wales's constitutional role, was considered at a diary meeting but turned down because "it is not her practice to discuss the royal family." The staff of the press office of Buckingham Palace have, meanwhile, been as helpful and courteous as ever. I am grateful for the assistance of the Prince of Wales's current press secretary, Philip Mackie, and his lady clerk, Kiloran McGrigor. Among previous press secretaries to the Prince of Wales who have over the years been close colleagues and friends to me, I warmly thank John Dauth, Warwick Hutchings and the late Victor Chapman.

Among experts in the Prince's specialist fields, some of them his close friends, who have helped me to a better understanding of his recent preoccupations, I must thank: Peter Ahrends, Ashley Barker, Christopher Booker, Tony Clegg, Phil Collins, Theo Crosby, Dan Cruickshank, Sir Philip Dowson, Trish Evans, Paul Greetham, Ernest Hall, Stuart Lipton, John Lockwood, Jules Lubbock, Michael Manser, John Simpson, Deyan Sudjic, John Thompson, Richard Wade, Dr Elizabeth Whipp and Lady Roisine Wynne-Jones.

Among writers, journalists and photographers, some of whom earn their living watching the Prince's every move, I have benefited from (and much enjoyed) the company of: Harry Arnold, Michael Barratt, the late Basil Boothroyd, Tina Brown, Nigel Dempster, Arthur

Edwards, Fred Emery, Donna Foote, Tim Graham, Anwar Hussein, Robert Lacey, Suzanne Lowry, Suzy Menkes, Peter Osnos, John Pearson, Howell Raines, Anthony Sampson, Andrew Stephen, David Thomas, Hugo Vickers and James Whitaker. I am also grateful to the editors of the *Observer*, the *Sunday Times*, the *Daily Mail* and *Today*, whose readers responded helpfully to some of the ideas in this book when I floated some sections of it in draft form.

John Holland, formerly the royal specialist at TV-am, was good enough to help with my research, conducting many of the preliminary interviews and compiling copious dossiers on the Prince's charitable activities and other public work. John has also worked as associate producer on the ITV biography of Prince Charles which I have made for London Weekend Television in conjunction with this book (produced and directed by Chris Ralling; executive producer Robin Paxton).

For their private and professional support I am especially indebted, as ever, to Hilary Rubinstein, Juliet Gardiner, Perry Knowlton and Lord Weidenfeld. Linda Osband's meticulous editing completed a ten-year cycle of friendship and professional collaboration, as indeed did Lynda Marshall's picture research. For many hours of listening and talking, both patient and wise, and for many other things besides, I owe a great deal to Cynthia Blake, to whom this book is cryptically dedicated. My sons Sam, Joe and Ben – the joint dedicatees, at a very young age, of my previous biography of the Prince of Wales – have been more than tolerant of their father's changing moods while writing this one.

"It must be hell writing books," the Prince of Wales once said to me. "They're so *long*, aren't they?" Yes, indeed, but compiling a fair and accurate public portrait of Prince Charles is a particularly complex, demanding and at times infuriating business for both parties. Michael Shea, until recently the Queen's press secretary, once paid me the dubious compliment of saying how much trouble I had caused him with my public utterances on the Prince – "as everyone seems to believe they're true." I have in my time received death threats, as well as many letters thanking me for helping the Prince's future subjects to a better understanding of his difficulties. My continuing hope in all that work, as in this book, is to maintain the happy medium divined in one of the reviews of *Charles, Prince of Wales*: to be "sympathetic without becoming sycophantic."

Chiswick, London, 1988

PART ONE

In Search of a Role

"The pleased incredulity with which the
public reacts to the elementary
demonstrations on the part of Royalty that
they are, after all, like other people is
matched only by the public's firm refusal to
accept them as such."

The Duke of Windsor,
formerly Prince of Wales
and King Edward VIII

ONE

Prince and Prime Minister

"There is no doubt of the young man's
capacity for goodness."
From a letter to Prime Minister Stanley
Baldwin regarding the last Prince of Wales

I N THE early hours of 12 June 1987, after winning her
third successive term as Prime Minister, Margaret
Thatcher's first thought was of winning a fourth. Stung by
her party's electoral losses in the most deprived urban
areas of Britain, for all the euphoria of a victory unprecedented in this century, Mrs Thatcher's first public act that
night was to make the plight of Britain's inner cities the
most urgent priority of her new government. When she
gave this emotional pledge to party workers from the
staircase of Conservative Central Office, even as the votes
were still being counted, the Prime Minister's words could
be taken to represent a remarkable political victory for,
among others, the Prince of Wales.

The voice of Britain's next King was not the only one
which had been raised in concern about the rapid social
decay around Britain's major conurbations, and the dis-
mal, often unhealthy, at times dangerous conditions in
which many of the less fortunate of his future subjects
were compelled to live. But it was one of the most

significant, one of the most compelling and one of the most informed.

For ten years Prince Charles had made it his business to travel to areas of the greatest deprivation in the United Kingdom, to talk to those whose lives could not be a starker contrast to his own, and to offer comfort and assistance. He was not only anxious to draw attention to the plight of the unemployed and the homeless, of racial and religious minorities, of young people otherwise bereft of hope for the future; he was also keen to devise ways of providing the emotional and financial support they so often seemed to be denied by local or central government. Via the Prince's Trust, Charles had long been administering grants to youth projects throughout the land – followed up by personal, often private visits to see for himself that the money was being put to good use. Ten years later, in the absence of any effective political opposition in Britain, he was steadily advancing into much more ambitious terrain.

The Prince's first full decade in public life had seen conditions in Britain's inner cities grow steadily worse. As hard-line monetarist policies raised unemployment to record levels, biting deeper into the lives of those on or below the poverty line, he was prevented by the nature of the British constitutional monarchy from voicing any overtly political protest. But he was acutely aware, as much from the example of some recent predecessors as from his own close study of British history, that he was in a unique position to appeal to the consciences of politicians. The heir to the throne may have no political power, but he has considerable influence.

He can speak, in short, for the people. He must do so in the most circumspect style, avoiding the slightest hint of involvement in party politics, but he is uniquely well informed and has a uniquely conspicuous platform. As heir apparent, this Prince of Wales sees confidential Cabinet papers and so is utterly *au fait* with day-to-day political issues. As a Privy Counsellor, he can air his views confidentially to senior politicians of the day. But he can never make any public statement even remotely susceptible to charges of political bias. For a man who cares passionately about the nation over which he will one day reign – and, through his constant travels, is in much closer touch with its problems than most ministers – the inhibitions placed upon him can prove very frustrating.

At times, perhaps too often, he is capable of letting his frustration show. A recent leak from a private luncheon, at which he complained to a group of newspaper editors of his lifelong struggle against royal protocol, recalled an even more poignant leak ten years ago from a dinner held in his honour by the Callaghan Cabinet. Not long before, Charles told them, a Qantas air hostess had had the *chutzpah* to come over and say to him: "What a rotten, boring job you've got!" Government ministers laughed sympathetically. "But you don't understand," said the Prince urgently. "She was right!"

Unlike his companions that night, Charles has not sought public office, even public prominence, let alone stood for election to a position of power and influence. It has been thrust upon him by the accident of his birth, and made much less palatable by the failure of the British constitution to define a public function for the Prince of Wales. Its unwritten rules are eloquent on what he must not do, but silent as to what he should.

What (as someone once asked, rather less politely, of his Aunt Margaret) is the Prince of Wales *for*? The only explicit purpose of his life, put at its bleakest, is to wait for his parent to die. For many of Charles's predecessors, excluded by their royal parent from any involvement in affairs of state, this proved a licence for princely dalliance and dilettantism. The history of the twenty English Princes of Wales before Charles is not, as a result, a particularly distinguished one. But the latter half of the twentieth century finds itself confronted by a Prince determined to change all that.

By the late 1980s Charles was placing himself squarely

at the centre of the contemporary political battleground. As his own personal philosophy has matured, so has his public work; as the scale of his vision has grown, so has that of his determination to improve living and working conditions in post-industrial Britain. As he reaches forty, the many disparate strands of his private and public life seem to be converging in this one central mission. After years of intellectual dabbling, he has developed a cohesive world view which he is anxious to put to practical use. In the decline of the quality of life for many Britons he has finally found a public purpose to his own. With some relish the Prince has mounted his political tightrope and set forth into the unknown.

If he courts controversy, ruffles complacent feathers, angers vested interests or arouses professional hostility, so be it. "I like," he had declared, "to stir things up, to throw a proverbial royal brick through the inviting plateglass of pompous professional pride and jump feet first into the kind of spaghetti bolognaise of red tape which clogs this country from one end to the other." Charles is a man of high seriousness; since his days as a Cambridge undergraduate, he has felt a deep consciousness of his place in history and a powerful ambition to make his mark. It is tempting at times, when his sense of his position makes nonsense of his human relationships, to say even that he has developed ideas above his station. Heir to the throne since the age of three, he was brought up by his parents to feel a deep sense of duty; to Charles, his birthright is now a sacred trust of which to make what he will. The vivid recent example of a Prince of Wales who betrayed that trust – his great-uncle David, briefly King Edward VIII before surrendering his throne for the woman he loved – has concentrated his mind enormously. He will go down in history, he is determined, as a Prince of Wales who used his office to enhance the common good.

Everything else in his life is now subordinate to that goal. At times, when he is misunderstood or his actions misinterpreted, he can grow angry and dejected, even show his mere mortality with thoughts of "packing it all in." But those moods quickly pass. His private life, his wife and children, his offstage enthusiasms from music to sport all take second place to his public ambitions. Only in the last few years has Charles finally defined this focus both for his personal philosophy and for his public role; now that at last he has, he is putting his confused past behind him and pursuing his future with an almost missionary zeal.

At the core of that psychological breakthrough, and at the heart of much public misapprehension, is the crucial constitutional truth that he has much more freedom of movement as Prince of Wales than he will have as king. Charles, like his great-great-grandfather King Edward VII, is doomed to spend most of his life waiting in the wings. Edward was the son of a mother who came to the throne early and lived to a ripe old age; Charles, like him, will most likely be a grandfather in his mid-sixties before he inherits the throne. For years he found this prospect an intolerable burden. Only recently has he perceived its advantages.

As appreciation of his public work has grown, Charles has increasingly been said to have the makings of "an innovative King." The simple truth, however, is that an "innovative" monarch is a contradiction in terms. As sovereign Charles could, should he so choose, reform the administrative machinery of the Crown itself, but he cannot reform the working of the nation. That is very much more in the province of the Prince of Wales. As monarch, his public statements will have to be utterly anodyne; King Charles III, for instance, would certainly not be free to pre-empt planning procedures by condemning proposed public buildings as monstrous carbuncles. As heir to the throne, however, he can speak his mind, court political controversy and relish the constitutional dangers involved. He cannot – as his immediate predecessor famously, idly and hypocritically did – say "Something must be done"; but he has enormous scope, while choosing his public words more carefully to see that something actually does *get* done.

In March 1988, at the age of thirty-nine, Prince Charles had achieved enough in one area of his public work for the President of the United States to write to him:

> I share your deep concern for the rehabilitation of our older urban and industrial areas. Your efforts to call attention to urban revitalization have greatly assisted the drive for partnerships among government, private enterprise and local citizens. I fully support the idea that we can use these partnerships to lead the way to a better life for all our fellow countrymen.

The story of Prince Charles's life so far, as he embarks upon middle age, is one of constant struggle against the limitations placed upon him by the genetic accident of his birth. It is the story of an introverted, contemplative figure anxious, unlike many of his predecessors, to make the most of his unenviable birthright. Privately, his is the story of a confused and tortured soul trying to come to terms with a claustrophobic, if comfortable life of inherited imprisonment; publicly, it is that of a caring and thoughtful man in search of good to do – not merely a prince on search of a role, but a crusader in search of a crusade.

TWO

The Frog Prince

"I didn't suddenly wake up in my pram one
day and say 'Yippee.'"

ON THE drawing-room sofa of the Prince of Wales's
apartment in Kensington Palace is a cushion embroi-
dered with a frog, which is wearing a crown and croaking:
"It's no fun being a prince."

The unkindness of fate has been a dominant theme of
Charles's life since 1953, his mother's coronation year,
when he encountered one of her private secretaries in a
Buckingham Palace corridor and asked his standard, four-
year-old question: "What are *you* doing here?"

"I'm going to see the Queen," explained the secretary.

"Oh yes?" said Charles. "Who's she?"

On being told the Queen was his mother, the young
Prince looked so bemused that the courtier felt a sudden
pang of guilt – "as if I had given away the secret of Father
Christmas."

It was to take Prince Charles many years to come to
terms with his unique destiny – the awful truth that, by
some quirk of genetic fate, he had been born to a life of
compulsory public service, with little privacy, less freedom
of choice and no escape-routes – a life sentence of solitary
confinement in a gilded cage. He described the feeling
with painful candour in the first interview he ever gave, at

the age of twenty: "I didn't suddenly wake up in my pram one day and say 'Yippee.' It just dawns on you, slowly, that people are interested. . . . " They certainly are.

When first you meet him, it is hard to concentrate on what he is saying. The face before you is a contemporary icon, familiar from postage-stamps and biscuit tins, banknotes and T-shirts. You have eaten off it and drunk out of it, dried your face with it, maybe even wiped your feet on it. High on the left of those ruddy, countryman's cheeks, resisting the remorseless advance of the crow's feet of middle age, is a deep scar – the price of fierce competitiveness on the polo field. When talking to the future King Charles III it is difficult to take your eyes off it, symbolizing as it does the violence with which he can vent his frustrations.

Then there is the voice. Through his father's high-pitched huskiness comes the unmistakably regal vowel sounds of his mother. Whatever he is saying, however ponderous or flippant, those vowels have an unfortunate tendency to undermine it, to pigeon-hole his every word in some remote eyrie of inherited privilege. They carry a curious note of apology for being who he is, as if he knew that a world in which houses are "hyses" is not the one the rest of us inhabit.

At five foot ten, a shoeless half-inch less than his wife, Prince Charles is slightly shorter than you expect; but there is not an ounce of fat on his 160-pound frame. The shoulders may be sloping, the chest surprisingly slight, the hips rather bulky and the legs too short; but this is one very fit, strong, muscular man, and every sinew is visibly tense. Offstage as on, he lives on his nerves. He licks his lips, he strokes his nose, he twists his three-feathered signet ring around his little finger. His mouth has an involuntary tic, dragging one side down towards his chin, unhappily giving an impression of disapproval. He smiles as he advances across the room to greet you, but his eyes are already wary, darting hither and thither for signs of potential danger. He is never off his guard.

But Prince Charles is that rarity among his gender, a good listener. Although he dislikes small-talk, he is very adept at it. Polite platitudes go with the job, but he prefers to make something concrete out of every encounter. The Prince is well aware that for most who meet him, however briefly, it will be a treasured highlight of their lives. The strain of living up to expectations is a constant pressure, merely one among many which make being royal such hard work.

We are all the victims of our parents' genes, but none more so than Charles, heir to the loftiest position on earth still determined by heredity. He is proud of his destiny, but at times appalled by it. It brings him wealth and glamour, access and influence, and a deep sense of failure. "Yes," he recently admitted, "I have changed in the last few years." But still he feels, through the mists of self-doubt, that he has not done enough to merit all the attention paid to him. He suffers, as would anyone so self-critical, bouts of deep depression, which he likes to work out alone – whether fishing in Scotland or painting water-colours in Italy.

In anyone else, it might be called a mid-life crisis. To Charles, who has no chance of changing his job or his aspirations, his home or his lifestyle, let alone his wife, it is merely the "middle period" – as defined by the Swiss psychologist Carl Jung, of whom he has become a devout disciple, under the tutelage of the South African-born writer and explorer Laurens van der Post. An introspective man, with a pessimistic streak, Charles believes that the modern world is on a downhill slope and thinks it only logical to explore alternative solutions.

This is not just the public Charles; it is the real one. His high seriousness is quite as evident in private. Visitors in search of the man behind the icon hear little but long catalogues of his concerns – inner-city blight, the London skyline, racial prejudice, drug abuse, youth unemployment, the rape of the environment. "He's going to inherit this country's problems, so he's trying to solve them now, by getting the youth of Britain back on their feet," says an admiring Phil Collins of the rock group Genesis, who helps organize concerts for the Prince's Trust. Other friends say Charles feels it all too personally, takes too much blame upon himself for failing to improve the social conditions of his future kingdom. He worries too much, they say, for his own good. One day it will make him ill.

The fun-loving streak of his youth certainly seems long gone. Even at home Charles wears a permanently worried air, from the moment he wakes and notes down on the pad beside his bed all he can remember of his dreams. It is a habit he has picked up from van der Post: "One can learn a considerable amount from dreams," says the Jungian Prince. His day begins with BBC Radio 4's farming programme (as does Mrs Thatcher's) and a bath drawn by one of his two valets, who will also have laid out his clothes for the morning; Diana, more often than not, will have been up earlier and driven over to Buckingham Palace for her morning swim while Charles still sleeps. Fruit, toast and Lapsang Souchong tea fuel the Prince for an hour or so's paperwork before his regular 10 a.m. meeting with his private secretary, Sir John Riddell, to discuss business which may lay hours or months ahead. "I hate having to plan so far in advance," he will always say when notified of the latest batch of invitations. Any decision which he can postpone, he will – preferably until the six-monthly planning meetings at which he and Diana arrange each day of their lives for the year and more stretching ahead.

In 1987, on the recommendation of a firm of management efficiency consultants, the Prince of Wales's office was moved from Buckingham Palace to St James's Palace. Here Riddell, a fifty-four-year-old former banker, is supported by two assistant private secretaries, David Wright and Rupert Fairfax (on secondment from the Hanson conglomerate to add some business expertise to the Prince's team). For a world figure of such proportions, with so celebrated a wife, the Prince's media operation is laughably amateur. The one press secretary assigned to "look after" Charles and (since 1981) Diana has tradition-ally been a Commonwealth diplomat; during 1987-88 the post was temporarily filled by a former Scottish journalist, Philip Mackie (since followed by another poacher-turned-gamekeeper, Dickie Arbiter, former court correspondent of a London radio station). The job description, in proto-col terms, is assistant press secretary to the Queen, one of two based in Buckingham Palace. For the purposes of his day-to-day London operations, therefore, Charles has his study in one palace, his office in another and his public relations representative in another. The result can be con-siderable confusion. There have been several misunder-standings under the new regime, to be examined later in these pages, which have caused the Prince some embar-rassment and enormous irritation.

At such moments he has a violently angry streak, of which his staff live in fear, though it rarely shows through in public. At Kensington Palace Charles apparently scatters angry handwritten notes everywhere, reprimand-ing staff for random shortcomings. Some were even leaked to the journalist Andrew Morton. For instance: "I didn't mean you to remove that glass for my toothbrush. It was a particularly nice glass. Please bring it back. If they have removed it I shall be very angry indeed. C." Or: "Please ask housemaid not to fiddle with radiators – especially in bathroom, where I had turned radiator off to prevent it becoming like a greenhouse. C." The underlining is a long-standing royal habit inherited from his grandfather, King George VI. But it needs no graphologist to tell us that the Prince's impatience turns all too easily to anger if he feels that his time is being wasted. There is always so little of it, and so much he wants to do.

His presence in a room tends to make the atmosphere stiff and formal. He likes to dress for dinner, even at home; and when he dines out, hosts must be careful: the Prince dislikes red wine and prefers fish or vegetables to meat and tea to coffee. His favourite dish is smoked salmon with scrambled eggs. He prefers Bach to the Beatles, Schubert to Springsteen. There is a passage in Berlioz's *Symphonie Fantastique* which can still, as it has for many years, reduce him to tears. He is a sentimental man, with a soft heart and a pronounced romantic streak.

However hard he has tried to understand "how the other half live," the Prince has never had a chance to live in the real world. He has never had to worry about his mortgage, wash his treasured Aston-Martin on Saturday mornings, pack his own suitcase, let alone lose it on long-haul flights. Rush-hour traffic parts for him like the Red Sea; he has never travelled on a bus. He does not carry money; when in need of some for politeness' sake, he will borrow it from an aide and probably forget to pay it back. He need not fret about his sons' school fees, or indeed their job prospects. Were he, for that matter, to have a daughter, the Lothario who tried to go too far would be liable by ancient statute to a charge of treason, still punishable by death.

No one beyond his family calls Charles by his first name. Though he would like to be thought a man of his times, the Prince is locked in a royal upbringing which requires him to take his position very seriously and expect such deference as his due. He shudders visibly when anyone refers to the Queen as "Your mother," a gross breach of royal etiquette. He expects a bow, and protocol decrees that you must wait for him to extend a hand. The ensuing shake is disappointingly limp, but then he has to get through so many in a day. These rituals can make a naturally warm man appear rather cold. They build around him an invisible barrier which many wish to penetrate, but few do. Most visitors come away feeling sorry for him, as he undoubtedly does for himself.

Constant politeness is one of his life's most exhausting demands; even for so fit a man, he seems permanently tired. Supplicants granted an audience are often dismayed to be told: "Do wake me up if I doze off." Much of his life is insufferably boring. His only release lies in rather desperate upper-class pleasures, from polo to the extensive collection of lavatory seats in which he still takes great pride. His sense of humour, once so promising, is now stuck in a teenage groove of practical jokes and silly voices. Even the genial self-deprecation has grown somewhat arch; asked by David Frost how he would describe himself, Charles replied: "Sometimes as a bit of a twit." He is always on the defensive.

Until recently there was an unworldliness, at times a naïvety about his yearning to tackle the problems of Britain and the Third World; he tended to choose somewhat eccentric advisers and to be too easily swayed by the last person he talked to, with the result that his grasp of the issues did not always match the depth of his concern. Recently he has become much more his own man and developed a sounder understanding of the most complex contemporary issues. But he can still seem blissfully unaware of the contradictions between his public work and his own comfortable lifestyle. On a celebrated visit to London's East End in 1987, the Prince proudly presented a cheque for £3,000 to a group of young blacks to launch a new small business – apparently oblivious to the irony that the night before his wife had worn a £5,000 dress to the première of the new James Bond movie.

Such confusions litter his life. In March 1988 he attracted much publicity – himself, for once, distracting attention from some more serious remarks – by announcing that he had banned aerosol cans in all his homes. Yes, he said with a male chauvinist grin, even hair-spray. The same week, he was filmed for television chatting with young blacks who had received a princely grant to decorate their surroundings with graffiti – sprayed, of course, from aerosol cans. It did not take the world's press long, meanwhile, gently to inform the Prince that thanks to long concern about the ozone layer, "safe" aerosol cans for domestic use had been available for several years. Among the stores which sold them, indeed, was The Body

Shop chain, famous as a happy retail hunting-ground for his wife.

It was nothing new of Charles to seem "out of touch." He has never really embraced the values of young Britons his own age; for most of his life the generation with whose aspirations he has been least in touch is his own, now approaching the seats of power rather faster than he is approaching the throne. "I am proud to be square," the teenage Prince declared when his contemporaries were hippies, and he is just as distant from them now that they are aging yuppies. Marriage came as a shock to the system of a thirty-two year old very set in his ways. Diana may have spruced him up, but the exterior Charles, like the interior, remains stubbornly conservative. Beneath each better-cut double-breasted suit is a defiantly military pair of black shoes, toecaps polished and gleaming. He is said to own a pair of jeans, but they have never been seen. Even when pottering about his country estate, Highgrove in Gloucestershire, he tends to wear tailored trousers and tie – the uniform of the gentleman-farmer he would like to have been.

He is most at home at Highgrove; apartments 8 and 9 of Kensington Palace are as much an office as a residence. The furnishings of both are those of a bygone British opulence, typified by the loose covers on the sofas and the framed family photos on the grand piano. Most royal residences have a faded antique grandeur to offset their draughty corridors and inadequate central heating; but despite the odd dash of Laura Ashley, Highgrove and "K.P." have the more impersonal chintz-and-mahogany decor of Embassy Row. They are elegant and mature, as befits his station, but neither feels like a lived-in home. At Highgrove he has designed himself a garden, the heart of which is a gazebo where he sits to read or deal with paper-work. He will roam the grounds, checking the progress of his beloved plants – perhaps, as he has rashly admitted, talking to them – or go for long walks on the private estate, though that will involve an escort of bodyguards. A Prince of Wales is never truly alone.

In the more macho days of his youth, Charles tried to please his father by embracing the adventurous, outdoor spirit of such projects as the British Transglobe Expedition. "If there were anything left to discover," the Queen Mother then said of her supposedly favourite grandchild, "he would have been an explorer." But Charles now tells friends that he would really like to have been a farmer; and some of his happiest recent experiences have been his incognito trips to share for a few days the lives of Highland crofters or his tenant farmers in the Duchy of Cornwall. These therapeutic visits, ridiculed by a wilfully mischievous tabloid press, have about them almost an air of penance. Charles seems to think a few days of sackcloth and ashes a fit price to pay for the otherwise very luxurious life he leads, largely at public expense.

Only in his mid- and late-thirties, since marriage liberated him from the shadow of his parents, has Prince Charles discovered the freedom to be himself. Hitherto, since the moment that courtier robbed the four-year-old Prince of his innocence, he had been too busy learning to be someone else. "Gradually," he said in that first interview, "you get an idea that you have a certain duty and responsibility. It's better that way, rather than someone telling you you must do this or you must do that because of who you are. It's one of those things you grow up in."

Growing up took him a long time. It is not surprising that a child brought up in a world of adults, predominantly female, whose view of the world was fashioned through the lace windows of royal palaces and castles, turned out to be a late developer. Even at school he was a somewhat solitary figure, slow to make friends, anxious not to make enemies, confused by his sudden inability to assert his rank when it suited him. The purpose of his schooling, without precedent in the history of heirs to the throne, was supposedly to give him a taste of life as a "normal" child; when he came home for the school holidays, however, he was again surrounded by all the familiar deference he had come to take for granted.

It is no wonder he grew confused. Already of meditative mien, Charles spent most of his teens and twenties riddled with understandable doubts and uncertainties. Having a pronounced sense of irony did not help. In his bearskin and scarlet uniform, before going out on public parade, the Prince would look at himself in a mirror and desperately wonder just who this absurd-looking person could be. In time he would make valuable friendships with a series of much older people, who would help him make sense of it all. But for the first twenty years of his life, his closest friendships were inevitably with his sister and brothers.

Charles was only three, and Princess Anne still a baby, when their mother inherited the throne. But the Queen did not let affairs of state get in the way of her plans for a big family. Students of the royal family *qua* soap opera tend to forget the size of the age gap between the royal siblings. Charles is twelve years older than Andrew, sixteen years older than Edward. One day, he will be their King; even between brothers, the royal awareness of rank is ever present. To both of them, especially Edward, their elder brother has always seemed very grown-up – an affectionate figure of wisdom and authority, even an object of hero-worship. All three boys underwent the same education, but they have turned out to be three very different characters. Encouraged by their father, they have always relished a particularly virulent strain of sibling rivalry, which now looks like fuelling their adult lives.

Why, for instance, did supposedly sensitive, artistic Prince Edward choose to join the Royal Marines, notoriously the toughest of all military units? Because his brother Charles had served a spell in each of the armed forces, ending up with his own naval command, while Andrew the career sailor had enjoyed a rare opportunity to see active service in the Falklands. It was Edward's only chance to outshine them. But the mindlessness of army life became claustrophobic; Edward's agonized, all too public decision to quit in 1987 took quite as much guts as finishing the arduous training course he had started. It braved the wrath of his father, who is desperately ambitious for his children to succeed, and who also happens to be Captain-General of the Marines. Edward's public baptism by fire, and some of his subsequent over-enthusiasms, have proved him to be the vulnerable accident-prone figure a youngest child often is.

These are also among Charles's predominant traits. But Edward is in fact much closer to Princess Anne – closer, despite the age gap, than either of his older brothers. It is at Anne's Gloucestershire home, Gatcombe Park, that Edward most enjoys relaxing, away from the pressures of the royal goldfish bowl. It was to Gatcombe that he fled from the pursuit of the press during his Marines ordeal. But Prince Charles, though Highgrove is just down the road at Tetbury, is a rather less frequent visitor to Gatcombe. He has never forged much of a friendship with Anne's husband, Captain Mark Phillips; it was Charles, with uncharacteristic cruelty, who gave Mark the family nickname of "Fog" – "because he's thick and wet." But his relationship with his sister has also, over the years, been somewhat volatile. It is a thinly veiled secret that for long periods, especially during their teens, Charles and Anne did not get on at all well.

Once Anne married, however, and had her first child, things changed. Charles doted on young Peter Phillips, his godson, until the chance came to have children of his own. Now his own wife, Diana, has found it hard to get on with her sister-in-law – recently elevated to the status of Princess Royal to set her apart from the two *arriviste* Princesses who have stolen much of her thunder. Given Diana's penchant for upstaging her fellow-members of the royal *dramatis personae*, there has inevitably been some awkwardness. "No one ever talks or writes about what *I'm* wearing," said Anne recently, with disarming candour, but more than a trace of bitterness. It is not as easy, of course, to be born and grow up a princess as it is to become one by choice – especially if Nature has not blessed you with cover-girl good looks.

The Princess Royal's outstanding work for the Save The Children Fund has recently rehabilitated her reputation with the public and transformed her into one of the royal family's most popular members. In a recent worldwide "phone-in" on the BBC's World Service, she displayed a mastery of Third World issues which belies the traditional airs and graces of royal patronage. For the ugly duckling to become a regal swan suited the British press; it was a new angle to an old story. But Anne still has not achieved her older brother's relaxed way of dealing with the Fourth Estate. Once, when abroad, news of the latest Anne incident reached him: about to go hunting, she had come up against a group of anti-blood sports protesters. An exchange of abuse climaxed with the Princess saying: "Who's paying you to do this?" As the story was told to him, Charles groaned. He knew exactly what was coming next: "Well, *we're* paying *you* to do that!" from angry taxpayers. It is a cardinal royal sin to fall into such traps. Avoiding them requires a politician's skill in periphrasis and evasion, which Charles has long since perfected. Today he admires his sister's public work enormously – even, at times, seems to envy it, as it is so clearly defined while his as yet remains so apparently random.

The wild card in the royal sibling pack is of course Prince Andrew, whose rumbustious youth caused his parents some very contemporary headaches. The Queen grew anxious when Charles took so long to marry, but more so when Andrew started to bring home one or two girlfriends with rather dubious pasts. But it was again the tabloid press who grew much more indignant than the Queen herself when her second son fell in love with a soft-porn movie star. Ever shrewd in these matters, the nation's first mother happily invited Koo Stark to Balmoral for the weekend, letting the affair burn itself out rather than stoking it up with protests. Charles looked on with mixed feelings. Though he had by then made the most spectacular match himself, he had always been jealous of Andrew's better looks and the fact that the second in line can behave much more naturally – be much more his relaxed and grinning self – when out and about. "Ah, you mean the one with the Robert Redford looks?" he used to sneer, when asked about Andrew's early progress in the navy. At the time he himself was self-conscious about a growing bald patch, as now is Edward. Tonsorially as in other ways, Andrew has again – as yet – proved the lucky one.

It was little consolation to Charles that Andrew was semi-publicly branded the family's black sheep. On his eighteenth birthday, when it is customary for Household staff to start addressing royal offspring as "Sir" or "Ma'am," the Queen told them to continue calling Andrew by his Christian name. Charles himself had never displayed quite the dash and suavity which were, and still are, his younger brother's hallmark. More introspective, more cautious, he allowed their different personalities to build a youthful barrier between them. Now, at last, Andrew's marriage to one of Diana's best friends has seen a high-spirited rapprochement. Charles may wince as much as many royalists at the giggling jolly-hockey-sticks antics of "Fergie," Duchess of York, but her presence as a sheet-anchor in the lives of his wife and brother have mercifully freed him to devote himself more to his own concerns.

The enclosed and sheltered nature of their childhoods inevitably placed an undue strain on all these sibling relations. Unable to form friendships with people their own age as freely as their contemporaries, the royal children relied on each other's company to an unusual degree. But the heir to the throne was obliged, of course, to take especial care over his own choice of friends. The result was that for years they tended to come from the "safe" worlds of polo, the forces and the British aristocracy – a

world which endorsed the status quo and rarely challenged him or his values. Of necessity, to some extent, the
Prince cultivated conservative-minded, rather hearty,
knockabout chums more than the kind of soulmates on
whom most mere mortals hope to rely. The sad result, to
this day, is that Charles has scarcely any intimate friends
of his own age to whom to turn in moments of difficulty
or stress. His private circle beyond his family tends to be
drawn from an array of much older acquaintances –
figures of wisdom and authority, inevitably dubbed gurus.

Lord Mountbatten and the Queen Mother, it is well
known, were pillars of his childhood and youth, often
recipients of confidences he could not share even with this
parents – especially, during his bachelorhood, on matters
of the heart. Mountbatten, especially, was a major figure
in the Prince's development, dubbed "honorary grandfather" after the premature death of his real one, King
George VI, when Charles was only three. The swashbuckling Earl's murder at the hands of the IRA in 1979 left a
gaping hole in the Prince's life which has never really been
filled, for the mentors who have since taken his place have
been of rather more philosophical mien. In his early and
mid-twenties, a late developer intellectually as in other
ways, Charles began to form a series of friendships with
much older men, who could offer the experienced, at
times spiritual help he needed in coming to terms with his
unique fate. The Conservative politician Lord Butler – by
then Master of Trinity, Charles's Cambridge college – was
one of the first. Another, less well-known mentor at that
time was Sir John Miller, an elderly crown equerry, who
first encouraged the Prince to go hunting despite the controversy it was bound to cause. Then came John Higgs,
secretary of the Duchy of Cornwall, who shared his interest in community architecture and organic farming.
When Higgs was suddenly struck down by cancer in 1986,
the Prince romantically and emotionally knighted him on
his death-bed.

In their different ways, all these sage older men perceived that their prime duty was to boost Charles's shaky self-confidence. No one has been more instrumental in that process, however, than Laurens van der Post, to whom Charles had been close for several years before it became common knowledge. It was to this contemplative but very worldly figure that Charles took his only previous philosophical enthusiasm, the works of E.F. (*Small is Beautiful*) Schumacher. Van der Post managed to dovetail Schumacher with the teachings of Jung, with a force which is still present in Charles's every public pronouncement. Under the heading of inner-city blight or the disasters of post-war British planning, there will always be a reference to the mutual support offered within a *small* community to the less talented or fortunate; and an exaltation of the individual qualities of every human soul. Now knighted for his pains, and a godfather to Prince William, van de Post did not just help Charles come to terms with the role to which he was born, and begin to see ways in which he could make the most of it. He developed his natural interest in the troubled world around him and encouraged him to explore the alternative values on offer. Above all, he helped Charles to reconcile the Prince he had learnt to be with the true self he was only now discovering.

Charles's *curriculum vitae* to the age of thirty amounted to a combination of royal tradition and princely "firsts" which were little to do with his own interests and inclinations, more evidence of his ambition to carve his own niche in history. Charles was the first heir to the throne in British history to have won a university degree; the first to have captained his own ship; the first to have flown helicopters and supersonic jets; the first to have made a parachute jump and trained as a commando. He was the first English Prince of Wales in seven-and-a-half centuries to have taken the trouble to learn a bit of Welsh.

This was the somewhat gung-ho track record he brought to his first conversations with van der Post, who quickly sensed the thoughtful spirit behind the obligatory public braggadocio and helped Charles to discover the inner man it had been obscuring. The results, in the last five years, have been dramatic. As the proverbial frog turned into a prince, so the Prince now discovered the freedom to turn into a human being.

THREE

The "Loony" Prince

"As far as I can make out, I'm about to
become a Buddhist monk, or live halfway
up a mountain, or only eat grass. I'm not
quite as bad as that."

IN BETTER days for the Glasgow shipbuilding industry,
James MacDonald and Wallace McCracken could have
expected a lifetime of steady employment in the Govan
shipyards beside which they grew up. In 1983, both in
their early twenties, both unemployed, tired of scratching
around for ways to make ends meet, they put their heads
together to find a way of improving on the dole queue.
The only expanding industry, it seemed, was the local
bakery, which had just invested millions in new plant to
feed the growing demand from supermarkets and chain
stores. Where, it occurred to these two enterprising young
men, in the dehumanized era of market forces, did the
corner shops now get their bread from? There, they
suspected, was "a gap we could fill."

All they possessed was a hotplate, a second-hand mixer,
an empty garage on an industrial estate and the friendly
help of a retired baker. With no capital at all, they
managed to produce only crumpets, pancakes and potato
scones. Things were not looking too promising until the
day they heard through the Glasgow district council of the

"bursaries" dished out, unlikely though it seemed, by the Prince of Wales. With a grant of £1,000 MacDonald and McCracken were able to buy the ovens they needed to bake profitable bread. Five years later, in 1988, Macs' Bakery was producing 7.5 million potato scones a year and twenty-one other lines from coffee biscuits to pizzas; with contracts from over 250 corner shops and an increasing number of supermarkets, they were employing thirty-five staff, contemplating the export market and confident of achieving their 1992 target of a £5 million annual turnover well ahead of schedule.

In 1987, as a gesture of gratitude, the two "Macs" repaid their £1,000 grant in the form of a donation to the Prince's Youth Business Trust, which had by now superseded the Youth Business Initiative, the pilot scheme of which they had been pioneer beneficiaries. Formally launched at the end of 1986, the PYBT is but one of a labyrinthine chain of enterprises conceived and launched by the Prince of Wales in his personal mission to the disadvantaged young people of Britain.

No. 8 Bedford Row, an anonymous building in the elegant hear of London's Bloomsbury, is today the national headquarters of an array of princely charities and trusts which have mushroomed in bewildering profusion since it all began, almost by accident, towards the end of 1972. One afternoon that December George Pratt, deputy chief probation officer for London, was pleasantly surprised to received a telephone call from Buckingham Palace. Pratt had been making a series of television and radio appearances to launch a new scheme of community service for young people in trouble with the law; on the line was the Prince of Wales's then private secretary, Squadron-Leader David Checketts, to say that the Prince had seen one of his broadcasts and was wondering if there was anything he could do to help.

Pratt was flattered but dubious. He knew from bitter professional experience that new community service schemes tended to complicate and obscure existing ones –

that layer upon layer of bureaucracy had to be consulted, informed, cajoled and convinced before any such projects could be launched. It was a lesson the Prince was soon to learn for himself, to his increasing annoyance.

But Pratt agreed to organize an exploratory meeting at the Palace, which was duly attended a month later by representatives of the probation service, the church, the social services, welfare organizations and police. From the chair Prince Charles, just twenty-four and still in the thick of his Service career, made an impassioned speech about the ideals of public service instilled in him at school and in the forces. He said how impressed he had recently been by seeing young army NCOs taking on responsibilities beyond their years. Surely there was some role the heir to the throne could play in helping delinquent youth?

More study meetings followed and the group, as Pratt had feared, grew larger. It was thought prudent to co-opt social scientists and officials from the Department of Education, the Home Office, the Welsh Office and the Scottish Office. The Prince was gently steered away from all notions of traditional youth work, with which it was thought he should not be seen to interfere. Nor was an incentive scheme like his father's, the Duke of Edinburgh's Awards, deemed appropriate. That was designed to inspire the already motivated to greater heights of accomplishments; Pratt and the Prince were at once in their determination that this scheme should somehow motivate the unmotivated.

At first, it did not occur to Charles to lend his support other than anonymously. Few beneficiaries of the first three years of pilot schemes, all of which he personally vetted and approved, knew of his involvement. In Cornwall a local policeman reported that a gang of unruly kids were plaguing his life; if they formed themselves into a lifesaving team, they were told to their astonishment, the police would pay all their expenses. In London a group of school drop-outs, up before the juvenile courts, expressed a desire to go camping; little did they know, as they returned dutifully to school, that the tents, pots and pans which had granted their wish had been borrowed from the army by the Prince of Wales, nor that the £37.50 each received to cover their rail fares were among the first grants to be handed out by the fledgling Prince's Trust.

It did not become so in name until 1976, by when Charles's secret had begun to filter out. He had hoped to remain in the background, selecting beneficiaries and monitoring their progress – but soon, through his young shyness, he began to see how encouraged these youngsters were by a princely handshake and a few words of royal encouragement. It still took some arm-twisting from Pratt. But by the Queen's silver jubilee year of 1977 the Prince's Trust was a fast-growing full-time operation, with seven regional committees distributing some £35,000 to 250 projects under the watchful eye of Pratt, its voluntary, unpaid founder-director.

That year also saw Charles take on the chairmanship of his mother's Silver Jubilee Appeal. Few yet perceived him as a social worker *extraordinaire*; despite a mention of the Prince's Trust in a rare speech in the House of Lords, it was as yet all rather hairy-chested stuff about the great outdoors, which scarcely struck a chord with the majority of young Britons. Even Charles's televised speech launching the Queen's Appeal had to be rewritten, after the few young people on his advisory committee had grimaced at his hearty references to Outward Bound-style ideals and the joys of community service. After all the euphoria, however, the street parties, the pervasive feeling that communities had not felt so united since the Blitz, the Prince was able to announce in the summer of 1978 that more than £16 million had been raised – an astonishing sum from a nation of only some fifty-six million people. The resulting fund was merged with that still invested from forty years before, when King George v's silver jubilee had equally remarkably raised £1 million from a country in the grip of depression – and the Prince of Wales became chairman of the Royal Jubilee Trusts.

Ten years on, this is but one of an ever-changing array of names on the discreet plaque in Bedford Row which conceals a veritable hothouse of charitable hard work in the Prince's name. The Queen had asked that the money raised by her Silver Jubilee Appeal be used "to help young people help others"; the interest on this huge investment is now devoted, under the Prince's personal supervision, to financing a variety of different initiatives reflecting his own personal ideals. The two "Macs" are but one example among tens of thousands of otherwise bereft young people who have been given a start in life by the Prince of Wales.

But the time-frame of their success story marks a period during which the Prince has been considered something of a crank by his future subjects and dubbed a "loony" by the popular press. Even his private secretary, Edward Adeane, astonishingly resigned his post in 1985 – thus breaking a century of unbroken royal service by his family – because of the new breed of advisers with whom Charles had begun to surround himself. From a brash young community architect called Rod Hackney to the insect expert Miriam Rothschild, they represented, to the old guard at the Palace, some alarming new streaks in the Prince: a tendency to espouse minority causes, to pursue "lunatic fringe" interests in his off-duty hours and to spurn the advice of those urging him down more ortho-dox channels. Charles had begun to ignore Adeane's advice so consistently and so determinedly that he felt obliged to quit the royal service, thus depriving himself of the certainty of becoming private secretary to the mon-arch, like his father and grandfather before him.

Though Charles has since stuck to his ideological guns and developed most of these private interests into con-structive public passions, the Prince is deeply hurt to this day by the carping. His defence mechanisms can be heard springing up like steel walls at the beginning of every major public pronouncement he makes, in an attempt to defuse the criticism before it rains down. In a disastrous outpouring to Andrew Stephen of the *Sunday Times* in

August 1985, he said: "You know, as far as I can make out, I'm about to become a Buddhist monk, or live halfway up a mountain, or only eat grass. I'm not quite as bad as that. Or quite as extreme." The following year, in the thick of architectural controversy, he began a speech by anticipating "a barrage of criticism that I don't know what I'm talking about; that I have got my facts wrong and clearly haven't done enough research ... [that] I am a deranged masochist." In 1987, accused of surrounding himself with architectural gurus, he snapped back: "If I had sat at these people's feet as often as disciples are supposed to do, I would probably end up by developing architectural haemorrhoids. Anyway, here I am: robed, sandalled, shaven and with a rather faraway look in my eyes."

By 1988, however, these self-conscious preambles had taken on a new edge of self-confidence, especially on the subject of architecture:

> Having been told so firmly what was good for them, what was fashionable and intellectual acceptable, what was artistically correct and contemporary, most of us were cowed into feeling that we were frightful reactionary imbeciles even to consider that what was being produced was often nonsense and thoroughly inhuman. Now, however, there is a growing awareness that it is all right not to be ashamed of such feelings.

The process which turned the apologetic Prince into the new, unashamed "Prince of Conscience," as he was dubbed by a 1988 BBC-TV profile, is the substance of the later chapters of this book. Back in 1985, it seemed to be a point he might never reach.

Long before outraging British architects (and feeling free, in his new-found self-confidence, to pre-empt the nation's public planning procedures), the Prince had confounded medical orthodoxy by championing various brands of "alternative" or "complementary" medicine, which professional institutions under royal patronage had fought for centuries to outlaw. The royal family has long been devoted to the principles and practice of homoeopathy; even today, to the hollow laughter of the British Medical Association, there is a court homoeopathist – about as contemporary a figure as the Poet Laureate or the Master of the Queen's Music, conspicuously unproductive courtiers whose annual stipend is paid in barrels of sack. But Charles's espousal of medical unorthodoxy in 1982 seemed almost wilfully eccentric. It was an intriguing pre-echo of his subsequent assault on British architects when the Prince, invited to address the BMA's 150th anniversary dinner, chose to abuse their hospitality with a few tart remarks:

> I have often thought that one of the less attractive traits of various professional bodies and institutions is the deeply ingrained suspicion and outright hostility which can exist towards anything unorthodox or unconventional. I suppose that human nature is such that we are frequently prevented from seeing that what is taken as today's unorthodoxy is probably going to be tomorrow's convention. . . . I would suggest that the whole imposing edifice of modern medicine for all its breathtaking success, is like the celebrated Tower of Pisa, slightly off balance. It is frightening how dependent upon drugs we are all becoming and how easy it is for doctors to prescribe them as the universal panacea for all our ills. Wonderful as many of them are, it should be still more widely stressed by doctors that the health of human beings is often determined by their behaviour, their food and the nature of their environment.

Quoting Paracelsus, the "renowned sixteenth-century healer," as a previous champion of unorthodoxy, Charles was on a high. Having found, as he thought, a charger fit to ride him a crusade, he proceeded to open an "alternative," drug-free cancer clinic in Bristol, the Bristol Centre, which proposed to treat the disease via diet, positive thinking and "support therapy." Orthodox cancer specialists wrote outraged letters to *The Times*, and indeed to the Prince, eliciting a highly defensive, even apologetic reply.

Such is the power of royal patronage that the BMA, mean-while, felt obliged to institute an official inquiry into "complementary" forms of medicine, the case for which was found distinctly unproven in its 1986 report. Some "alternative" treatments – herbalism, for instance – were denounced as "positively harmful."

Thrashing around in his search for a mission, Charles had rather publicly burnt his fingers. Little more was heard from him on the subject of alternative medicine, though a defiance of orthodoxy arises to this day in his more philosophical public pronouncements. The famous Harvard speech of 1986, for instance, after a rambling celebration of Greek, Roman, Judaic and Hebrew think-ing, climaxed with the suggestion that "the natural science of psychology" be introduced to university curricula (where, of course, it had held a respected place for many years). In a barely intelligible coda, filtered through his embryonic understanding of the teachings of Jung, the Prince bared his tortured and cliched soul:

> We are, to all intents and purposes, embarked upon a per-ilous journey. The potential destruction of our natural earth; the despoliation of the great rain forests (with all the untold consequences of such a disaster); the exploration of space; greater power than we have ever had or our nature can per-haps handle – all confronts us for what could be a final settle-ment. But if we could start again to re-educate ourselves, the result need not be so frightening. Over Apollo's great temple was the sign "Man know thyself.' . . . Could man at last, begin to learn to know himself?

It was small wonder that another speech that autumn, in which he had talked at some length to rural Canadians about "the mirror of the soul" – a Jungian reference which few of his listeners grasped – was pilloried as "a load of mystic mumbo-jumbo delivered to a bemused bunch of lumberjacks." There was not, as it happened, a single lumberjack in his audience; but the Prince's impenetrable reflections were way beyond the travelling press, his attendant tribunes of the British people. Charles has never again made so revealing an exposition of his developing personal ideals. Instead, he much more sensibly began to put them to practical use. In this sense, 1986 was to prove a crucial year of transition.

Thanks, in the public mind, more to his wife than Charles himself, the involvement of leading rock stars that summer lent the Prince's Trust some glamour it sorely needed. Its tenth birthday concert at Wembley Arena on 20 June 1986 raised more than £1 million, given that stars of the order of Mick Jagger and Elton John, David Bowie and Paul McCartney, Tina Turner and Rod Stewart, Eric Clapton and George Michael all gave their services free (as they have done again since, in what seems to be becoming an annual event). But the mosaic of Charles's other preoccupations, in the public mind, remained unhappily rooted in abstruse reflections across the Atlantic and unappreciated, little publicized "good works" at home.

The Prince's Committee, based in Cardiff, continued its painstaking, piecemeal work to improve the environment of Wales, offering grants to needy cases and awards to those who used them best, to the tune of some £150,000 a year. Charles has an especially soft spot for the Committee, one of the first charities he founded, which he has now neatly dovetailed into his broader campaigns in the field of conservation. All year round, then as now, he made a point of paying regular visits to projects fostered by the Committee – as indeed he promoted the interests of another of his earliest passions, the United World Colleges, in virtually every country to which his travels took him.

When Charles inherited its presidency from Lord Mountbatten in 1978, UWC was a group of three sixth-form colleges in Wales, Singapore and Canada seeking to promote international peace and understanding by educating young people of all races, nationalities and creeds side by side. Community service takes the place of sport, an international baccalaureate that of more conventional national examinations. A major role had been played in the colleges' foundation, in 1962, by Kurt Hahn, founder of Gordonstoun, whose influence still permeates the Prince's every public purpose. By implementing Hahn's fundamental thesis – that prejudices evaporate in disciplined communities facing constant challenges and occasional stress – UWC aims to raise generations of "multipliers" to carry its message throughout the world. The emphasis of that message, in the words of the Prince of Wales, is on "the things which unite us all rather than those which divide us."

His ten years as president have seen UWC's operations double in size, with three more colleges added to the chain – in Italy, the USA and Venezuela – entirely thanks to his efforts. A visit to Caracas in 1978 was typical of his work as a determined lobbyist of governments and philanthropists; the Prince's request for a second meeting with the President of Venezuela resulted in the opening of the Simon Bolivar College of Agriculture eight years later. The Armand Hammer United World College of the West, in Montezuma, New Mexico, opened its doors in a former hotel in 1982, after Charles had convinced the elderly American tycoon that UWC's ideals would provide him with a fitting monument. The royal lobbying continues still, according to UWC's Director-General, Sir Ian Gourlay, in Indian, China, Hong Kong, Australia and sundry Third World countries.

Said the Prince on UWC's twenty-fifth anniversary in 1987:

> I believe firmly in a type of education which tries to encourage the development of self-reliant young men and women who are able to take the initiative when necessary, and who have the moral courage to stand up for those qualities of human decency and integrity which matter so much.

With growing self-awareness, he took the conscious risk of adding: "I am not in favour of an elite if it is solely based on birth and wealth, but I am certainly in favour if it is based on high standards which provide the student with a challenge that is really worthwhile."

Other interviews in previous years had shown Charles woefully paper-thin on the complex world issues which troubled his caring heart. To the popular press, it all added to the picture of an eccentric soul in torment, as unsure of himself as of the world around him. In his own future kingdom, however, the Prince's pronounced practical streak was at last beginning to assert itself over his half-hatched metaphysics.

Nowhere, for instance, did the mockery have a hollower ring than around the hills and dales of the Duchy of Cornwall, where the Prince was known as an enlightened landlord who had stewarded long overdue reform of his massive estates. The man who was dubbed a crank for taking time off to share the rural tranquillity of his tenants was, in fact, fast becoming an authority on the complexities of agricultural development and land reform. In an era of rapid change which proved a daunting challenge to most of Britain's farming community, long set its ways, Charles spearheaded an enlightened response to the economic revolution of the time. The Duchy was to prove an unlikely springboard for the jump between the worlds of illusion and reality which Charles so badly needed to make.

He had good reason, besides, to want to learn how to milk cows. "Two-thirds of Prince Charles's income," as one Duchy executive was fond of saying, "comes out of the udder of a cow." Since he inherited it at the age of three, the Duchy of Cornwall has provided the Prince with his income, mercifully sparing him in recent years any part in the annual controversy about the Civil List (the public money voted by Parliament each year to maintain individual members of the royal family). As Duke of Cornwall, Charles pockets the net profit of this massive enterprise – these days averaging towards £2 million per annum – though he surrenders one-quarter to the Treasury as a voluntary form of income tax.

In 1987, the latest year for which figures are available, this gave him an income of £1.94 million out of which to finance his staff, residential expenses and running costs, not to mention everything else from his polo ponies to his wife's clothes. Though Diana has received financial help from her father, she too receives nothing from the Civil List. The Duchy also provides the Prince with a holiday home in the Scilly Isles, Tamarisk, which he very rarely uses; other members of the royal family, however, tend to use it to "get away from it all" more frequently than is realized.

Charles, like his mother, has a reputation as a penny-pincher, even though he was estimated by a *Money* magazine survey in March 1988 to be the fourteenth wealthiest individual in Britain, with assets totalling some £340 million. The Queen is reputed to walk around Buckingham Palace late at night, switching off all the lights before she goes to bed. Charles himself has been known to organize deals with fashion houses for Diana – the world's best mobile advertisement – to receive their wares at cost price.

He thought it might be "a good idea," he told the writer Penny Junor in 1987, "if the royal family stopped receiving money from the Civil List and lived instead on the income from the Crown Estates." His figures, of course, were wildly out, indicating either that he had been badly advised, or had spoken off the top of his head, without first doing his homework. Statistics issued next day by the Treasury showed that Charles had not taken into account the "hidden' expenses of the monarchy, such as the upkeep of the royal flight, the royal yacht and the royal train, not to mention all the Queen's horses and all the Queen's men, which between them bring the total cost of the monarchy to the British taxpayer to some £30 million, rather than the £4 million of Charles's estimate.

When it comes to running his own business, the Prince is more careful with his figures. He is also concerned to run the source of his income as a philanthropic business, with attention to the needs and rights of his tenant-farmers as much as the maximization of his assets. The Duchy of Cornwall now comprises some 126,000 acres of property in twenty counties, 70,000 of them farmland. The Prince is landlord, for instance, of 50,000 acres in the Forest of Dartmoor; 3,000 acres of woodland; 1,500 dwellings in London and the country; office and shop investments; a large number of small leased properties – garages, school sites, golf courses – and such landmarks as Dartmoor Prison and the Oval cricket ground. The Duchy owns 230 miles of foreshore and 14,000 acres of fundus. There are 240 farms ranging from ten-acre holdings on the Scilly Isles to 900 acres in Dorset and 1,600 on Dartmoor. With 2,400 tenancies in all, it provides employment for some 700 people.

Like many royal institutions, the Duchy had lagged behind the times for decades, taking little note of the "second agricultural revolution" which followed the Second World War. Asset management – a grim necessity for most of Britain's larger landowners in an era of agrarian economic reform – was a concept unknown to the Duchy until 1972, when Sir Anthony Gray gave up managing the estates of the wealthiest of Oxford colleges, Christ Church, to take its creaking machinery in hand.

Gray saw his central task as the establishment of an aggressive investment fund, to secure a larger, more stable income for the Prince, while maintaining his reputation as a responsible landlord whose property was conscientiously maintained and whose tenants were decently treated. Over the ensuing decade, the sprawling Duchy's capital investment was concentrated into farmland in the southwest of England, while its extensive holdings in the Kennington area of South London were strengthened. Younger and more business-minded land "stewards" (or agents) were appointed, surplus properties were sold off and rents increased – though still carefully held at comparatively moderate levels – as a mini-boom resulted from, Britain's accession to the European Economic Community. By the time Prince Charles felt the need for a country house – having spurned the offer of Chevening, in Kent, now made over to the Foreign Secretary – the Duchy was able to buy him one in the shape of Highgrove House.

Highgrove proved a base from which Charles could, as he devoutly wished, intensify his interest in the Duchy. Until the Prince left the navy his tours of inspection had necessarily been sporadic, rather formal affairs – lightning visits, primarily to see and be seen. Now he could afford the luxury of spending whole days in one area, taking lunch on one farm, tea on another, inspecting crops on a third, newly renovated buildings on a fourth. Some of the more antique privileges conferred on him by the Duchy, meanwhile, were reformed at his specific request. Proceeds from the ancient tradition of *Bona Vacantia*, whereby the Duke inherited the estates of those dying intestate and without next-of-kin, were devoted instead to the Duke of Cornwall's Benevolent Fund. A pension fund was set up for Duchy staff. The Prince Council, the body of eminent advisers on Duchy policy, was meanwhile rejuvenated; among those to join it was John Higgs, Estate Bursar of Exeter College, Oxford, a friend of Gray's who was soon to become very close to the Prince.

In 1981, on Gray's retirement, Higgs took over as the Duchy's Secretary and Keeper of the Records. A former agrarian officer for the United Nations, his special interest was in rural development. But Higgs was also an expert in estate management, a practising farmer, and a cannily wise man whose thinking dovetailed with Charles's emergent philosophy. During his five-year stewardship, the modernizing of the Duchy continued apace. The commercial management approach was intensified, investment policy overhauled and internal administrative machinery streamlined. Under an investment policy adopted in 1984, more sales of assets (especially in Kennington) took place, to swell the investment fund, while the Duchy purchased new property in London, Southern England and – at the Prince of Wales's special request –

Wales. For years there had been criticism that Charles owned no land, let alone a home, in his principality. Now, as Duke of Cornwall, he was the proud possessor of 700 acres at Boverton in the Vale of Glamorgan, devoted primarily to beef and corn, which the Duchy runs as a partnership with a local farmer, Michael Price.

Today the Duchy is a thriving business, run very much like any other company with extensive assets. The Prince, or Duke, functions as chairman, with the Secretary as managing director, and a board comprised of non-executive directors (the Prince's Council) headed by the Lord Warden of the Stannaries (at present Sir Nicholas Henderson, the former British Ambassador to Washington). Since January 1987 the Secretary has been David Landale, the former chairman of Timber Growers (UK) Ltd, which represents the interests of private woodland owners throughout Britain. Its offices are a handsome Pennethorne building in Buckingham Gate, directly opposite the Palace, as well as six regional headquarters in London, the south-west and the Scilly Isles. As part of the Crown, the Duchy is subject to Acts of Parliament only if specifically provided; it is subject, for instance, to the Agricultural Holdings Act, but not to compulsory purchase.

For over a century, its activities have been controlled by a sequence of special legislation known as the Management Acts. The most recent, the 1982 Management Act, gave the Duchy (in the summary of Martin Argles, acting Secretary after Higgs's death) "greater flexibility in the use of its capital." But life "beyond the law," he argued, is not always as attractive as it might sound:

> The Duchy has to abide by the spirit of the law, but cannot benefit from the formal appeal procedures available to the private citizen.... Recent changes have made the Duchy subject to the Rents Act and to parts of the Town and Country Planning Acts. Until the latter change was made, the Duchy could not obtain a formal planning permission for

development of land before it sold; that made sales difficult to organize.

With the closure in 1984 of the Home Farm, Stoke Climsland in Cornwall, the Duchy parted with the last of its "model" farms, long used for training, teaching and experimentation. The following year, however, 420-acre Broadfield Farm, near Tetbury, was purchased and amalgamated with the 300 acres already adjoining Highgrove, which had hitherto been let to local farmers. The new 720-acre farm was recalled under the Prince's control: a manager was appointed and techniques such as organic farming introduced. Though it has become something of a bogey phrase to the Prince's critics, all "organic" farming really means is using no nitrogenous fertilizer and no herbicide or insecticide sprays; only 240 of Broadfield's acres are currently "going" organic, of which only fourteen have been officially classified as such by the agricultural authorities. The Highgrove enterprise, in which the Prince loves to get involved at weekends, is otherwise devoted mainly to dairy, beef, sheep and corn.

In 1987 Argles said:

> The Duchy is stronger today than twenty years ago. Its investment is better spread, its farms better equipped and repaired, its other property no longer poor. It is not so dependent on farm rents, which may be static or fall, for its income. But all concerned with it, whether as tenants, managers or outsiders, still have to come completely to terms with its present form.

Acknowledging recent unease among some Duchy tenants, especially about rent increases, he argues that the sudden change in 1984 from forty years of agricultural expansion to a policy of quotas, constriction and falling profits has been as traumatic for the Duchy as its tenants. "The Duchy," he says, "may be seen by some tenants as mainly responsible for the difficulties they face, whereas national policies are primarily to blame."

David Landale adds that current policy in Kennington is to dispose of properties in the domestic rented sector, as they become available, in favour of more ownership of commercial investment properties. One of his main headaches during 1988 was the Duchy's extensive conservation programme on Dartmoor, which was being undermined by the local practice of winter-feeding sheep on the moor, a gradual cause of damage to its ecological structure. Talks with local farmers were continuing through the summer, with "especial tact and diplomacy," but the Prince might have to consider banning farmers from leaving fodder on his property unless greater co-operation could be achieved before winter.

Charles, says Landale, is very much a "hands-on" Duke of Cornwall, interested in every aspect of the Duchy's work. He has now personally visited "virtually every one" of the farm tenancies throughout his massive estates. Says the Prince himself:

> This is a period of rapid change. The Duchy is not immune from this, and it has to take a business-like approach to the management of its assets and estates. But I am concerned that at the same time it should provide an example of the best kind of stewardship of the land. This means acting responsibly and sympathetically towards all those directly and indirectly concerned with the Duchy and towards its environment; and it means taking initiatives to help solve problems in housing, farming and employment which are intensified in this time of change. The Duchy is above all a landed estate and it will continue to be so. Its relationship with the people who work on its land is of paramount importance, and it is the farmer who is the backbone of the whole operation.

The Prince's supervision of the Duchy's reform, throughout his late twenties and thirties, was to pioneer his growing mastery of other areas of modern British and international life. Still, however, the frustrations of his position held him back. In the wake of the extraordinary success of the Live Aid concerts, which raised huge amounts of money in a bid to alleviate famine in Ethiopia and elsewhere, Prince Charles became an admirer and friend of the man who had inspired it all. "I wish I could be like Bob Geldof," he felt moved to say at the time – an honest, chance remark at a reception to a woman he had never met before. Since it became public three years later, the Prince's candour has been widely misunderstood.

Charles was not just expressing a wish to be hailed, like Geldof, as a champion of the oppressed, using his position to raise money from unlikely sources for the worthiest of causes – and, if only temporarily, actually to make an impact. He was again lamenting the inhibitions of his office – envying Geldof his freedom to cajole, bully, even insult and abuse politicians, including the Prime Minister herself, who chose to leave such problems to be tackled by caring citizens rather than government.

Charles must tread a middle course which draws attention to social problems, encourages individuals and the private sector to help, and fosters government aid wherever possible. It is not implicit criticism of government policy to show concern about the conditions of the less privileged; it *is* out of order, however, for him to talk of a "divided Britain," a "North-South gulf" in urgent need of government attention. As yet it has been the Prince's advisers rather than the man himself who have let slip such unfortunate asides. For it is, moreover, in the Prince's interests to stay on the right side of the Prime Minister; he or she, as will be seen, can do much to improve the Prince's lot and offer tantalizing scope for enhancing his role in the national life.

By the mid-1980s and his own mid-thirties, however, thanks to some false starts and a lousy press, the Prince of Wales had reached the low point of his personal graph of private unhappiness and public under-appreciation. The man with a new-found freedom to explore unfashionable ideas was again branded a "loony"; the Prince in search of a role himself believed, though few else did, that he had found it; and the bulk of his daily life was devoted to improving that of others. Just around the corner lay two developments which were to alter his public life entirely, giving it the shape and focus it so conspicuously lacked. That he possessed the wherewithal to seize those opportunities, and to run with them in style, is a tribute to all the agonies which had dogged his life hitherto. It was his own reward for the years of diligent study and troubled soul-searching.

For the strength of character which he now began to display had emerged despite – rather than thanks to – the traditions of his family and the circumstances of his upbringing. The positive sides of Charles's character seemed at times to be in open defiance of his genes. It was "extraordinary luck," a friend said to Lord Mountbatten, shortly before his death, that in Charles we had a Prince of Wales so conscientious, so responsible and so intent on making the best of his unenviable fate. "It's not luck at all," replied Mountbatten, the family historian. "It's a bloody miracle."

FOUR

A Palace Revolution

"I've learnt the way a monkey learns
– by watching its parents."

P RINCE Charles's great-grandfather, King George V,
once told his friend Lord Derby: "My father was
frightened of his mother, I was frightened of my father,
and I am damned well going to see to it that my children
are frightened of me."

Though no forerunner of Dr Spock, George was, in fact,
just reciting the existing royal rule-book – reiterating what
had through three generations become the standard royal
approach to the raising of children. Since the days of
Victoria and Albert royal offspring had been burdened
with impossibly demanding training programmes, well
away from the company of their peers, while expected in
private to be paragons of decorous virtue, seen but not
heard. Many, as a result, had gone right off the rails.

Life was always especially hard on the oldest boy,
groomed from birth to inherit the throne. The pattern
stopped only because Elizabeth II's father – a gentle-
hearted man with no sons to bully, anyway – was not born
to be King. Only the abdication of his brother thrust this
reluctant monarch on to the throne, quite unexpectedly,
when his elder daughter was already ten. By the time she

herself had children, Elizabeth had determined to do things differently.

With the strong support of her down-to-earth, no-nonsense husband – whose traditionalism has always been enlightened by a maverick, iconoclastic streak – the Queen planned what amounted to a quiet revolution in the upbringing of her children, especially the heir to the throne. Even before they were old enough, she had conceived the daring notion of sending them to school with other children, in the hope that they could grow up as "normally" as possible.

There were, as shall be seen, immense obstacles. And there were constitutionalists who advised against, arguing that members of the royal family neither can nor should attempt to lead "normal" lives – while duly commending the Queen's determination that Charles should, unlike herself, see as much as possible of the lives of other children his own age. But Elizabeth was adamant. The lessons of recent family history were awesome; and her own childhood, though a very happy one, had scarcely prepared her for what lay in store.

In the early years of her own reign, the Queen's sense of inadequacy to the task suddenly thrust upon her was capable of reducing her to tears. For the first ten years of her life, after all, there had been no prospect of her inheriting the throne; she was taught the decorum befitting a King's grand-daughter and niece, not the sophistication and know-how required of a King's daughter and heir. Even after her father's accession, when his daughter's prayers that he might yet have a son proved vain, King George VI thought *Punch* magazine the best way of introducing Elizabeth to political arguments and personalities. Occasionally he would mark an article for her to read in the Palace copy of *The Times*, in those days still a special edition printed on superior paper.

From the governess assigned to Elizabeth and her sister Margaret, the late Miss Marion Crawford ("Crawfie"), we have received a chatty and detailed account of the little Princesses' upbringing, which makes it clear that preparations for the burdens of monarchy were the last thing on the then Duke and Duchess of York's curriculum for their children. "I had the feeling," wrote Miss Crawford, "that the Duke and Duchess, most happy in their own married life, were not over concerned with the higher education of their daughters. They wanted most for them a really happy childhood, with lots of pleasant memories stored up against the days that might come out, and later, happy marriages." Even their grandfather, King George v, was bothered about little more than their handwriting. "For goodness sake," he told Crawfie, "teach Margaret and Lilibet to write a decent hand, that's all I ask you. None of my children could write properly. They all do it exactly the same way. I like a hand with some character in it." Their mother's aspirations for them summed up the Princesses' education: "To spend as long as possible in the open air, to enjoy to the full the pleasures of the country, to be able to dance and draw and appreciate music, to acquire good manners and perfect deportment, and to cultivate all the distinctively feminine graces."

After thirty-six years on the throne, however, Elizabeth has become the shrewdest and most deft of monarchs, inching the institution closer to its people while preserving the essential, almost mystical gulf between the two. As the Queen has seen eight prime ministers come and go, such skills have come to seem innate in her. They certainly owe little to the token lessons in the constitution which she started at the age of thirteen with Sir Henry Marten, Vice-Provost of Eton, and which became a correspondence course while she was sequestered at royal country residences during the war. Marten religiously imbued the teenage Princess with the precepts of the constitutional historian Walter Bagehot, on which George v had been raised. Bagehot's definition of the British constitutional monarchy – with its famous summary of the monarch's rights *vis-à-vis* the Prime Minister, "to be consulted, to encourage and to warn" – remains largely unchallenged. But the representative family monarchy of the later twentieth century, as acclaimed by it people in her silver jubilee year, 1977, is much more than the personal creation of Elizabeth II.

When pondering the education of their eldest son, the Queen and her husband pooled their own very different experiences, hers the traditionally sheltered royal education at the hands of governesses and tutors, his a disrupted progress through private schools in France, England, Germany and Scotland. They were determined to make a bold departure from the pattern of private tutors and isolated home education established by their forebears; and their every effort with the young Charles was directed towards it. The young Duke of Cornwall at first showed little of the self-confidence needed by one of his rank to survive in the brutal, amoral world of young schoolboys away from home. But so do many sons of the privileged. Elizabeth and Philip were determined that the heir to the throne should be educated outside his home, in the company of other boys his own age, from the earliest possible moment.

It had never before been considered possible. The education of Princes of Wales has throughout British history provided a forum for argument, experiment and even intrigue, resulting as often as not in unhappiness and failure. From the time of Edward I, who was sent to France to be educated, most monarchs have tried to create super-monarchs in their own image; others, such as the Hanoverians, have been more intent on defusing the threat posed to their rule by their own heir. But it was the last hundred years which provided the most instructive examples, all too familiar to Queen Victoria's two great-great-grandchildren in the 1950s. Elizabeth II and her consort were above all concerned to learn from the mistakes made by Victoria and hers.

"Who Should Educate the Prince of Wales?" was the title of a provocative and anonymous pamphlet published

in 1843, when Bertie, Prince of Wales – the future King
Edward VII – was just two years old. Bertie's mother,
Queen Victoria, was as intent as the pamphleteer and his
wide readership on producing a model prince – ideally, to
her, a working model of her beloved husband Albert. The
Queen was aware of the inadequacies of her own education, thanks in part to the plain speaking of her uncle, the
King of Hanover: "She was more ignorant on her accession than any girl of her age in the world." But she was
more anxious, as were her subjects, to eradicate the memory of George III's lecherous sons, her other uncles, of
whom she shared Shelley's view ("the dregs of their dull
race") rather than Lord Melbourne's ("jolly fellows"). The
plans she and Albert laid for their son's upbringing, even
before he had been born, were partly by way of atone-
ment. More important, they constituted an elaborate
effort to resecure a shaky, discredited monarchy and to lay
the foundations for its survival into a more democratic
age.

The educational treadmill they devised for poor Bertie
was founded on a fundamental misreading of history,
swallowed wholesale from their overtrusted German
confidant, Baron Christian von Stockmar. He persuaded
Victoria and Albert that the mistakes of George III's sons
were caused by their inadequate education, and that this
had been largely responsible for the gradual shift of executive power from the monarch to the monarch's ministers.
In fact, their education had been excellent: George IV, if
not William IV, was one of Britain's most cultured kings.
The alteration in the unwritten constitution owed much
more to the industrial revolution, and the nineteenth-
century electoral reforms which followed it, than to the
character of the sovereign. It was the growth of diverse
political parties, and the alternatives thus available to a
more broadly enfranchised nation, which forced the monarchy into its now familiar non-political role. The alternative, and the only way to retain executive state powers,
was for the King to identify himself with political factions,

which would have ensured his downfall with theirs. He could not, as Sir Lewis Namier observed, "in turn captain opposite teams."

The uneducated Victoria was plainly surprised by the limits to her constitutional powers and constantly attempted to exceed them. Prince Albert was himself a man of considerable ability, whose intellect and imagination were quite the match of most of his wife's ministers. He was, as Lord John Russell put it, "an informal and potent member of all Cabinets", and he believed that his son would need similar qualities to ensure the monarchy's survival. So, with Stockmar, Prince Albert personally devised a comprehensive programme designed to drum them into him.

At the age of seven, the Prince was handed from the nursery to a formidable team of tutors. Their principal, a thirty-year-old Eton master aptly named Henry Birch, was instructed quite simply to fashion an "executive Governor of the State . . . the repository of all the moral and intellectual qualities by which it is held together, and under the guidance of which it advances in the great path of civilization." Lessons in the Palace lasted at first six, then seven, hours a day, six days a week. Bertie worked longer hours, and enjoyed shorter holidays, than any of his schoolboy contemporaries. Birch had orders to ensure that he was thoroughly exhausted by the end of each day; among other physical pursuits, he was drilled daily by an army sergeant to deflect his budding skills at dancing. Even the tutors began to think the regime too demanding. "You will wear him out too early. . . . Make him climb trees! Run! Leap! Row!" the French master, Dr Voisin, urged Birch's successor. "In many things, savages are much better educated than we are." But Albert and Stockmar would have none of it. The results were disastrous.

Before he was ten, the Prince was on the edge of a nervous breakdown. Days of utter lethargy began to follow a few of intense activity. There were outbursts of destructive rage. He would stand in a corner screaming and stamping, or hurl things against walls and through windows, before falling into a state of complete physical collapse. His father devised a series of punishments for this behaviour, but none, however severe, could curb it.

The young Bertie's world was entirely one of adults. At one stage he was sent to attend meetings of Pop, the Eton debating society, but behaved with such boorishness, and displayed such ignorance, that he was quickly withdrawn from the society of his fellows. When he was finally sent out into the world, to Oxford, his father was insistent that "his position and life must be different from that of other undergraduates." He wrote the distinctive gown and gold-tufted cap of the nobleman; professors came to his home to teach him and six handpicked aristocrats; students had to rise whenever he entered a lecture hall or common room. Prince Albert at this time dismissed him as "a thorough and cunning lazybones," and Queen Victoria even told friends that he was mentally deficient. But his tutors found in him powers of application, and qualities of openness and honesty, which his regimented life had all but suppressed.

Thanks to a liberating tour of America in 1860 and a happier time at Cambridge, Bertie gradually began to escape the shadows of his youth and adolescence. He grew from an overweight, oversexed, utterly repressed Prince of Wales into a mature, diplomatic and immensely popular King. For over forty years as the pillar of a glittering London court, in the absence of his eternally mourning mother, he eroded memories of the gambling and marital scandals with which his youth had besmirched the monarchy. On his thirtieth birthday, soon after giving evidence in the Mordaunt divorce case, he lay apparently dying from typhoid; his sudden recovery six weeks later had the nation, surprised at its own fickleness, demanding a day of national rejoicing. Bertie's innate strength of character finally overcame his childhood brainwashing – ensuring his security and success, thirty years later, on the throne. Some legacies of his upbringing, notably those fits of rage, never left him. But he was aware of it and took pains to see that his own sons were spared such suffering.

King Edward VII was a grandfather four years before he acceded to the throne. As Prince of Wales, he had had to cope with his widowed mother's intransigence when setting about the education of his own heir. His initial plan was to send Prince Albert Victor ("Eddy" to his family) to public school and university, and his second son George to Dartmouth and a naval career. But at only seven months Prince Eddy was diagnosed a weak baby and soon showed himself a backward child. The tutor engaged by their father, the Rev. John Neale Dalton (father of the Labour politician Hugh Dalton), found that only Prince George's company could inspire Eddy's constitutional lethargy to any interest in anything. He advised that they should on no account be separated.

Their grandmother had set her heart on sending Prince Eddy to Wellington, a school with a military slant of which the Prince of Wales was a governor. She was content for George to enter the navy, but Eddy was to be King and should not be allowed to acquire the rough habits and nationalistic attitudes of Service life. It took all her son's and Dalton's ingenuity to dissuade her; the Palace memos that flew on this subject are themselves full of cautionary tales for anyone contemplating the education of a monarch. The Prince of Wales's first concern was that his sons should grow up, unlike him, with people rather than books, out of doors more than in classrooms, left to find their own levels rather than be programmed for perfection. But thanks to Dalton, he was now even more intent on keeping them together. Victoria was coaxed into permitting them both to attend Dartmouth "as an experiment."

King George V later recalled:

It never did me any good to be a prince, I can tell you, and many was the time I wished I hadn't been. [Dartmouth] was a pretty tough place and, so far from making allowance

for our disadvantages, the other boys made a point of taking
it out on us, on the grounds that they'd never be able to do
it later on. There was a lot of fighting among the cadets, and
the rule was that if challenged you had to accept. So they
used to make me go up and challenge the bigger boys – I was
awfully small then – and I'd get a hiding time and again. . . .

It may have made a man of George, but it just about
destroyed poor Eddy. Dalton reported to the Prince of
Wales that Eddy "fails not in one or two subjects, but in
all." His "abnormally dormant" disposition made it
impossible for him "to fix his attention to any given subject for more than a few minutes consecutively." Even that
was only achieved thanks to the reassuring presence of his
young brother. Plans to part their ways were again abandoned, and Eddy was sent to join George aboard HMS
Bacchante. Between 1879 and 1892, accompanied by Dalton and a team of tutors specially chosen to assist his
backwardness, Eddy joined George on three extended
world cruises, the one still fading away, the other growing
to the full flush of manhood. Those years, wrote King
George V's biographer, Harold Nicolson, developed in
him "a quality more forceful than ordinary manliness – a
categorical sense of duty . . . which became the fly-wheel
of his life."

In 1892 the brothers' paths did at last part. After a brief
sojourn together in France, George was back in the navy
as a midshipman, while Eddy was being crammed for
Cambridge. "I do not think he can possible derive much
benefit," the head tutor reported to Dalton. "He hardly
knows the meaning of the words 'to read.'" After Cambridge, Eddy served a bored term in the Hussars, then
began to devote what energies he had to a life of somewhat
scandalous dissipation; to this day, theories survive that
the heir to the throne was Jack the Ripper (or that the
Ripper was a royal surgeon acting on the Prince's behalf,
to silence the friends of a prostitute he had made pregnant). For once, Queen Victoria and the Prince of Wales

were agreed: his only chance of salvation was "a good sensible wife with some considerable character." She was found in Princess May of Teck, to whom Prince Eddy proposed in December 1891. A month later, aged twenty-seven, he was dead of pneumonia.

For all his lack of promise, Prince Albert Victor in death stirred his family and the nation to paroxysms of grief. His brother George, robbed of the only human being with whom he could enjoy an absolutely equal friendship, was desolated. "No two brothers could have loved each other more than we did," he wrote to his mother, Queen Alexandra. "Alas! It is only now that I have found out how deeply I have loved him." George's devastation was compounded by the fact that he was now heir to the throne and would have to abandon his naval career for a study of the constitution. His standard of education, as he himself readily admitted, was "below that of the average country gentleman educated at a public school." The navy had given him a strict sense of duty, orderly habits, a strong instinct for command and obedience and a deep feeling for conservative orthodoxy. But he was woefully ignorant, for instance, of contemporary domestic and foreign politics; his main interests were yachting, shooting, stamp-collecting and the management of the Sandringham estates. Even after falling in love with and marrying his brother's fiancée, Princess May (who later became Queen Mary), he remained emotionally immature.

His father came to the rescue. Edward VII took a great delight in endowing his virtuous son with all the fatherly companionship he himself had been denied. "We are more like brothers than father and son," he wrote to him. He made George, once Prince of Wales, privy to all state secrets – again a reversal of his own parents' policy – and instructed him in the ways of the world. But he could do nothing about that emotional deficiency. As a result, King George V conspicuously failed to recreate this happy and productive relationship with his own children.

Throughout his life, King George V treated his family as

if it were a ship's company, of which he was both master and martinet. His eldest son, when Duke of Windsor, recalled in his memoirs:

> We were, in fact, figuratively speaking, always on parade, a fact that he would never allow us to forget. If we appeared before him with our Navy lanyards a fraction of an inch out of place, or with our dirks or our sporrans awry, there would be an outburst worthy of the quarter-deck of a warship. Another greeted the appearance of one of us – it may well have been me – with hands stuffed into trouser pockets. Lala [their nanny] was immediately summoned and ordered to sew up the pockets of our sailor suits, a royal command which, despite some inward reservations, she did not dare to disobey.

The King deeply detested change and decreed that what had been good enough for him would be good enough for his sons. A senior tutor, H.P. Hansell, was therefore engaged to prepare Prince Edward and Prince Albert (known to their family as David and Bertie, later respectively King Edward VIII and King George VI) for entry to Dartmouth. Hansell urged that they be sent to preparatory school, where, he argued, they would benefit from the stimulus of competition and gain valuable early experience of community life. "My brother and I", George replied, "never went to preparatory school. The Navy will teach David all he needs to know."

This time it was the younger brother who lagged behind. Prince Edward, though slight, was physically robust; his natural charm combined with his quick brain to ensure easy success. Prince Albert was more diffident, suffered from a stammer and was invariably bottom of his class. "One could wish," wrote his tutor to the King, "that he had more of Prince Edward's keenness and application." King George VI's biographer, Sir John Wheeler-Bennett, quotes a contemporary's judgement that "it was like comparing an ugly duckling with a cock pheasant." Through a characteristic effort of will, however, Bertie later began to make up lost ground, and was to enjoy a happy and successful naval career after his elder brother had been diverted to training for kingship.

Edward was sent to France and Germany, to learn their languages and study their politics, and thence, reluctantly, to Oxford. At Magdalen he insisted on living in his own rooms in college – to prove a happy precedent for his great-nephew, Prince Charles – and was soon known around the university as "the Pragger-Wagger." He beagled, kept a string of polo ponies, played roulette and frequented the college bar. This routine Edward recalled in his memoirs as "tranquil, sober and serious" days. "Bookish he will never be," reported the college president, Sir Herbert Warren, to the King, "not a Beauclerk, still less a British Solomon." George V was not in the least concerned.

Edward VIII, in fact, seemed in later life to consider education a positive disadvantage for a prince. Remembering how little he learnt from his tutor, Mr Hansell, and being "unable to recall anything brilliant or original that he ever said," the Duke of Windsor commented: "No doubt, in view of the restraints laid upon the Monarchy, this was all for the best. To have put a Prince in the direct line of succession under a bold and opinionated teacher might well have led to the one conflict with which the constitutional system cannot cope." At least Oxford taught him something of his fellow-man. "All the time," according to Warren's report, "he was learning more and more every day of men, gauging character, watching its play, getting to know what Englishmen are like, both individually and in the mass. . . . " This stood him in good stead at Dartmouth, where he was mercilessly ragged. The other cadets were fond of dyeing his hair red, and on one occasion "guillotined" him in a window-frame to remind him of his heritage. "Nothing I had ever learnt under Mr. Hansell," he wrote, "seemed to supply a solution" to such problems.

Prince Edward did not risk taking a degree at Oxford. Nor did Prince Albert when he spent a year at Cambridge after the First World War – in which both saw service, though not as active as either would have wished. In the early 1920s Albert was content to build up a solid reputation at home, particularly in industrial welfare and youth work, while the Prince of Wales scored a series of dazzling personal triumphs overseas. It was this cautious, determined conscientiousness which stood the Duke of York in such good stead in 1936, when his brother's abdication suddenly pitchforked him into a job for which he was totally unprepared. Thanks also to the creative devotion of his wife, King George VI became an inspirational figurehead to Britons through the extreme demands made on them by the Second World War.

George VI's daughter and her husband thus came to the unexceptional conclusion that a contemporary constitutional monarch needs a good, all-round education much than any form of special training. Prince Philip, characteristically, went further:

> The art of education is to combine formal training with as wide a variety of experiences as possible, including some which involve a calculated risk. I think education is intended to produce intelligent, morally strong, self-sufficient human beings willing and capable of improving the machinery of living which man has created for his enjoyment.

If this was intended as a manifesto for the upbringing of any child, it was also founded on the determination of Charles's parents to learn from recent family history and avoid the mistakes of their recent ancestors. Elizabeth's own father provided a valuable object lesson.

Since the death of George IV in 1830, when monarchs have reigned rather than ruled, the one essential required of a sovereign has been that he command the respect of his people. It would be absurd to expect consistent ability, even competence, of any office passed on by heredity. Given a character which his people can respect, from a distance, any sovereign can survive; without it, the monarchy would be in its nearest danger of collapse, as it was in 1830, and as it would have been in 1936, had not the Duke of York so quickly grown into the breach left by his brother's abdication. King George VI was an historic example of a monarch who started out with respect, if few other qualifications, and was subsequently enlarged by his office. Prince Charles himself understands this. "There isn't any power," he has said. "There can be influence. The influence is in direct ratio to the respect people have for you."

Of his upbringing Charles has also said: "I've learnt the way a monkey learns – by watching its parents." Philip has always taken a different line on this from Albert, his most celebrated predecessor as Prince Consort: "Training isn't necessary. They do on-the-job training, so to speak, and learn the trade, or business, or craft, just from being with us and watching us function, and seeing the whole organization around us. They can't avoid it." In a striking conclusion, Philip added: "What is much more difficult is bringing them up as people."

The more Elizabeth and Philip tried to raise Charles as a "normal" boy, the more they realized it was neither possible nor, perhaps, entirely desirable. Even their youngest son, Prince Edward, only recently came a cropper when trying to prove himself a self-styled "ordinary person like anyone else" via his 1987 television spectacular, *It's a Royal Knockout*. When the assembled press politely signified their embarrassed disappointment, through a muted response to his question "Well, what did you think?" Edward lost his composure and stalked out of the room. Accustomed to deference, he was not able to deal with disapproval, however courteously expressed.

The ineluctable truth is that, because of their constitutional role and position, the royal family can no more be "normal" or "ordinary" people than most Britons would wish them to be. However hard Prince Charles has tried to understand the everyday dilemmas of his future subjects, and however much sympathy he has displayed with the least fortunate of them, a full understanding of such problems is inevitably denied a man who has never had to experience any of them himself. Charles, in turn, has unique problems – explored elsewhere in this book – to which few Britons can have any access; they are part of the price of privilege. But the very security of the British monarchy, and its continuing preeminence in a century when so many others have fallen, is entirely dependent upon its lofty, exalted status above and apart from politics and people – living life at a symbolic distance which few loyalists would wish to see reduced. Were they to lead more "normal" lives – like, for instance the "bicycle-kings" of Scandinavia, more accessible to their people but mere puppets of their governments – the fabric of the British monarchy as now so successfully constituted would quickly begin to crumble.

Prince Philip was thinking on a more pragmatic plane when discussing "normality" and the thinking behind Charles's upbringing with his biographer, the late Basil Boothroyd:

> People talk about a normal upbringing. What is normal
> upbringing? What you really mean is: was I insisting that
> they should go through all the disadvantages of being
> brought up in the way other people are brought up? Precisely
> that – disadvantages. There's always this idea about treating
> them exactly like other children. In fact it means they're
> treated much worse, because they're known by name and by
> association. . . . It's all very well to say they're treated the
> same as everybody else, but it's impossible. I think that what
> is possible, and in fact necessary, is that they should realize
> they're not anonymous. This has got to come at some stage.

The first step with Prince Charles – and, given recent family history, an innovation of more consequence that the common sense behind it suggests – was to treat him exactly the same as his younger sister and brothers. All four were introduced at the earliest ages to the widest possible choice of pastimes: swimming, sailing, shooting, fishing, go-karting, polo. In Charles's case, fishing, shooting and polo became abiding passions, at all of which he in time became more proficient than his father. "I've always tried to help them master at least one thing," said Philip, "because as soon as a child feels self-confidence in one area, it spills over into all the others. You even notice that if they feel they've made a real personal accomplishment of that kind, then this is immediately reflected even in their academic performance."

Philip never cared too much, however, about academic prowess. He went through school reports as carefully as any other parent, but there were rarely recriminations. "I don't really take them frightfully seriously. I say: "Look, I'm only going to bother if you're permanently bottom. I really couldn't care less where you are. Just stay in the middle, that's all I ask.""" Charles's father has always, anyway, disapproved of the importance attached to examinations:

> Children go through enormous changes. For a time they're in phase with life around them, then they go out of phase and become unlivable with, and everything they do is wrong and cross-grained and maddening. Then suddenly it all comes right for a bit. Then they go off on another tack. It's impossible at any point to say "This is what they're going to be like." The pendulum's got to swing a lot more before it settles down.

Philip, unlike most fathers, seems to have grown more tyrannical with age. In his sons' childhood, he was not always the strict, disciplinarian parent that has been painted. His idea of a major family crime in the early stages of Charles's life was dishonesty – "by which I mean that if you ask them a question, they must give you an honest answer." Nor was he at that stage an over-intrusive father: "There are often questions you'd like to ask, but it's much better not to unless it's really necessary." His children's behaviour, he said during their childhood, had been "averagely good. . . . I think they do silly things occasionally, but it's nearly always satisfactorily resolved, more by discussion than anything."

Once the children were old enough, most family decisions were taken on a committee basis: one member, one vote. In this Elizabeth was again making a deliberate departure from recent family history, but she was also acknowledging the strength of character of her husband, a strong-minded man with forthright views compelled in many areas of his life to play second fiddle to his wife. He may have to walk a pace behind her in public, play merely a walk-on role in her support on such occasions as the State Opening of Parliament, but in matters domestic Elizabeth has always acknowledged her husband as head of the family. He rules the roost, for instance, behind closed doors at Windsor.

Philip's philosophy, while the children were children, ran:

> It's no use saying do this, do that, don't do this, don't do that. You can warn them about certain things – that's the most you can do – or you can say this is the situation you are in, these are the choices, on balance it looks as if this is the sensible one, go away and think it over, and come back and let me know what you think.

There were times, of course, when the children's wishes were overruled. "It's very easy, when children want something, to say no immediately. I think it's quite important not to give an unequivocal answer at once. Much better to think it over. Then if you do eventually say no, I think they really accept it."

Clearly, Charles's parents had thought long and hard about how to raise him. They were anxious to point up those aspects of his childhood which could approach those of other children – alias the notion of "normality" – while trying to offset the creature comforts, privilege, deference and other obvious abnormalities which he might otherwise have come to take for granted. For all his parent's hard-wrought good intentions, however, the main effect of

Charles's schooldays were to leave him lonely, quite unhappy and more confused then ever.

It is not just that a "normal" life, to a Prince of Wales, is a contradiction in terms. There is also the increasingly irresistible argument that too much education – and thus, perhaps, too informed an intelligence – can, for the heir to the throne, be as much a liability as an asset.

PART TWO

The Student Prince

"From his childhood this boy will be
surrounded by sycophants and flatterers by
the score, and will be taught to believe
himself as a superior creation."

Keir Hardie
on the birth of the future
King Edward VIII

FIVE

A "Normal" Childhood

"Mummy has an important
job to do"

IT IS given to few mortals to be the object of global
attention before they are born. Even in embryo, the
child growing inside twenty-two-year-old Princess Elizabeth, Duchess of Edinburgh, managed to excite the world
and its press to fever pitch in May 1948.

In the reign of her father, King George VI, however,
pregnancy was still a word which Buckingham Palace
could not quite bring itself to utter of a royal princess. A
coded announcement on 4 June, the eve of Derby Day,
simply stated that "Her Royal Highness The Princess Elizabeth, Duchess of Edinburgh, will undertake no public
engagements after the end of June." Official confirmation
that an heir to the throne was on the way came with equal
obliqueness later that summer, when it was further
announced that King George VI had decided to abolish
the ancient custom – deeply embarrassing for all concerned – whereby the Home Secretary of the day attended
and verified each royal birth.

By 14 November 1948, the comings and goings of a
posse of distinguished doctors at Buckingham Palace were
the only clue that the birth was imminent. Crowds
lingered outside the Palace throughout that rainy Sunday,

the lack of news all day doing little to dampen their ardour. Some spirits within the Palace itself, however, did begin to flag. By early evening the expectant father had grown impatient; Prince Philip took his private secretary and close friend, Lieutenant-Commander Michael Parker, for a game of squash in the Palace court. After a swim in the adjacent pool, they were back on the squash court at 9.15 when the King's private secretary, Sir Alan Lascelles, ran in with the news that a prince had been born.

Twenty-one gun salutes were fired, bonfires blazed from one end of the country to the other, and the fountains in Trafalgar Square turned blue for a week. The 7lb 6oz infant was the first royal child to be born at Buckingham Palace for sixty-two years, and the first royal baby in direct succession to the throne since the birth of the future King Edward VIII in 1894. Princess Elizabeth was only the fourth heiress presumptive in British history to have given birth to a male child.

The Prince, as yet unnamed, was fifth in descent from Queen Victoria, thirty-second from William the Conqueror and thirty-ninth from Alfred the Great. He was the most Scottish prince since Charles I and the most English since Henry VIII; eleventh in descent from the Electress Sophia, through whom the present royal family's title to the throne is established under the 1701 Act of Settlement, he could claim descent from the Yorkist kings through William I and the Lancastrian kings through John of Gaunt. Thirteenth in descent from James I and VI, his Scottish ancestry included Robert the Bruce and St Mary of Scotland through James's mother, Mary Queen of Scots; through Henry Tudor, his Welsh ancestry could be traced back to Llewelyn-ap-Gruffydd, the last native prince of all Wales. Through his maternal grandmother, he was the first potential Prince of Wales ever to be a direct descendant of Owen Glendower; through his father, he had the blood of Harold, last of the Anglo-Saxon kings. Genealogists stretched the line almost to the crack of doom: on one side Charlemagne, Cadwallader and Musa ibn Naseir, an Arab sheikh born in Mecca in 660; on the other plainer names such as John Smith, Frances Webb, Mary Browne and Peter Checke, a sixteenth-century Essex innkeeper (see Appendix B).

The names chosen for the Prince by his parents – Charles Philip Arthur George – caught out the experts. Though said by the Palace to have been made for "personal and private reasons," the choice of Charles caused widespread surprise. The two English kings who had borne the name had enjoyed such miserable reigns that it had been abandoned by the royal family for nigh on 300 years; its only other royal holder, Bonnie Prince Charlie, was notorious for his insurrection against the House of Hanover.

The new Prince Charles's first few years were to be acted out against two stark backdrops, which were to make a deep and lasting impression on his psyche: the constant absence of his parents on official duties and the worsening health of his grandfather, the King. The boy's first Christmas and New Year, for instance, were the last for several years that he would spend with both his parents at his side. It was the first – and hardest – lesson in learning that he had not been born as other boys.

Though the infant Prince's daily routine has been described in meticulous detail, it comes down to an unsurprising round of playpens, teddy bears, torn-up books and regally soiled nappies. Only for the first year of Charles's life was his mother spared most royal duties, while his father was based at the Admiralty in London rather than on active naval service. By Charles's first birthday in November 1949, however, the normal working life of what the King called "the family firm" had been resumed. His father was away for Christmas, which was spent with the King and Queen at Sandringham.

Charles was one year and nine months old when his mother bore her second child the following summer, on 15 August 1950. Photographs of the period show the tiny signs of bewilderment on the face of a young child no longer the epicentre of his parents' intermittent attention. Charles was scarcely yet aware that straits and islands around the world had been named after him, though he took more than a usual childish interest in the sheets of stamps which bore his face. But his young world was already, as it was to remain throughout his childhood, one much more of adults than of children his own age.

With two children installed, and their parents' lives again busy and public, the royal nursery settled into a rigid daily regime in the care of two nannies, Mabel Anderson and Helen Lightbody. Charles and his sister Anne were got up each day at 7 sharp, dressed, fed and played with in the nursery until 9, when they enjoyed a statutory half-hour with their mother. They rarely saw her again until teatime, when Princess Elizabeth would hope to have cleared two more hours in her day. She liked to bath the children herself whenever her schedule permitted, after which they were often dressed up again to be introduced to distinguished visitors. Even before his third birthday, Charles had learnt to bow before offering his cheek for a peck from "Gan Gan," Queen Mary, and not to sit down unbidden when in the presence of his grandfather the King. It was a formidable introduction to the complexities of any child's life – bathed only sporadically, and unpredictably, in the natural warmth of his mother, with his father all but a stranger.

Charles's third Christmas in 1950 saw Prince Philip stationed in Malta, now with his own naval command. For some reason Elizabeth chose to spend the holiday alone with her husband, leaving her children back home in the care of their grandparents at Sandringham. Even their attention, however, was frequently denied him. The young Prince enjoyed an early and somewhat brutal experience of constitutional monarchy that Christmas, when the Lord President of the Council, Herbert Morrison, shut the door of a Privy Council meeting in his face. "Sorry, young fellow-me-lad," said Morrison, "but I'm afraid you can't go in there. We've got a meeting with your grandfather, and it's very, very secret."

Charles was visibly happier when the domestic routine settled back to what passed for normality at Clarence House that spring. And so might family life as he knew it have continued, as his mother dearly hoped, for another ten or fifteen years before being blighted by the burden of monarchy. But the King's health was growing worse. His wife and daughter knew, though as yet he did not, that he had cancer. By July, an increase in the young couple's royal duties on the monarch's behalf forced Prince Philip to give up his one brief naval command. In October, their departure delayed for two weeks by another operation on the King, Charles's parents left a tour of North America and Canada. Included in Princess Elizabeth's luggage was a sealed envelope of documents she would have to sign if her father died during her absence.

So Elizabeth and Philip now missed their son's third birthday, which was again spent with his grandparents and Aunt Margaret at Buckingham Palace. On their return the King made the Duke and Duchess of Edinburgh members of the Privy Council. It was all by way of momentous preparation, which to Charles only meant another Christmas spoilt by the news that his parents would soon be off travelling again. His mother took him to visit Father Christmas at Harrods, perhaps meditating that a particular wheel had come full circle. At the time of her son's birth, her father's health had forced him to cancel a Commonwealth tour; by Christmas 1950 it had been re-scheduled for early 1952. Now, again because of the King's increasingly rapid decline, it was to be undertaken for him by his daughter and her husband. The pictures of George VI waving them off at London Airport, a frail and shadowy figure seemingly buffeted by the breeze, were a shock to his affectionate subjects.

On 6 February 1952, in a hunting-lodge called Treetops overlooking the Sagana River in Kenya, Charles's mother learnt that she had become Queen during the night. Monarch at twenty-five, Elizabeth had suddenly lost even what there was of her restricted freedom and family life. Her father was dead at only fifty-six – fourteen years younger than his own father George V and (as it was to prove) twenty-two years younger than his brother Edward VIII, though both were equally heavy smokers. Less prepared for accession than on her last tour, Elizabeth left for the urgent flight home in a brightly patterned dress and hat. As she said goodbye to the grief-stricken servants at the door of the lodge, her chauffeur knelt on all fours to kiss her shoes.

Heir apparent at three years old, Prince Charles was now Duke of Cornwall, Duke of Rothesay, Earl of Carrick and Baron of Renfrew, Lord of the Isles and Great Steward of Scotland. "That's me, Mummy," he was heard to whisper when the Duke of Cornwall's name was mentioned in church among the prayers for the royal family. But from his point of view, little else had changed. He was scarcely aware that flags would now fly throughout the land on his birthday. His daily routine was much the same, apart from the absence of his grandfather – from whose funeral rites he was carefully excluded, though he had been staying with him at Sandringham on the night the King abruptly "disappeared." (When told only that his grandfather had "had to go away." Charles had not unnaturally asked why he had not said goodbye.)

The young Prince saw no difference in the mother who still supervised his bathtime – to which end the new Queen had asked the Prime Minister, Winston Churchill, to put back his weekly audience by one hour. After Easter 1952, however, a subdued holiday with the court still in mourning, Charles was confronted with the first outward sign of change. His grandmother and aunt moved into Clarence House, the family home refurbished only two years before for him and his parents, who in turn moved back into Buckingham Palace. The second-floor nursery suite had been carefully redecorated, to seem as much like the Clarence House nursery as possible. There was his box of toy soldiers, his cuckoo-clock, his ten-foot-high mock-Tudor dolls' house, his toy cupboard; he had a new, full-size bed, made for him by students of the Royal College of Art. But his mother's study on the floor below was now declared out of bounds.

Passing it one day, Charles urged his mother to come and play. "If only I could," said the Queen, gently closing the door against him. As the months went by, this was not the only reason Charles had to think his childhood different from that of other little boys. When he joined his family on the Palace balcony, or at the Trooping the Colour, his eyes were those of an excited member of the crowd, watching the colourful displays. The puzzling thing was that some people seemed to prefer to look at him.

As far as they could, Charles's parents tried to mitigate the potential corruptions of privilege. All the Palace staff, at the Queen's insistence, called the Prince simply "Charles" (as they continued to, indeed, until his eighteenth birthday). When the Prince misbehaved, he was duly punished, the palm being administered to the royal hindquarters as much by his nannies as by his father. He had to learn to take his toffee out of his mouth before the royal car stopped, and not – as he once did, to general popular delight – to press his half-sucked sweet into his mother's hand. Prince Philip once spanked him for sticking his tongue out at the crowd watching him drive down the Mall. In such painful ways did Prince Charles begin to learn about the unusual accident of his birth.

Nor was he allowed to take deference for granted. When the Prince omitted to call his detective "Mister," simply using his surname – as he heard his mother and father do all the time – he was rebuked and told to apologize. When he slipped an ice-cube down a footman's neck, he was punished. Once, when he left a door open and a footman rushed to shut it, Philip stopped the servant, saying: "Leave it alone, man. The boy's got hands." His father also found Charles pelting a Sandringham policeman with snowballs, while the hapless officer silently took his punishment, unsure whether to reply in kind. "Don't just stand there," shouted Philip. "Throw some back." It was also at Sandringham that the Queen once sent Charles back out of the house, not to return until he had found a dog lead he had lost in the grounds, with the memorable royal rebuke: "Dog leads cost money."

Such was the pattern throughout his childhood. But in the later months of 1952, as he began to master the rudiments of the Queen's English, Prince Charles began almost by accident to discover the meaning of the lavish home life he otherwise took for granted. No longer could he ride around London in the back of the family car, with his father at the wheel. These popular excursions had suddenly stopped, and now – aged three – he had his own car with his own chauffeur. He also had his own footman, an eighteen-year-old Palace servant called Richard Brown (whom Charles once "knighted" with his knife when he stooped to pick up some food the young Prince had dropped). "Why haven't you got a Richard?" asked Charles when out to tea with a friend. His friend didn't have a Mister Kelly, either – Sergeant Kelly, to be precise, Charles's newly assigned private detective, the first in a long line who would shadow him for the rest of his life. It was thanks to Kelly that Charles soon met another change of routine. No more could he go for walks through Green Park and St James's Park, across the road from his home. Already the bars of his gilded cage were being erected.

Part of growing up, as Charles's distinctive character began to emerge, was to develop some sort of working relationship with his sister. The Queen, looking back, is emphatic that all four of her children showed very different personalities at the earliest ages, and it was already clear that Charles and Anne were totally unalike. He was much more like their father in appearance, already aping some of Philip's public mannerisms: the hands behind the back, the erect bearing, the habit of looking an interlocutor fixedly in the eye, often causing a certain unease. Anne was much more like their father in character: extrovert, self-confident to a fault, occasionally temperamental. Charles took after his mother, who in turn took after George VI: instinctively shy and retiring, yet overcoming it with a deliberate effort of will, which in time sowed the seeds of a driving sense of duty. The solemnity on Charles's face in some early photographs, contrasting with the mischievousness on Anne's, is that of the camera-shy, not of the humourless, child.

It was Anne, the crowds in the Mall noticed, who waved confidently, after the fashion of her mother, long before her elder brother could summon the self-confidence to do the same. It was Charles, by contrast, who kept reminding his sister, often in vain, that she must curtsey when entering their grandmother's drawing-room. It was Charles who pulled Anne along the platform to say thank you to the engine driver when the royal train delivered them to Sandringham. But it was Anne who first discovered, and exploited, the wonderful Palace game discovered by her mother and aunt before her: if you walked past a sentry, he would make a very satisfying clatter coming to attention and presenting arms. To walk back and forth past a sentry box provided hours of childish entertainment, to the chagrin of the long-suffering guards on duty. Charles, when he discovered that he too was one of the privileged few who could produce this startling effect, steered clear of sentry boxes. It was somehow embarrassing.

The Prince's fourth birthday was the first he had ever known his father to spend with him. Preparations were already under way for the Queen's coronation the following June. Ancient ritual called for the Duke of Cornwall, as senior royal duke and head of the peerage, to take an oath of allegiance to the new monarch; but it was the first time in British history, at least since the creation of the Dukedom in 1337, that a sovereign with so young an heir was to be crowned. With his mother reluctant to put Charles through such an ordeal, he simply watched from a gallery of the Abbey. That afternoon, when his parents returned home after a triumphant progress through London, they led their son on to the balcony of Buckingham Palace, to a wave of renewed cheering. It was Charles's first experience of mass adulation, which might be thought to have turned the head of a four-year-old child. But scarcely anything of that day has lodged at all vividly in his memory.

For the bewildered young boy, all the coronation really meant was that his parents would soon be going away yet again – this time, for much longer than before. For a few months, the Queen's presence at home was interrupted only by excursions around the country to show herself to her new subjects. But in late November, soon after Charles's fifth birthday, she and Prince Philip were again to undertake that postponed and interrupted Commonwealth tour, this time in their own right. They would be away for six months.

The coronation had led to the first full flush of publicity about the royal children, which their mother decided was not in their best interests. Charles and Anne had never, anyway, been allowed to see too many of the newspapers which carried their photographs; but now the Queen began to impose further restrictions, for her children's own good. In late June, following an absurd number of requests for his presence, the Palace officially announced that Prince Charles – still only four – would not yet be undertaking any official engagements. By way of confirmation, the Queen cancelled plans for the youngest member of the Duke of Cornwall's Light Infantry to present Charles with a set of model soldiers to mark the regiment's 250th anniversary.

No more photographs of the royal children were issued for several months. There had been criticism that they were already becoming over-exposed to the public's unremitting interest; the *Daily Express* calculated that in the twenty-three weeks of 1953 up to June, it alone had published fifty pages of royal pictures (proving, *en passant*, that today's tabloid obsession with the royal family, especially its younger members, is nothing new). Nor was there any special celebration of Charles's fifth birthday in November. His parents stayed away at Sandringham, finalizing their plans for the tour, while the crestfallen boy spent the day at Windsor with his grandmother and Aunt Margaret.

A week later – once the Queen had ordered some toys from Harrods, to be stored away for her son's Christmas presents – came the moment of parting. The night before, as the Queen tucked up her children, Charles had spontaneously promised "to look after Anne." Once out of the room, Elizabeth II – yet to come to terms with the role so suddenly thrust upon her – melted into tears. Though the Queen had now been on the throne almost two years, she was not yet the monarch of whom Churchill would proclaim "a glorious new Elizabeth era"; Elizabeth was still the twenty-seven-year-old girl whom the Prime Minister feared might crack under the strain.

Charles too wept copiously; but as much as he disliked these separations, he was already aware of the need for them. "Mummy has an important job to do," he told a friend who asked where the Queen was. "She's down here." He pointed out Australia on the globe newly installed in the nursery, on which he followed his parents' progress around the world. His nannies testified that he felt her absence very keenly. Upon their joyous reunion at Tobruk, on the royal yacht, it was only with difficulty that Charles was restrained from joining the line of dignitaries waiting to shake hands with the Queen, as she was piped aboard. "No, not you, dear," were mother's first words to son after their six months apart. The young Prince seemed to have grown up beyond recognition during their long separation. As they sailed home, the Queen decided that it was time for her son's education to begin in earnest.

On his fifth birthday the previous November Prince Charles had reached the age at which the law requires every English child to begin a formal education. Although the Queen and Prince Philip had long since decided to alter the traditional patterns of royal tutelage, their revolutionary plans remained as yet strictly secret. Charles did not seem quite ready to be sent to school – let alone, as some Labour Members of Parliament were demanding, to the state primary school around the corner. For a five-year-old, the rather plump little boy was socially mature, as was only to be expected of one living in a world of adult and formal behaviour. But he did not seem particularly bright.

He could write his own name, in carefully etched capital letters; he could count to a hundred; and he could tell the time. His mother herself had taught him that much. But he could scarcely read at all, despite hours of enjoyment being read – and committing to memory – the works of Beatrix Potter and A.A. Milne, and the *Babar the Elephant* books (all of which he now enjoys reading to his own children). The Prince enjoyed his dancing classes, for which a mixed group of young aristocrats joined him at the Palace each week, and his riding lessons at Windsor, though he was already displaying less enthusiasm than his sister. He attended a London gym class and had started piano lessons, showing promise of some musical aptitude. But the only formal instruction Charles had received for the arduous royal years ahead, as yet, was to be made to stand still for long periods of time.

Before leaving for her Commonwealth tour, the Queen had engaged a governess for her son: a small, spry Scotswoman in her mid-forties named Catherine Peebles. Though Miss Peebles had previously had charge of the widowed Duchess of Kent's two younger children, Princess Alexandra and Prince Michael, she had no formal training, no university or college degree, and no revolutionary ideas on the upbringing on children. It was enough for the Queen to have noticed in "Mispy" a mixture of common sense and kindly strictness which echoed her own gentle instincts. The one rule Charles's mother imposed on her son's governess, knowing the child's growing uncertainty of himself, was "No forcing."

The Queen had considered inviting other children to join Charles's classes, but decided that his temperament urged against it. If the boy's world so far had been one of adults, it had also been one of female adults – and distinctly genteel ones at that. Apart from his father, who was so often away, Charles had spent most of his time with the Queen, the Queen Mother, Princess Margaret, his two nurses and his sister. The difficulty of establishing normal dealings with other children just now might distract him. It was decided that Charles would have his lessons alone. Even Anne was forbidden to disturb his morning with Miss Peebles in the Palace schoolroom, where a desk and a blackboard had now joined the more familiar globe. When the time came for "Mispy" to teach Charles's three young siblings, other children did join the classes. Looking back, the Queen is sure she judged the difference in Charles correctly.

Miss Peebles became one of the select few to receive a copy of the Queen's daily engagement card. Each morning, when possible, Charles still spent half an hour with his mother at 9. Then the day's instruction began, lasting initially until 11.30, noon when he was a little older. Miss Peebles confirmed the Queen's own concern that Charles's unnatural start in life had already rendered him a nervous, highly strung child of unpredictable sensitivity. "If you raised your voice to him, he would draw back into his shell and for a time you would be able to do nothing with him." His nurse, Mabel Anderson, agreed: "He was never as boisterous or noisy as Princess Anne. She had a much stronger, more extrovert personality. She didn't exactly push him aside, but she was certainly a more forceful child." Anne could always find some way to amuse herself, while Charles always needed to be entertained. She was also better with her hands; Charles was all "fingers and thumbs."

Charles's shy, almost timorous nature was due in part to his dawning awareness of his position. He knew how he was expected to behave, if not yet exactly why. When he visited a friend's farm, it was noticed that he took a polite interest in everything to be seen – almost as if he were on a royal visit – rather than showing a child's quick and selective enthusiasms. At times the spectacle of a little boy so aware of proprieties became almost pathetic: when encouraging his corgi or another of his many pets to perform its tricks, he would always add a most polite "please."

On a rewards-for-effort system, Miss Peebles began to draw out the boy's special interests. After beginning each day with a Bible story, Charles was allowed to indulge his fondness for painting, at which he has since developed much of his father's skill. Geography was another natural source of fascination; it was Miss Peebles who installed the globe on which Charles followed his parents' travels, and he was soon able to tell visiting ambassadors the precise whereabouts of their country. History was more of a problem, when trying to educate a future king to think of himself as a normal child. But Miss Peebles thoughtfully developed a course she called "Children in History," in which great figures were traced right back to their origins, whether regal or humble. The only subject which completely baffled him, as it pretty much has done ever since, was maths.

The afternoons were taken up with educational excursions: down the Mall to the shipping offices in Cockspur Street, for a talk from Miss Peebles on the trade routes; up Highgate Hill to trace the steps of Dick Whittington and his cat before a visit to the pantomime; to the Tower, to be shown round by the Beefeaters; to St George's Chapel, Windsor, to see Winston Churchill installed as a Knight of the Garter; to Madame Tussauds, to laugh at the wax effigies of himself and his parents.

In that first year, Charles quickly learnt to read, but still had some difficulty with his writing. After Christmas

1955 – celebrated with a party for forty children at the Palace, and a visit to Harrods to ask Father Christmas for a bicycle – he began to learn French. The afternoon excursions became more rigorously instructive, with visits to the various London museums. But by now the press had caught on to the routine, and the outings had to be abandoned for a straightforward nature walk through Richmond Park. Even they, in time, became uncomfortable obstacle courses.

The Queen began to doubt whether it was possible for her son to enjoy anything approaching a normal education. If the press would not allow him to visit the British Museum in peace, what chance of privacy would he have at a "normal" school? And would his presence disturb the education of the other children? Her cherished plans seemed in danger, but she was determined not to abandon them lightly. On 11 April 1955 her press secretary, Richard Colville, sent the first in what was to prove a long series of such messages to British newspaper editors:

> I am commanded by the Queen to say that Her Majesty and the Duke of Edinburgh have decided that their son has reached the stage when he should take part in more grownup educational pursuits with other children. In consequence, a certain amount of the Duke of Cornwall's instruction will take place outside his home; for example, he will visit museums and other places of interest. The Queen trusts, therefore, that His Royal Highness will be able to enjoy this in the same way as other children without the embarrassment of constant publicity. In this respect, Her Majesty feels it is equally important that those in charge of, or sharing in, the instruction should be spared undue publicity, which can so seriously interrupt their normal lives.

The request caused a lull – if only a temporary one – in press attention. Charles and "Mispy" remained unmolested when they visited London Zoo and the Planetarium; the boy was soon an expert in recognizing constellations, proof to his mother that, like her, he was "at heart a country person." They even managed a ride on the underground, the Prince passing unrecognized as the son of inconspicuous parents (Miss Peebles and Sergeant Kelly). Extra-curricular activities now included charades, field sports, more riding and Charles's first games of cricket and soccer – neither of which, though the national sports of his future subjects, was to prove an abiding enthusiasm. Team sports, apart from polo, have never much appealed to him. It is striking that, even at so young an age, he took with much more passion to the solitary pursuit of fly-fishing, under the guidance of one of the Balmoral stalkers. His father also began to teach him boxing – but reluctantly, and with some irritation, abandoned the idea after a chorus of public protest.

By the autumn of 1956 the Queen was sufficiently pleased with Prince Charles's progress to take the next major step she had in mind. In October, soon after the start of the school term, Colonel Henry Townend, founder and headmaster of a smart London day-school for boys, was pleasantly surprised to find himself invited to tea with Her Majesty at Buckingham Palace. Hill House, the Colonel's small establishment in Hans Place, just behind Knightsbridge (conveniently near the Palace), had been recommended to Charles's parents by friends and acquaintances who had sent their own sons there. One Hill House mother had particularly pleased the Queen by informing her that it was the only school in London outside which the pavement was washed and the railings dusted every day. The school's rather Spartan manifesto – very much that of Charles's father – was trumpeted on the busy notice-board beside its front steps, open for inspection to any casual passer-by:

A sense of rivalry has to be encouraged and a boy must be led to discover something in which he can excel. He must be trained to react quickly in an emergency, have a good sense of balance and control, have the strength and ability to extract himself from a dangerous situation and the urge to win.

Though naturally flattered when the Queen asked him to accept her son as a pupil, Colonel Townend was alarmed by the daunting double responsibility, both to the heir to the throne and to his other pupils. It was mutually agreed that, for the present, Charles would join the other boys only for their afternoon recreation. Lessons with "Mispy" continued in the mornings; Charles would then don his school uniform and be taken to Hill House to join the crocodile along the King's Road into Chelsea. School games were played in the grounds of Duke of York's Headquarters, the military depot named after that very Duke who marched his men to the top of the hill and marched them down again. Newspaper editors, of course, also marched their men towards the playing fields, once the Prince's new afternoon schedule – which had been successfully kept secret for several weeks – was discovered. But one picture of Charles playing soccer looked much like another, especially as he did not join in with much enthusiasm, and the novelty soon wore off.

As the Queen and Colonel Townend had hoped, Charles quickly merged into the crowd of schoolboys walking in line down the street, recognizable only when politely raising his school cap to passers-by. It was not as if he were a fully-fledged schoolboy. That, again amid tight security, was being planned for the New Year. Over Christmas, meanwhile, official duties again took Prince Philip abroad, so it was thought necessary to provide Prince Charles with some male company to offset the petticoat regime. Michael Farebrother, a thirty-six-year-old former Guards officer and headmaster of St Peter's School, Seaford, joined the Royal Household at Sandringham as "tutor-companion" to the Prince.

They roamed the estate together, visited Brancaster Beach, kicked a rugby ball around the Sandringham gardens and talked about the great figures of history. Farebrother's special subjects were Latin and history, but little academic work was done that Christmas. Charles's favourite occupation, according to his new companion, was again a solitary one: watching *The Lone Ranger* and *Champion the Wonder Horse* on television. Much though the Prince warmed to his new friend, Farebrother could prove no substitute for a father whose forcefulness transcended his absenteeism.

Farebrother's brief spell in charge coincided with Catherine Peebles's Christmas holiday, but it also marked the end of her supervision of Prince Charles. Though "Mispy" would stay at the Palace to take charge of Princess Anne, Charles was to miss her solely. With the retirement not long after of Helen Lightbody – Miss Anderson also stayed on to look after Anne – he was suddenly deprived of the two main guardians of his childhood, with whom he had spent considerably more time than with either of his parents. As he moved into a suite of his own in the Palace, Charles kept in close touch with both, but the shock of their departure renewed his sense of isolation. The approach of that first day at school with other children, away from the security of home, is tough enough for any child, most of whom face it at the age of five. For eight-old Charles the prospect became positively awesome. Although his parents had striven to prepare him for it, the young Prince was simply not equipped to be wrenched from his sheltered environment.

SIX

Still A Little Shy

"I wish they prayed for the other boys too."

NOT LONG before the news of Colonel Townend's establishment was broken to him, Prince Charles had asked the Queen: "Mummy, what are schoolboys?"

For all his mother's thoughtful care, for all the down-to-earth influence of his father, by no stretch of anyone's imagination was eight-year-old Prince Charles an ordinary child. He had grown up in palaces and castles. Ships and soldiers, objects of fantasy and imagination to other boys his age, were to Charles everyday realities. He had seen his parents, often himself, treated with awe and reverence even by the high and mighty. People became nervous and ill-at-ease in the presence of his family. At the ring of a bell, his nanny – and he had no reason to suppose that all children did not have nannies – would drop whatever was happening and take him to see his mother. At the age of four he had been named one of the world's Top Ten Best Dressed Men, alongside Marshals Tito and Bulganin, Adlai Stevenson, Billy Graham, Fred Astaire and Charlie Chaplin.

The Prince had never handled money; when occasionally he saw some, this supposedly potent substance turned out to be curious lumps of bronze and cupro-nickel bearing a picture of his mother. He had never been shopping.

He had never been on a bus. He had never got lost in a crowd. He had never had to fend for himself.

Nevertheless, on 28 January 1957, Prince Charles made British history by becoming the first heir to the throne ever to go to school. At 9.15 a.m. a black Ford Zephyr driven by a Palace chauffeur, with Charles and Miss Peebles in the back, pulled up at the school entrance, where Colonel Townend was waiting to greet him. In the school uniform of cinnamon-coloured jersey and corduroy trousers, Charles ran up to the man he had previously known as a football referee. Inside he hung up his coat – distinctive for the velvet collar so admired in his Best Dressed Man citation – and plunged with stiff upper lip into the morning's routine.

The new boy was No. 102 on the school roll of 120, the sons of well-to-do professional men, lawyers, doctors, military men and politicians. One fellow-pupil was the grandson of the new Prime Minister, Harold Macmillan. There were a number of foreign children, the sons of diplomats stationed in London. Hill House was a school for privileged children, still young and self-confident enough not to be in awe of him. The headmaster had warned them to make no special fuss of the familiar new face in their midst, but their upbringing had anyway taught them otherwise. The Prince's new peers were more than equipped to take his arrival in their stride. All this was of little comfort to Charles, who, as far as he was concerned, might as well have been arriving at Dotheboys Hall.

Opened only five years before, the school very much reflected the personal philosophy of Colonel Townend, a former Gunner officer of forty-seven who had been an Oxford football blue and England athlete. There was no corporal punishment, and the predominantly female staff taught a syllabus broad by pre-preparatory school standards. It even included elementary anatomy lessons from Mrs Townend, a state-registered nurse who had once been theatre sister to Sir John Weir, an assistant at the Prince's birth. The school doors were equipped with automatic devices to prevent trapped fingers. All the furniture had rounded edges. The school motto was taken from Plutarch: "A boy's mind is not a vessel to be filled, but a fire to be kindled."

It had been decided that the new boy, to his understandable confusion, would be "Prince Charles" to the staff, but plain "Charles" to his fellow-pupils in Form Six of Middle School. Given no special escort that first morning, but left to make his own way, he declared the highlight a visit to the school "madhouse," a gymnasium with padded walls, for a game of basketball. After lunch he painted a picture of Tower Bridge and signed it Charles. At 3.30 it was time to go home, and the black Zephyr was waiting at the door. As the Prince told the Queen all about it that evening, she felt a great sense of relief. The experiment, it seemed, was going to work.

Next morning, however, the crowd outside Hill House was so enormous that she hesitated to let him go. It was not just that the press had set up a constant vigil; local residents who had read of the new recruit in their morning newspapers were all but choking the street. After telephone consultations with Townend the Queen relented, and Charles arrived at school thirty-five minutes late. He had to run a gauntlet of sightseers and photographers to get inside. It was the same when he left, and again the next morning. Already it was clear to both the headmaster and the royal parents that this could not go on. Unless the newshounds and thus the gawkers could be moved on, the monarchy's bold experiment in liberal education would have to be called off.

The Queen kept her son at home, while her press secretary again went into action. A detective reported back to him with the identities of all pressmen waiting outside the school, and the news that they intended to wait all day. Colville then personally telephoned each of the newspaper editors involved, reminding them of the Queen's plea of eighteen months before. Within an hour Fleet Street had recalled its hounds, and Charles was able to get on with his schooling.

Before long he had settled into everyday school routine more smoothly than those watching over him dared to hope. Swimming and wrestling (which took the place of boxing at Hill House) became his favourite pastimes, and he continued to show promise with water-colours. In the classroom he remained something of a plodder, which worried nobody. The purpose of sending Prince Charles to school was not to sow the seeds of a giant intellect, but to help him meet people his own age and learn to live among them.

Just as important, it was also to help him develop normal relationships with people older than himself, other than courtiers and fellow-aristocrats. In this it seemed to be succeeding admirably. Charles was, if anything, politer to the staff than most of the other children; if not yet wholly aware of his station in life, he had been sufficiently drilled at home to treat those around him with the utmost respect, however deferential their behaviour towards him. Townend's philosophy, moreover, was to instil discipline in a family rather than an institutional context. Though the boys called the headmaster "Sir," and though he did not eat his meals with them, the geography of the cramped, converted building was such that they constantly ran in and out of his private quarters at will. It all helped Charles to understand status as a functional necessity, rather than a matter of arbitrary rank and privilege.

Perhaps, thought his parents, the heir to the throne could, after all, grow up like any other little boy from a "good" family background. His end-of-term report was certainly ordinary. Hill House made a practice of not sending exam results to parents; they were posted on the board and could be viewed by those who wished to. The royal parents refrained, but it is the unenviable fate of princes to have their school reports preserved for posterity. Apart from arithmetic, where the verdict was "below form average, careful but slow, not very keen," Charles's report for the Lent Term of 1957 contained the standard quota of "fair," "good," "shows keen interest" and "made a fair start." Behind the familiar vernacular of the school-teacher, anxious not to cause too much trouble at home, was what appeared to be a reassuringly average start.

By the end of the following term the assessment remained much the same: determined but slow. Charles was, perhaps generously at that stage, credited with "above average intelligence," and showed signs of a creative bent scarcely evident in either of his parents. Arithmetic was still a major problem, painting his favourite pursuit. At Balmoral that summer, twenty-seven-year-old Mlle Bibiane de Roujoux was imported from Paris to help with his French, which for a while was the only language spoken at the royal dining-table. Charles parents were reassured that their experiment was worth continuing, and that summer it was announced that HRH Prince Charles of Edinburgh was soon to be sent away to board at a preparatory school.

Well aware that she herself had met few beyond the Palace walls before the age of eighteen, when she had persuaded her father to let her sign on as a second subaltern in the wartime ATS, the Queen was conscious of the disadvantages of sequestering her eldest son at home. But she and her husband had equal evidence that it was no use expecting him to melt inconspicuously into the life of a boarding-school, like any other child. Simpering royal commentators were cooing in column after column that Charles and Anne were "ordinary" children being brought up in a "normal" way, but it was now obvious to their parents that this was impossible.

The best they could hope for was to guide their son, by their own fond attentions, into sharing the lives of other, more ordinary children without himself unduly suffering. On a visit to the USA in 1956, his father was rather more specific: "The Queen and I want Charles to go to school with other boys of his generation and learn to live with other children, and to absorb from childhood the discipline imposed by education with others." The royal couple had already been making a series of visits, private and public, to British boys" schools and had entertained a number of headmasters socially at Buckingham Palace. But Philip's announcement brought forth a predictable shower of advice.

In the forefront was the then Lord Altrincham (now John Grigg), whose attack on the monarchy in the August 1957 edition of his journal, the *National and English Review*, earned him a televised slap in the face, excrement through his letter-box and lasting public obloquy. Though his subsequently disclaimed title became all but synonymous with treason, it is now generally forgotten that Altrincham was in fact a self-declared monarchist, protesting that he made his loyal criticisms in the Queen's own interests. There were few, however, who bore this in increasingly apoplectic mind as they read how the monarchy had "lamentably failed to live with the times" and that the court, unlike the society it was supposed to reflect, remained "a tight little enclave of English ladies and gentlemen."

The Queen's decision that her son would go to a private preparatory school was another topic to which Altrincham addressed himself:

> Will she have the wisdom to give her children an education very different from her own? Will she, above all, see to it that Prince Charles is equipped with all the knowledge he can absorb without injury to his health, and that he mixes during his formative years with children who will one day be bus-drivers, dockers, engineers, etc., not merely with future landowners or stockbrokers?

A minority of Labour MPs used Altrincham's strictures to renew their plea that the heir to the throne should attend a state school, to mix with the less wealthy and privileged of his future subjects. The feeling at the Palace was that such a course was impossible. Although it had obvious cosmetic advantages, at a time when Elizabeth II was concerned to bring the monarchy into closer touch with a broader cross-section of her people, would not the pupils, perhaps even the staff, at a London secondary or grammar school be even more in awe of the heir to the throne than the sons of the well-to-do? Would not a private boarding-school, enclosed in its own grounds, afford a greater chance of privacy and immunity from the press than a school open to the streets of the capital? If Charles were to be the first heir to the throne in British history to be sent away to school so young, might it not be done by degrees, rather than by so abrupt and melodramatic a gesture towards social democracy?

Besides, the Queen and Prince Philip, like most middle- and upper-middle-class British parents, were convicted that the standards of private education were still higher than those of state schools. They were about to make their son suffer quite enough, they could tell, without risking substandard tuition to undermine his future. Given a system which, then as now, permitted freedom of educational choice to the wealthy, they had as much right as any other well-heeled British couple to make their own decision.

A boarding-school, and a private one, it was to be. Prince Charles was too young to be consulted about the choice of his first boarding-school, and had anyway made it more than clear that – like any other child his age – he was reluctant to leave home at all. But the Queen and Prince Philip had looked over a number of preparatory schools, including the one Philip had himself attended. It had moved since the 1930s and was scarcely the same place, but it seemed to provide everything they were looking for. And Philip, again like many other conservative-minded British fathers, found the idea of sending his son to his old school downright satisfying.

Charles's father was also pleased to offer a posthumous salute to a favourite ancestor. Just before the First World War Prince Louis of Battenberg, then First Sea Lord, had occasion to be impressed by the polished manners of two midshipmen under his command. On discovering that they were both ex-pupils of Cheam preparatory school, the Duke of Edinburgh's grandfather decreed that hence- forth all male members of the Battenberg family would go there. When Philip enrolled at the school in 1930, it had been established for more than 200 years in the Surrey town from which it takes its name. But in 1934, the year after his departure, Cheam moved to the village of Head- ley, near the Hampshire Downs, where a reluctant Charles arrived in September 1957.

At the Queen's request the joint headmasters, Peter Beck and Mark Wheeler, continued the style established at Hill House: the new pupil would be "Charles" to his fellow-pupils and "Prince Charles" to members of staff, whom he in turn would address normally as "Sir." Charles had already visited Cheam with his parents and his sister. "You won't be able to jump up and down on these beds," his mother had told him as he gazed with dismay upon the springless wooden frame and its unyield- ing hair mattress. As the royal family roamed the tranquil school grounds, the peace disturbed only by jets from the nearby US air-base, they felt reassured that Cheam's sixty- five acres should offer the required insulation from the outside world of sightseers and pressmen. Its copious undergrowth, however, would also provide excellent cover for intruders, so it was decided that the young Prince's detective should accompany him and live in the grounds.

Before term began Beck and Wheeler had sent a letter to all parents, passing on the Queen's unremarkable wish that there be "no alteration in the way the school is run." Charles was to be treated "the same as other boys. . . . It will be a great help if you will explain this [to your sons]. His parents" wishes are that he should be given exactly the same education and upbringing as the other boys at the school." Once again, however, it was impossible to expect Charles to merge naturally into the beginning-of-term throng. He remembers those first few days at Cheam as the most miserable of his life.

His mother recalls him shaking with horror as they

began the long overnight train journey from Balmoral to London, to be followed by the sixty-mile drive to Headley. On arrival, in his grey school uniform, Charles raised his blue school cap politely to Mr Beck, then watched his parents drive away. A few hours later the maths master, David Munir, who had been detailed to keep a special eye on the Prince, looked out into the school grounds. One small boy, "very much in need of a haircut," stood conspicuously apart, a solitary and utterly wretched figure.

Cheam boys were just that much older than Charles's fellow-pupils at Hill House. Despite – perhaps because of – their parents" urgings, they simply could not accept the heir to the throne as just another of the twelve new boys. Charles himself had no experience of all of forcing his way into a group of strangers, winning the acceptance of his peers. The Cheam boys could not quite believe that Prince Charles was among them. Nor, for that matter, could he.

For the first time in his life, Charles was sharing an uncarpeted room with other boys, making his own bed, cleaning his own shoes, waiting on others at table and keeping his clothes in a wicker basket under his bed (known to the boys as "the dog basket"). Cheam had 100 pupils between the ages of eight and fourteen. The day began at 7.15 a.m. with the rising bell, followed by prayers at 7.45 and breakfast at 8. Lessons began at 9 and continued, with one break, until lunch at 1. There were half-holidays on Wednesdays and Saturdays, and on Sundays there was an extra half-hour in bed before the school parade to the nearby parish church of St Peter's.

Charles wrote the compulsory minimum of one letter home per week, and was always among the first to snap up his weekly half-pound allowance of sweets. Though he was losing his puppy fat, the Prince was still a plumpish boy. When the change to a school diet prompted a few stomach upsets, he confided to his first-year teacher, Miss Margaret Cowlishaw, that he wasn't used to "all this rich food" at home.

No "tuck" boxes were allowed at Cheam, as at most

such schools, but sweets were bought out of the boys"
recommended pocket-money of 25 shillings (£1.25) a
term. In fact, the boys did not handle the money themselves, using instead a system of credits. So the young
Prince was still denied any experience of coin of the
realm, itself enough to render apocryphal one of the first
Cheam revelations to make the British newspapers.
Charles, so the story went, was kept short of pocket-
money by his parents, so he had held an auction of his
personal belongings to raise money for more sweets. For
once, the Prince learnt that newspaper fictions can have
their rewards. As the story wended its way into the American press, the Association of Retail Confectioners of
America, then in conference in San Francisco, voted to
send over a massive food parcel containing everything
from bubble gum and jelly beans to peanut butter and
tootsie rolls. "We were told the Prince was short of candy,"
said the accompanying note, "so our committee unani-
mously passed a resolution to the effect that we ought to
pitch in and help him out of a jam."

It did him no harm in the school popularity stakes.
According to Peter Beck, Charles's unwonted need to fend
for himself soon helped him become a good mixer. A
special friend was the headmaster's daughter, Mary Beck,
the only girl at the school. Charles's supposed loneliness –
a sensation not unknown to eight-year-old boys in their
first term at boarding-school – may indeed have been
partly in his own mind. He was already aware that other
children might befriend him for the wrong reasons. It was
often the nicest boys, he recalls, who hung back, not wishing to be seen "sucking up" to him; those who forced their
attentions on him were often those whom he liked least.

The experience proved the beginning of a lifelong need
to make an extra effort in such company. The Prince
knows that the heir to the throne is by definition the focal
point of any room's attention; to justify that attention, he
has to try to appear more than usually interesting. It is a
tricky psychological problem, which must account in large

degree for the painful shyness of the eight-year-old school-boy. As he strove to overcome this, his fellows marked him down as a bit of a lone wolf.

At Cheam, furthermore, Charles began to be haunted by another shadow which has pursued him ever after: that of his father, an outgoing, gregarious man who had never had to cope with such problems. At Cheam, after all, Philip was Prince of Greece and Denmark, not of England or Wales. The press were not pursuing him from bush to bush, and the other boys looked on him with no awe. While academically undistinguished, Philip had shone on the sports field – First XI goalkeeper and captain of the cricket team – and Charles knew all too well that his father was looking for similar achievements from him.

The Prince's lessons at Cheam were geared to the Common Entrance Examination taken before admission to most British public schools (although, as it transpired, he was to attend one which did not require it). History remained an abiding interest, not least because he now knew that it largely concerned his ancestors and was uneasily aware that it was already preparing to receive him. In geography he also shone, again because his parents" tours had made the globe a familiar place. Maths remained an utter mystery, closely followed by Latin and Greek. Before the afternoon lessons there were games, about which he remained unenthusiastic (despite evidence to the contrary in his end-of-term reports), or other out-door activities such as camping or wildlife study, very much modelled on the precepts of the Boy Scout movement, though the school had no troop as such.

As at Hill House, the Cheam gymnasium became one of his favourite haunts, where athletic rough-and-tumble often developed into a mild schoolboy fracas. Charles soon had a reputation for giving as good as he got. He was particularly sensitive to jokes about his plumpness and took days to recover after hearing the boy beneath him in a collapsed rugby scrum cry "Oh, do get off, Fatty." The school was visited regularly by a barber from Harrods,

Cecil Cox, who once saw an older boy douse Charles's head under a cold tap; the visitor watched impressed as the Prince filled a bath with cold water, wrestled with his assailant and finally forced him in fully clothed – only to be pulled in himself.

This was one of many Cheam anecdotes, some truer than others, which found their way into the press during Charles's first term. "Even the school barber was in the pay of the newspapers," snorted Prince Philip. It did not help the "normality" of Charles's education, nor his standing among his peers, that all too often there had to be complex inquiries before school crimes, apparently to be laid at his door, were found to be the work of others. Within a week of his arrival, for instance, Charles's name had been deeply carved in the back of a pew in the parish church. This was one story the newspapers did get hold of, but Beck, with help from the Palace, persuaded them to print corrections when other boys eventually admitted their guilt.

In an attempt to head off journalists' intrusions, Beck and Wheeler had held a press visit to the school before term began and made a special plea to be left thereafter in peace. But of the eighty-eight days of term, there were stories in one newspaper or another on sixty-eight. Again the effects were unpleasant, not least for the hapless pupil at the centre of it all. Rumours abounded of boys and staff accepting bribes from pressmen. They were never proved true, but a tense atmosphere of mutual suspicion developed and morale at the school began to suffer. Although the Prince's detective coped with most intruders, there were occasionally more dramatic incidents. One night he aroused the head-master after seeing a prowler on the roof of Charles's dormitory; a lengthy search was conducted, but no one found. Only much later did a young friend of Charles's, David Daukes, confess to getting back into bed seconds before the search-party arrived. Even schoolboy pranks were becoming worthy of the police incident book.

Once again, the Queen decided to safeguard her son's education, not to mention his sanity, by direct action.

In the Christmas holidays her press secretary invited all British newspaper editors to a meeting at Buckingham Palace. Peter Beck told the gathering of the disruption their employees were causing at his school. Bribes had been offered, though none to his knowledge accepted. Everyone felt themselves under constant surveillance. The Prince's first term had ended unhappily for all, not least Charles himself. Recalling the pleas he had made before and during Charles's time at Hill House, Colville spoke plainly to the editors. Either it stopped, and the press printed only those stories of genuine significance, or the Queen would abandon her cherished plan to educate her son at normal schools and withdraw him behind the Palace walls to the care of tutors. History would record that the failure of the great royal educational experiment was entirely the fault of the press.

Duly sobered, British editors ensured that Cheam was little more molested during Charles's four years there. Only the foreign paparazzi photographers persisted, climbing over the newly heightened walls and building hides in the undergrowth; on one occasion Mary Beck, drawing her father's attention to an unseasonal firework display in the garden, unwittingly assisted in the capture of one intruder, who had been using infra-red equipment to take pictures after dark.

Six months later, however, British newspapers did have a story "of genuine significance" to publish. It was the summer term of 1958, the end of Charles's first year at Cheam, and Commonwealth Games were being held in Cardiff. The Queen had been due to perform the closing ceremony at Cardiff Arms Park on 26 July, but a sinusitis operation enforced her absence. The Duke of Edinburgh took her place and introduced a tape-recorded message from Her Majesty, which was played over the loudspeakers of the packed stadium.

Charles and a few friends, who had filed into Peter Beck's study to watch the event on television, heard the Queen's disembodied voice say:

> I want to take this opportunity of speaking to all Welsh people, not only in this arena, but wherever they may be. The British Empire and Commonwealth Games in the capital, together with all the activities of the Festival of Wales, have made this a memorable year for the principality. I have therefore decided to mark it further by an act which will, I hope, give as much pleasure to all Welshmen as it does to me.

There was a buzz of anticipation as many in the arena had guessed what she was going to say. "I intend to create my son Charles Prince of Wales today."

The tape had to be stopped as an enormous cheer convulsed the stadium and 36,000 Welsh voices broke into "God Bless the Prince of Wales." When the clamour died down, the Queen's voice continued: "When he is grown up, I will present him to you at Caernarvon."

The scene in Beck's study at Cheam might have given the Queen a moment's pause. The headmaster, who with Charles had known what was coming, watched a look of dire unease cloud his face as the other boys spontaneously joined in the clapping and cheering. Charles's own memory of the occasion is vivid:

> I remember being acutely embarrassed when it was announced. I heard this marvellous great cheer coming from the stadium in Cardiff, and I think for a little boy of nine it was rather bewildering. All the others turned and looked at me in amazement. And it perhaps didn't mean all that much then; only later on, as I grew older, did it become apparent what it meant.

For a mother trying to bring her son up as much like other boys as possible, aware that his own emergent character was still far from self-confident, far from mastering its environment, it was an odd piece of timing. The Queen has since confessed that she now numbers this moment among the few mistakes she made in the upbringing of her son and heir.

In the headmaster's study that afternoon, Charles also automatically became Earl of Chester and Knight Companion of the Most Noble Order of the Garter. They go, as it were, with the job. Reflecting that her son was still young for his years, a chastened Elizabeth decided that it was too soon for the formal ceremony installing Charles in his Garter stall at Windsor; this ancient ritual was, in fact, to wait ten years – by which time it was part of the build-up to another major ordeal, his formal investiture as Prince of Wales at Caernarvon, and thus his emergence into full-time public life.

Those days remained mercifully far off as Charles continued his steady but undistinguished progress at Cheam. "He is still a little shy," his first end-of-term report had read, "but very popular ... passionately keen on and promising at games ... academically, a good average." Beck later summed up with the verdict that the Prince was above average in intelligence, but only average in attainment. By this he did not mean that the boy was bright but idle; rather, he was pointing out the natural advantage Charles possessed in general knowledge. The new Prince of Wales was much better informed about the world, the outside world and its ways, than his contemporaries; by this time, after all, he had met many of the people who ran it and engaged them in polite conversation.

This strange species of maturity, fostered by the formal conduct around him at home, also meant that Charles spoke and wrote the Queen's English with above-average clarity and style, at times tending to a precocious use of long words. In other ways, he was much less mature than his fellows and remained so for many years. He joined in their schoolboy crazes – at that time for pogo sticks, hula-hoops and roller skates – with the intense enthusiasm of one unaware of such excitements at home. But the Queen's caution in not providing everything he requested led to embarrassments. When he asked for a boat to sail on the school pond, his was conspicuously the smallest to be seen. At least he had the good sense not to waste his time sharing his friends'' love of stamp-collecting; at home, he knew, the collection he would inherit from his great-grandfather, George V, was the finest and most valuable in the world.

Charles continued his piano lessons, the first steps in a love of music unparalleled in the royal family since Prince Albert. He sang in the school choir and piped a clear treble solo in the end-of-term concert attended by the Queen. He continued to show promise at painting and a passing talent at woodwork; Charles produced a coffee-table which for many years remained one of Princess Anne's most treasured possessions. He dominated one end-of-term exhibition with a grim construction entitled Gallows and Stocks. He also began to join with a will in many of the school entertainments; like his mother, who with her sister had starred in the wartime Windsor pantomimes, he seemed to find such enforced public display one method of conquering his shyness. In a way, it was an apt preparation for the many bizarre public roles required of royalty.

One such Cheam production certainly was: a Shakespeare compilation under the title *The Last Baron*, which told the tale of the Duke of Gloucester, later Richard III. The time-honoured understudy's dream came true when the boy cast as Richard fell ill and Charles hurriedly took over the part. In front of an audience of parents, he had to deliver with due gravity such lines as "And soon may I ascend the throne." The drama critic of the *Cheam School Chronicle* wrote: "Prince Charles played the traditional Gloucester with competence and depth; he had a good voice and excellent elocution, and very well conveyed the ambition and bitterness of the twisted hunchback." His "traditional Gloucester" was modelled on Laurence Olivier's celebrated performance as Richard III; before the Cheam production, the young Prince listened repeatedly to a recording of the Olivier production. (On hearing of this many years later Lord Olivier repaid the compliment, rejoicing that King Charles III would in time become "the first artistic king since Charles II.")

The Queen, unusually, was not in the audience that night, 19 February 1960. The headmaster interrupted the performance to come onstage and announce why: she had given birth to another son, Prince Andrew. Cheam staff were accustomed to boys being somewhat dashed by the news of the arrival of a younger sibling. They were struck by Charles's overt delight at having a baby brother, the almost excessive enthusiasm with which he relayed the latest news from home – evidence, to the teachers who now knew him so well, that the Prince would always be much happier secure in the bosom of his family. As Mabel Anderson said of Charles: "He felt family separation very deeply. He dreaded going away to school." His only link with home was the unlikely figure of his detective, Detective Constable Reg Summers, who provided a reassuring presence around the school grounds and behind the Sunday crocodile to church. The Queen felt the distance equally keenly and denied herself as well as her son much pleasure by resisting the temptation to bend school rules by calling him home for royal occasions. Later that summer, however, a special dispensation was granted for him to attend the wedding in Westminster Abbey of his Aunt Margaret to the photographer Antony Armstrong-Jones. The Earl of Snowdon, as he became the following year, quickly formed an especially warm friendship with Prince Charles, founded as much as anything else on mutual admiration, which lasts to this day.

The Queen was careful to visit her son no more frequently – three times a term – than other parents and to ask for no special privileges beyond the fact that cameras should be put away in her presence. Princess Anne enjoyed coming for the annual sports day and always entered the younger sisters' race, unfortunately achieving no higher a position than fourth. She could take comfort in her brother's generally undistinguished record on the sports field. Never much of a team player, he was bored by cricket, although he eventually made the First XI, and not the most mobile of rugger players: "They always put me in the second row," he complained, "the worst place in the scrum." His reluctant best was soccer, and in his last year at Cheam he was made captain of the First XI. Unhappily, the team lost every match that season, with a final tally of four goals scored against their opponents" eighty-two. This time, the *Cheam School Chronicle* was not so kind: "At half," wrote the soccer coach, "Prince Charles seldom drove himself as hard as his ability and position demanded."

Looking back, the staff remember Charles fondly for his uncertainty of himself and for a few little incidents which showed promise of the reflective man in the making. "Most of the time," said one of Charles's teachers, "he was very quiet. He never spoke out of turn. Sometimes his voice was so low that it was difficult to hear him. But he was a boy who preferred action to noise. When there was a task to do, he got on with it quietly. No fuss." David Munir remembered once catching Charles downstairs, finishing off his daily chores, when he should long since have been in bed. Munir warned him that he would be getting himself into trouble with Matron. "I can't help that, sir," the boy replied. "I must do my duties."

Charles's extreme gentility was particularly marked on the football field, where he caused general amusement by his habit of apologizing chivalrously to anyone he felled with a perfectly proper tackle. But it was endearing to find him so embarrassed by the standard prayer for the royal family, including the Prince of Wales, at Sunday morning service in St Peter's. "I wish," he said, "they prayed for the other boys too." When someone gave Charles a "doodle-master," a new-fangled drawing toy, he was happy to lend it around until every other locker had its own. And he took his corporal punishment with the self-discipline of one who "would rather get things over with."

By the end of his time at Cheam – despite such unnerving distractions as the discovery of an IRA plot to kidnap him, which had the school grounds swarming with police for days – Charles had emerged an utterly average pupil. But the school had never quite won his whole-hearted enthusiasm. The jolt of leaving home left bruises he still nursed. If he had grown accustomed to life away from home, he was still miserably aware that he was not – and never could be – one of the boys. Beck emphasizes that "the job of a preparatory school is what it says: to prepare and not to produce a finished product." But Charles had only just mastered his new environment when he was abruptly removed from it. The last thing Cheam had prepared this particular pupil for, in fact, was the unwelcome translation even further from home to the chilly wastes of North Scotland, and Gordonstoun.

SEVEN

He Hasn't Run Away Yet

"I did not enjoy school life as much as I
might have. . . . "

THE QUEEN and her mother had always taken it for granted that Charles would go to Eton. It was the natural breeding-ground of the English upper classes; it offered, in their view, the best education available; and above all it was right on the doorstep of the family's weekend home at Windsor. Charles's father, however, had other ideas.

"Every time you hiccup," Philip told his son, "you'll have the whole of the national press on your shoulders." His own *alma mater*, Gordonstoun, was much more strategically placed on the edge of the Moray Firth. "If you go to the north of Scotland you'll be out of sight, and they're going to think twice about taking an aeroplane to get up there. So it's got to be a major crisis before they'll actually turn up, and you'll be able to get on with things. . . . " Charles was content to do the bidding of the imposing parent he increasingly hero-worshipped: "He had a particularly strong influence, and it was very good for me. I had perfect confidence in his judgement." Again the young Prince seemed only too pleased to gratify his father's whims by following in his footsteps.

As we have seen, however, bringing up Prince Charles

in Prince Philip's mould was not entirely a logical exercise. Where Philip was outgoing, Charles was introspective; where Philip gregarious, Charles awkwardly sociable; and where Philip had been an obscure European prince, of the kind not unfamiliar to many British public schoolboys, Charles was the heir to the throne, the first in British history to be sent away to school so young. His fears that Gordonstoun sounded "pretty gruesome" were confirmed shortly before his arrival when Lord Rudolph Russell, younger son of the Duke of Bedford, ran away from the school, declaring: "Gordonstoun is no place for me."

Was it the right choice of school for a shy and hesitant child, in most respects a late developer? Those involved in the decision – among them the Queen Mother, Lord Mountbatten and Dr Robin Woods, Dean of Windsor – remained divided ever after. Charles himself, though in later life he decided that Gordonstoun had been "good for me," absolutely hated the place.

The school has been painted as a remote Spartan outpost providing some sort of Germanic assault course towards manhood. Its life is tough, to be sure, with an unusual emphasis on outdoor and physical attainment. Its pupils are drawn more heavily than those of most comparable schools from a curious mix of the old-school upper classes and the social-climbing self-made. But Gordonstoun's ways are, in ideological terms, far from brutish. Every time on the school curriculum, every eccentrically named rung up its all-important status ladder, is based on a rigorous educational code founded in pacifism. It was formulated in the wake of the First World War by Prince Max of Baden, last Chancellor of the Kaiser's Imperial Germany, and refined by his private secretary and disciple, Kurt Hahn. It may provide a more eccentric, narrowly aristocratic education than most other British public schools – including Eton – but Gordonstoun parents are well aware what they are letting their sons in for.

The school is modelled on that founded in 1920 by Prince Max in his castle-monastery at Salem, on the north

shore of Lake Constance, in Southern Germany. The
Prince who had been intimately involved in the collapse
of Germany, here set himself the personal task of rebuild-
ing his nation's manhood. "Let us train soldiers," he said,
"who are at the same time lovers of peace." Prince Max
was given to somewhat grandiose statements which, by
appointing his private secretary the school's first headmaster, he expected Hahn to put into effect: "Build up the
imagination of the boy of decision and the will-power of
the dreamer, so that in future wise men will have the
nerve to lead the way they have shown, and men of action
will have the vision to imagine the consequences of their
decisions."

What Max really sought, Hahn believed, was the combination of stamina and leadership which had defeated
Germany – the very combination bred in the English public schools, of which he himself had gained some experience when a Rhodes at Oxford before the war. Hahn's two
great influences were Plato (particularly *The Republic*)
and Dr Thomas Arnold of Rugby, both of whom he was
given to quoting copiously:

> I will call the three views of education the Ionian view, the
> Spartan view, the Platonic view. . . . Those who hold the first
> view believe that the individual ought to be nurtured and
> humoured regardless of the interests of the community. . . .
> According to the second view the individual may and should
> be neglected for the benefit of the State. . . . The third, the
> Platonic view, is that any nation is a slovenly guardian of its
> own interests if it does not do all it can to make the individ-
> ual citizen discover his own powers: and further, that the in-
> dividual becomes a cripple from his or her own point of
> view if he is not qualified by education to serve the commu-
> nity.

The selection process at Salem was quite as elitist as at
Eton. Only children from the upper layers of German
society were considered; even then, Hahn fiercely scrutinized their strength of character – far more important to

him than their academic prowess – before admitting them. In the Germany of the 1930s, after the death of Prince Max, Hahn was accused of anglicizing German education. He also happened to have been born Jewish. In 1933, when Hitler took power, he was arrested and the school closed. His stand was uncompromising. "It is a question now in Germany of its Christian morality, its reputation, its soldierly honour; Salem cannot remain neutral," Hahn wrote to the old boys of Salem. "I call on all members of the Salem Association who are active in the SA or SS to terminate their allegiance either to Hitler or to Salem." The rise of Nazism made Hahn feel more urgently "the need to educate young people in independence of judgement and in strength of purpose when following an unfashionable cause, to teach the protection of the weak, the recognition of the rights of the less fortunate, and the worth of a simple human life." The children of Germany at that time were surrounded by "three decays: the decay of adventure and enterprise, of skill and care, and of compassion."

On his release Hahn fled to England, where he fell ill. An Oxford friend, William Calder, invited him to recuperate on his estate in Morayshire, where he met up again with another university contemporary, Evan Barron, then owner and editor of the *Inverness Courier*. When Hahn told these sympathetic friends of his plans to recreate the Salem experiment in Britain, they took him to see the Gordonstoun estate, near Elgin. A lease was available on the eighteenth-century mansionhouse, complete with pepperpot turrets and balustrades, and its 300 acres. Hahn took it, and in the summer of 1934 opened the school with a clutch of masters and just thirty boys, one of them Prince Philip.

Though the Gordonstoun philosophy was overtly based on that of Salem, Hahn added two significant new dimensions. One was to carry across from Germany the altruistic traditions of the Cistercian monks, who had ministered to the vicinity of Salem centuries before. The other was to counteract the scholastic emphasis of other British schools. "I estimate," he said, "that about sixty per cent of boys have their vitality damaged under the conditions of modern boarding-schools." His aim was "to kindle on the threshold of puberty non-poisonous passions which act as guardians during the dangerous years."

Hahn was now accused of germanicizing English education, but all his philosophy came down to was a version, more literal than in most public schools, of Juvenal's *mens sana in corpore sano* ("a healthy mind requires a healthy body"). To protect his pupils from their increasingly urbanized home environments, he wanted them to pit their young physical resources against the forces of nature on land and sea. Like Baden-Powell, he aimed to inspire a sense of purpose and self-reliance, aligned with one of duty and service. Boys, said Hahn, should be taught "to argue without quarrelling, to quarrel without suspecting and to suspect without slandering." Apart from a special concern for late developers – a boon to its new recruit – Gordonstoun's purpose, enshrined in the school motto, PLUS EST EN VOUS ("There is more in you"), was not markedly different from the traditional British public-school ideal.

But its methods were. Physical fitness was something of a cult: it remains so with the Prince of Wales to this day. Boys were frequently despatched on testing expeditions, over land and water, designed to stretch initiative and physique to their limits. Public service was instilled by participation in four local activities: fire-fighting (the school's auxiliary is a recognized branch of the Elgin fire service); manning a coastguard station, complete with rockets and life-saving equipment; a mountain rescue team, which has in its time saved climbers" lives; and an ocean life-saving team. Hahn introduced the Moray Badge as a selective reward for achievement in these fields. It proved the inspiration for the Duke of Edinburgh's own international award scheme, whose silver medal Prince Charles was to win in his last term.

Hahn's precepts are now as evident in Charles's beliefs and pronouncements as his father's. It was a bold Prince of Wales, for instance, who suggested in 1987 that a form of compulsory community service might take place of national service in Britain, the only European country in which it had been abolished. As the leader-writers sharpened their pens that afternoon, none traced the notion back to the immense influence of Hahn on both father and son. On the very day that it was announced that Charles would be going to Gordonstoun, Hahn happened to be delivering a lecture in Glasgow. "A sick civilization," he said, "is throwing up five kinds of young people: the lawless, the listless, the pleasure and sensation addicts, the angry young men and the honourable sceptics." The antidotes were "simple physical training, expedition training and rescue service training."

Uncannily similar phrases can be found to this day – increasingly, in fact, as he grows older – in many major speeches made by the Prince of Wales. Back in 1962, with garbled versions of Hahn's philosophy and Gordonstoun's strenuous regime appearing in the British press, it was no wonder that the thirteen-year-old Prince felt daunted. On a private visit to the school with his parents, he found conditions even more Spartan than at Cheam: unpainted dormitories with bare floorboards, naked light bulbs and spare wooden bedsteads. Life appeared to be lived in huts, as exposed to the North Sea gales as were the boys' knees in their short trousers. It was a cheerless sight, and Charles remained unenthusiastic about what he called his "imminent incarceration."

His arrival at Gordonstoun, he remembers, was even more miserable than at Cheam. As he was shown to Windmill Lodge, the asbestos-roofed stone building he was to share with fifty-nine of the 400 other boys, the prospects seemed even worse than he had expected. Not only had he been rudely yanked from an environment to which had just grown accustomed, but all his dogged progress up the Cheam hierarchy had now come to naught. He

was an unprivileged new boy again, at a school where the
boy's older years altered their attitude to him. Where at
Cheam he had found diffidence, at Gordonstoun he came
up against adolescent malice. The only boys he knew,
apart from Lord Mountbatten's grandson, Norton
Knatchbull, were his cousins Prince Welf of Hanover,
whom he had visited with his father in Germany earlier
that year, and Prince Alexander of Yugoslavia. Even they,
for befriending him in his first few days, were labelled
"bloodsucker" and "sponge" by their contemporaries.

The Gordonstoun day began with the cry of the
"waker" at 7 a.m., followed by a run round the garden in
shorts and singlet. Then came the first of the day's two
cold showers; Charles and his fifty-nine housemates
shared a washroom containing six showers and one bath.
He had to make his own bed and clean his own shoes
before breakfast. The rest of the new boys' day, in an
official summary prepared for public consumption by the
headmaster, Robert Chew, went beyond the normal stint
of classwork to "a training break (running, jumping, dis-
cus and-javelin-throwing, assault course, etc.) under the
Physical Training Master' and "seamanship, or practical
work on the estate." They would also see active service as
coast guard watchers, sea cadets, army cadets and scouts,
with the Fire Service, Mountain Rescue and/or Surf Life-
Saving teams.

When not occupied by their formidable schedule, boys
were at liberty to wander at will around the countryside
and down to the sea, though the town of Elgin was strictly
out of bounds. Charles eagerly took full advantage of this
freedom; visitors noticed with interest that he tended to
take them for walks round the countryside rather than
show them round the school. He developed nodding
acquaintanceships with the fishermen and shopkeepers of
the nearby village of Hopeman, and occasionally – but
only occasionally, for fear of singling himself out –
accepted invitations to Sunday lunch or a day's shooting
with family friends among the local worthies. He

desperately wished that he could use his position to bend the rules and escape more, but this would have involved braving the wrath of his father as much as the staff and fellow-pupils. Conforming to the school regime, like any other unprivileged member of its society, was gradually to become doubly claustrophobic. It was, meanwhile, in the countryside that Charles preferred to relax; school games he did not much enjoy, and he felt obliged to shun his peers" illicit activities in Elgin's Pete's Cafe.

By the end of his first term, during which he was among the blue-suited new boys in charge of the school dustbins, Charles had qualified (in one of Gordonstoun's many unique, hierarchical rituals) to wear the standard school uniform of grey sweater and shorts. He had also qualified for a ritual ducking, fully clothed, in yet another cold bath; but the Prince, surprisingly, was spared this ordeal. It seems strange that Gordonstoun boys hesitated to put the Queen's son through a customary humiliation; but Charles's limited success at "blending in" – or the full extent, to put it another way, of what he was up against – was soon evident from the testimony of one school-leaver, who was not slow to sell his story to a Sunday newspaper:

> How can you treat a boy as just an ordinary chap when his mother's portrait is on the coins you spend in the school shop, on the stamps you put on your letters home, and when a detective follows him wherever he goes? Most boys tend to fight shy of friendship with Charles. The result is that he is very lonely. It is this loneliness, rather than the school's toughness, which must be hardest on him.

It was. "It's near Balmoral," his father had told him. "There's always the Factor there. You can go and stay with him. And your grandmother goes up there to fish. You can always stay with her." Charles did, whenever he could. At Birkhall, her home on the Balmoral estate, the Queen Mother heard from Charles of his homesickness, his loneliness, the impossibility of blending into school like other boys. She provided a sympathetic shoulder to cry on, literally, and was especially moved by all the qualities of her late husband so evident in her favourite grandchild. More than either of Charles's parents, perhaps, she understood the ordeal of the quiet and uncertain child in a harsh and alien world. "He is a very gentle boy, with a very kind heart," she said, "which I think is the essence of everything." But she would not, as he asked, intercede with his parents to take him away from Gordonstoun. She would try, she said, to help him through a trial he must face. It was another early lesson in the duty which went with his birth.

"Well, at least he hasn't run away yet," said Prince Phillip, asked how his son was getting on at Gordonstoun. At the end of Charles's first term, however, the headmaster was able to report to his parents that their son was "well up . . . very near the top of his class." The Christmas holidays provided further trials-by-press, as the crush of photographers drove him off the public ski slopes of Bavaria, but worse lay in store during the summer term back at school. The Cherry Brandy Incident, now a fondly remembered, amusing milestone in Prince Charles's childhood to most Britons, was much more than that to the boy at the time. It upset him deeply, leaving scars which lasted several years – notably a bewildered mistrust of the press which has never really left him, though it is not so bewildered.

On his arrival at Gordonstoun another appeal had been made for the press to leave him in peace – not least because "publicity . . . singles His Royal Highness out as different in the eyes of all other boys of the school" – and by his third term press coverage of his progress was minimal. By then, June 1963, he had won further promotion within the school, entitling him to more freedom of choice over outdoor training activities – one of which was the expedition aboard the school yacht, *Pinta*, which brought him to Stornoway, on the Isle of Lewis, on Monday 17 June. As usual his detective, Donald Green, accompanied the party of Charles and four other boys ashore. Green went off to make arrangements at the local cinema – Jayne Mansfield was to be the object of their scholastic attentions that evening – leaving the boys to wait in the Crown Hotel. Once word of the Prince's arrival got around, a crowd quickly gathered, and Charles soon found a sea of faces pressed against the hotel windows, peering and pointing at him.

I thought "I can't bear this any more" and went off somewhere else. The only other place was the bar. Having never been into a bar before, the first thing I thought of doing was having a drink, of course. And being terrified, not knowing what to do, I said the first drink that came into my head, which happened to be cherry brandy, because I'd drunk it before when it was cold out shooting. Hardly had I taken a sip when the whole world exploded round my ears.

Into the bar, as he took that first sip, had walked twenty-two-year-old Frances Thornton, a freelance journalist known ever after to Charles as "that dreadful woman." At fourteen, the Prince of Wales was under the legal age for purchasing alcoholic liquor. Within twenty-four hours, the story had gone round the world. Coming soon after other public criticisms – of Charles shooting his first stag and "invading the Lord's Day" by skiing in the Cairngorms on a Sunday – it caused uproar. Even the Profumo Affair, the Cabinet sex scandal then at its height, could not keep it off the front pages. To make matters worse, Buckingham Palace at first issued a denial, after misunderstanding Green's telephoned account of the incident. The following day, after further inquiries, the Palace press office was forced to retract it, thus keeping the story bubbling along. There followed the carpeting of Green by the Queen's senior detective and his subsequent resignation, while the entire nation felt qualified to discuss the question of suitable school punishment for Charles. *The Times* felt moved to inform its readers that the headmaster of Gordonstoun kept a cane in his study, at the ready, for just such moments.

As leading articles called on the Head to act, Mr Chew summoned Charles to his study and withdrew his recent school promotion. It was a punishment much more devastating than the cane. Reduced to the ranks, Charles had again had his life complicated by undue and unwelcome attention. For so trivial an incident to have had so disproportionate an effect now seems absurd; the Queen was able to laugh at the episode, later concluding that it was a salutary lesson in the necessary restraints on royal conduct. But Charles – though now, to many newspaper readers, a more human and endearing figure – was thoroughly unsettled and unable to laugh about it at all for several years. When boys made puns on the name of the school yacht, *Pinta* – "Drinka Pinta Milka Day" was then the Milk Marketing Board's popular slogan – he somehow failed to appreciate the joke.

The next year passed quietly enough, however, for the Prince to prove something to himself and his family by passing five GCE "O" levels, in Latin, French, history, English language and English literature (though maths and physics still eluded his grasp). By the time he returned to school that autumn, after a particularly happy summer holiday, his life seemed to have found a new equilibrium. But it was very soon to turn sour again, when an exercise-book went missing from his classroom.

That sort of thing had happened before: forgeries had been hawked around Fleet Street, and one genuine one, culled from a waste-paper basket, had turned out to be the work of another boy. Name tags from Charles's clothes had proved popular on the school's "black market," and textbooks inscribed with his name had disappeared. These were the everyday realities of his "normal" school life, with which he had learned to live, albeit uncomfortably. But this time the olive-green book in which Charles wrote his essays had been stolen from the pile on his form-master's desk. The headmaster issued an appeal for what he called "a collector's item."

It was too late: the exercise-book had already reached

Fleet Street. A Gordonstoun boy (who was never identified) was reputed to have got £7 for the book from an Old Boy, an officer cadet, who had then sold it on to a Scottish journalist for £100. Rumours of offers as high as £5,000 abounded in London for some time until the book was traced to St Helen's, Lancashire, and the offices of Terence Smith of the *Mercury Press*. It took Scotland Yard six weeks to get the book back, by which time the German magazine *Der Stern*, the French *Paris-Match* and the American *Life* magazine all possessed photostats. Convinced by the Scotland Yard seizure of the document's authenticity, *Stern* published the essays in full, in German – illustrated by the handwritten text in English, complete with the form-master's comment: "Quite well argued." It was "highly regrettable," said Buckingham Palace, "that the private essays of a schoolboy should have been published in this way."

So it was; but it could have been a great deal worse. Charles emerged with credit from worldwide exposure which would have daunted any schoolboy. Though published under the lurid headline "The Confessions of Prince Charles," what little the essays revealed showed the sixteen-year-old Prince a liberal and original thinker, reasonably mature for his age. *Stern* managed to miss the point of the piece about which it got most excited: a dissertation on the corrupting effects of power. Its views were not those of the future King of England, but of the nineteenth-century historian William Lecky, a section of whose *History of England in the Eighteenth Century* the class had been told to precis.

The Times quoted with approval from another piece on the subject of democracy. The Prince professed himself "troubled by the fact that the voters today tend to go for a particular party and not for the individual candidate, because they vote for the politics of a party." He thought it wrong, for instance, that a below-par Conservative candidate should win votes simply because he toed the party line against nationalization or the abolition of the public schools. In another, on the press, he emerged from his recent ordeals surprisingly unsoured, arguing that a free press was essential in a democratic society "to protect people from the government in many ways, to let them know what is going on – perhaps behind their backs."

The matter might have ended there, had not *Stern* thought of adding a last, gratuitous paragraph: "Prince Charles became short of pocket-money at Gordonstoun at the end of August. It then occurred to him that some collectors paid good money for original handwritten manuscripts and sold the work to a schoolmate for thirty shillings." *Time* magazine decided to follow up this intriguing titbit, and the following week published its version of the saga under the headline "The Princely Pauper." Now the Palace lost patience and issued one of its extremely rare denials. Colville wrote to *Time*:

> There is no truth whatever in the story that Prince Charles sold his autograph at any time. There is also no truth whatever in the story that he sold his composition book to a classmate. In the first place he is intelligent and old enough to realize how embarrassing this would turn out to be, and second, he is only too conscious of the interest of the press in anything to do with himself and his family. The suggestion that his parents keep him so short of money that he has to find other means to raise it is also a complete invention. Finally, the police would not have attempted to regain the composition book unless they were quite satisfied that it had been obtained illegally.

Far from printing a retraction, the editors of *Time* headlined the letter "Moneyed Prince Charlie," with the rider: "The Royal Family's press officer mounts a princely defence in his belated offer to clarify the case."

Though the affair dragged on for some time yet, it was mercifully forgotten by the following Easter, when Charles was confirmed at Windsor. Though his young seriousness took on, for the first time, a contemplative air which is today very familiar, the episode is primarily remembered more for the attitude of his father, who took a dim view of the entire proceedings. Prince Philip thought his son too young, at sixteen, for solemn acceptance into the Church of England, and had indeed been undergoing a period of doubt about his own religious beliefs. Philip's tortured progress from the Greek Orthodoxy of his childhood through Salem's German Protestantism to the formal Anglicanism of his adopted life had bred a disenchantment, even a cynicism; there had been a time, though he had now in middle age reverted to Anglican orthodoxy, when he had classed himself agnostic, perhaps an atheist. Again, Charles was in a different mould. During pre-confirmation talks with the Dean of Windsor, Robert Woods, he displayed a sound grasp of his undertakings, and his faith has not since wavered. His father, at the time, was intent on making his protest felt, and anyway considered the then Archbishop of Canterbury, Dr Michael Ramsey, a very tiresome preacher. Throughout his son's confirmation service in St George's Chapel, Windsor, Prince Philip conspicuously read a book. "Come and have a drink," said Woods to Ramsey afterwards. "Thank you," said an outraged Archbishop. "Bloody rude, that's what I call it."

Back at Gordonstoun, Charles finally managed to pass maths "O" level, graduated from the piano via the trumpet to the cello, and scored a local triumph as Macbeth – despite, inevitably enough, much merriment in the audience when the three witches cried: "All hail, Macbeth, that shalt be King hereafter!" It was the high point of a year during which school life had become, after those early trials, somewhat monotonous. Charles was in the mood for a change, and for once his parents agreed that his position might now be used to afford him a privilege allowed few other school boys. On condition that he would return to Gordonstoun to finish the work he had begun there, he could take a break at a school somewhere in the Commonwealth.

During her coronation tour of Australia, the Queen had

promised that she would "send my eldest son to visit you too, when he is older." The promise seemed long overdue in that autumn of 1965, when the Australian Prime Minister, Robert Menzies, seized the chance of a visit to London to persuade the Queen that the ideal choice would be Geelong Grammar School – the so-called "Eton of Australia," near Melbourne, in his own state of Victoria. It was the then Australian High Commissioner in London, Sir Alexander Downer, himself a Geelong old boy, who introduced the notion of Timbertop, Geelong's mountainside outpost 200 miles to the north, in remote but accessible foothills of the Victorian Alps.

Geelong sent all its boys for a year of exercise and "self-reliance" at Timbertop, which at first made Charles fear that it sounded like an Australian Gordonstoun. In fact, the school's philosophy is less heavy-handed, more homespun. By self-reliance, the school meant literally that: there was a handful of masters *in loco parentis*, but the boys were mainly younger ones in the charge of their seniors, who would appeal to the staff only in the event of emergency. Theirs was a rural life of comparative self-sufficiency, each boy having broad freedom to spend his time as he pleased. It was above all an exercise in getting to know people and displaying leadership qualities, from which the young Prince of Wales, still far from sure of himself, could only benefit. Being of the age of the older boys, he would undertake the responsibility of having a younger group in his direct care. Unlike his fellows, he would have to spend some time working for his GCE "A" levels in history and French, scheduled for his return to Gordonstoun, but the rest of the time would be more or less his own, in excellent fishing and walking countryside. Though made famous by Neville Shute in *The Far Country*, the gumtree forests around Mount Timbertop were otherwise undiscovered by the rest of humanity.

Charles flew out at the end of January 1966. Though just seventeen, he had still not entirely conquered his fear of new, unknown situations and again remembers feeling very apprehensive. He had heard that Australians were "critical" and expected a mixed reception. Even more unnerving, it was his first trip abroad without either of his parents, though he had reassuring company in the shape of two familiar figures: his detective, Detective Inspector Derek Sharp, and Squadron-Leader David Checketts, then the thirty-five-year-old equerry to Prince Philip.

A former public relations man with a distinguished RAF record, Checketts was to prove a mainstay of Charles's life for the next thirteen years. In Australia he set up home with his wife and family at Devon Farm, some 120 miles from Timbertop, and acted as a kind of business manager for the Prince. The farm became a headquarters for dealing with all press and administrative inquiries, and for entertaining Charles over many a down-to-earth week-end. The Prince would muck in like a member of the family, making his own bed, coming down to breakfast in his dressing-gown, doing his share of the household chores and acting as an elder brother to the Checketts' young children. It was the beginning of a lasting friendship: in time Checketts was to become his equerry and later his first private secretary.

Checketts has said of those seven months in Australia: "I went out there with a boy and returned with a man." Many others, including Charles himself, have since testified that this was the period in which he at last shed his perennial burden of "late development" and grew into manhood. If the Australian public did at first receive him with inquisitive caution, it was the acceptance of his schoolmates which the Prince was more concerned to win. One night at Timbertop, after taking a walk in the rain, he knew that he had succeeded. When returning to his dormitory duties carrying a rolled umbrella, he was delighted to be greeted by a chorus of "Pommy bastard!"

Timbertop boys live together in a compound of nine huts, each containing about fifteen, and each supervised by an older boy described as "a sort of NCO." One such was Charles, who shared a room in the masters" quarters with a sheep-farmer's son named Stuart Macgregor, a former head boy of Geelong who had come out to Timbertop to study in peace for his university entrance. Here Charles, too, studied for his "A" levels. He did not attend what few classes there were, but spent time supervising the younger boys in such chores as woodcutting, boiler-stoking and (again) dustbin-emptying. He joined in the strenuous hikes and cross-country runs which were compulsory most afternoons and weekends, and earned popularity by rather neglecting his studies for the life of the outback; a familiar figure silhouetted against the horizon, he was occasionally late with the essays he sent down to supervisors at Geelong. His Australian hosts were introducing him, quite deliberately, to a university style of tuition, not knowing whether he would ever again have the chance to enjoy this style of academic life.

Excursions further afield became more exotic: sheep-shearing and pig-swilling, gem-hunting and panning for gold. Charles felled trees, took part in a scheme to help war widows and was introduced to the local ornithology. He was thoroughly enjoying himself. Timbertop, he found, was as stimulating as Gordonstoun had become monotonous. He was popular among his fellows for himself, not his rank, and he had never known such freedom to wander the great outdoors at will. He had originally come to Australia for one term, but the Queen had privately directed that he might stay for a second if he so wished. The choice left entirely to him, Charles decided without hesitation to stay.

In a vivid account for the *Gordonstoun Record*, under the heading "Timbertop: or Beating about the Bush," Charles himself chronicled the joys of each day at Timbertop with boyish enthusiasm. Woodchopping, for instance, was

   essential as the boys" boilers have to be stoked with logs
   and the kitchen uses a huge number. The first week I was
   here I was made to go out and chop up logs on a hillside in

boiling hot weather. I could hardly see my hands for blisters. . . . Each afternoon after classes, which end at three o'clock, there are jobs which . . . involve chopping and splitting wood, feeding the pigs, cleaning out fly-traps (which are revolting glass bowls seething with flies and very ancient meat), or picking up bits of paper round the school. . . .

Of weekend expeditions into the bush, he wrote:

You can't see anything but gum-tree upon gum-tree, which tends to become rather monotonous. . . . You virtually have to inspect every inch of the ground you hope to put your tent on in case there are any ants or other ghastly creatures. There is one species of ant called Bull Ants which are three-quarters of an inch long, and they bite like mad! Some boys manage to walk fantastic distances over a weekend of four days or less, and do 130 or even 200 miles. The furthest I've been is 60 – 70 miles in three days, climbing about five peaks on the way. At the camp site the cooking is done on an open fire in a trench. You have to be very careful in hot weather that you don't start a bush fire, and at the beginning of this term there was a total ban in force, so that you ate all the tinned food cold.

An unexpectedly important moment in the Prince's life came at the end of that first term, when he joined a party of thirty other boys on Geelong's annual visit to the missionary stations in Papua New Guinea. They landed at Port Moresby – after a flight which had taken them over Prince of Wales Island – to find that an unexpectedly vast crowd had gathered at the airport to see the Prince, who had never before encountered such a throng in his own right. His instinct was to stay on the plane, in the hope that it would take off again as soon as possible. Checketts, as both remember it, had to "more or less kick the Prince of the plane"; Charles walked across the tarmac towards the ecstatic assembly in a state of high anxiety. Once he reached them, however, and found how easy it was to talk to people even in such difficult circumstances, he began to enjoy the experience. Since that day, he says, he has never again been nervous of big crowds.

Again the Prince wrote his own account of the trip, this time for the Geelong school magazine, and one extract reveals not only his dawning interest in anthropology, but also the beginnings of a personal philosophy which would later take firm root:

> I can't help feeling that less and less interest is being taken by the younger Papuans in the customs and skills of their parents and grandparents, because they feel that they have to live up to European standards, and that these things belong to the past and have no relevance to the present or future. . . . I was given one or two presents by young people, and when I asked if they had made them, they said their mothers or aunts had. No doubt, however, in the years to come, when there are new generations of Papuans, they will consider these ancient skills of use. . . .

In Sydney more than twenty years later, for Australia's 1988 bicentennial celebrations, Prince Charles told its people that his time at Timbertop had provided some of the most genuinely happy moments of his life. His second term there confirmed Charles in a lasting love for the Australian way of life, its penchant for the great outdoors, for ruggedly masculine pursuits and for a down-to-earth, no-nonsense attitude to friendship. He was to revisit the country very frequently, even attempt to spend a prolonged period there as Governor-General. "Australia," he said at the time, "opened my eyes. Having a title, and being a member of the upper-classes, as often as not militates against you there. . . . Australia conquered my shyness." By way of repaying the compliment, the headmaster of Geelong, Thomas Garnett, said that before the Prince's visit "most Australians had very hazy and possibly erroneous ideas of him . . . as just a distant and uninteresting figurehead. In future most of them will know him as a friendly, intelligent, natural boy with a good sense of humour, who by no means has an easy task ahead of him in life."

Three terms back at Gordonstoun were to seem an unwelcome extension to his schooldays, though he had the consolation of becoming head boy, or "Guardian" (like his father before him), and passing two "A" levels (a Grade C in French and a B in history, with a distinction for his optional special paper). To his relief as much as his satisfaction, Charles had proved that he could win a university place in his own right, the first heir to the throne in British history to do so. His last year at Gordonstoun, more than anything else, showed the ever more earnest young Prince developing a fondness for the arts; inspired by hearing Jacqueline du Pré play the Dvořák concerto, he started regular cello lessons, and he sang the Pirate King in Gilbert and Sullivan's *The Pirates of Penzance*. Unlike his father, he showed little interest in matters scientific or technological; his preoccupations seemed to lie in the past rather than the future, and the time he had spent in the caves of Morayshire, bats fluttering around his head, was to be followed up with a close interest in archaeology at Cambridge and thereafter. He had played his last team games – apart from polo, much more an individualist's sport, anyway – and had no more than a broken nose to show for his time on the rugger field. His natural introspection had much more to feed on.

At home, too, there had been significant advances. Prince Charles had spent his eighteenth birthday studying for his "A" levels, barely aware that bells were tolling all over the country in honour of the occasion and judges at the Old Bailey wearing their finest scarlet robes. Upon that day, he had reached the age at which he could reign as king in his own right. If any disablement befell the sovereign, there would no longer be any constitutional need for his father to act as regent in his place. Now he was chairing his first meetings of the Duchy of Cornwall and undertaking his first full-scale public engagements with his parents. A date had also been set, in the summer of 1969, for his investiture as Prince of Wales at Caernarvon.

Charles had just two more years before his emergence, fully-fledged and much trumpeted, into public life. He was to spend them sampling a brief taste of a unique kind of freedom, the freedom of university life, which to most who have known it retains a distinctive flavour throughout all their subsequent metamorphoses. Charles was more than ready for it. He may have declared himself "glad" that he went to Gordonstoun, but he was even more glad to leave. "He's looking forward to leaving school," said his father. "There comes a time when you've had enough of it."

For his own part, the Prince summed up that "I might not have enjoyed school life as much as I might have, but that is because I am happier at home than anywhere else." He gave thanks that Gordonstoun had "developed my will-power" and "helped me to discipline myself." For self-discipline, he declared – "not in the sense of making you bath in cold water, but in the Latin sense, of giving shape and form to your life" – was surely "the most important thing" any education could instil. He has since proved even more of a traditionalist than his parents in his attitude to bringing up his own children – seeing no problem, for instance, about abandoning them to nannies in the school holidays while going off to fish alone in Scotland. So there seems every reason to expect him, in the fullness of time, to subject his own sons – for their own good – to the same Moray Firth miseries.

EIGHT

The Packaging of a Prince

"I don't blame people demonstrating.
They've never seen me before. They don't
know what I'm like."

A S PRIVATE secretary to the Queen, Sir William Heseltine is today the most powerful figure in Buckingham Palace besides the monarch herself. The only man with the instant ear of both sovereign and prime minister, he advises on constitutional matters, liaises with government and presides over a massive nexus of power, influence and patronage.

In the mid-1960s, Heseltine was assistant press secretary to the Queen, a brash young Australian already on his second stint in royal service. Private secretary to the Australian prime minister at the age of twenty-five, he had then spent two years in London as an assistant information officer at the Palace, before returning to Australia as right-hand-man to the Governor-General. During those few years back home, in the heart of the Commonwealth, Heseltine pondered the striking difference between the reserved, po-faced, almost sullen monarch in the popular mind and the shrewd, jaunty, often witty lady he had come to know. On his return to her employ in 1965, he determined to do something about it.

Back at the palace, the new press secretary found David

Checketts deep in similar musings over the immediate
future of Prince Charles. Traditionally, royal press officers
had regarded their role primarily as keeping the press at
bay; they saw it as their function, unlike most press or
public relations officers, more to discourage journalists
than to assist them, more to prevent anything being
printed than to promote their corporate product. But
these two progressive thinkers, still young by royal standards for the positions they held, had more contemporary
ideas. As Heseltine set about improving the monarch's
"image" – itself a word new-fangled enough to bring a curl
to courtly lips – his thinking dovetailed with Checketts's
proposals for some gentle orchestration of the Prince of
Wales's launch into public life. Together they devised a
four-year plan which amounted to the unprecedented
"packaging" of a prince and was to pave the way towards
a bold, often volatile new era in relations between the
monarchy and its people. By the time Heseltine finally
unveiled the centre-piece of his new royal iconography –
the joint BBC-ITV film *Royal Family*, shown on the eve
of Charles's investiture in 1969 – he had opened up to an
insatiable public a Pandora's Box of royal goodies which
could never again be slammed shut.

His employers, as yet oblivious of the Palace revolution
being hatched below stairs, were meanwhile proceeding
along rather more orthodox lines. On 22 December 1965,
the Queen and Prince Philip hosted a dinner-party at
Buckingham Palace with the express purpose of discussing
the Prince of Wales's future. Gathered around the table
were the Prime Minister (Harold Wilson), the Archbishop
of Canterbury (Michael Ramsey), Lord Mountbatten
(representing the Services, as Admiral of the Fleet), the
Dean of Windsor, the chairman of the Committee of University Vice-Chancellors (Sir Charles Wilson) and the
Queen's private secretary, Sir Michael Adeane. Adeane
had briefed all the guests beforehand on the subject for
discussion – who was not himself invited, thus somewhat

giving the lie to Philip's proud protestations that his son was involved in all decisions over his upbringing.

At breakfast next morning, Prince Charles learned from his parents that the conversation had continued into the small hours. As Charles had already indicated his own wish to go to university, the dinner-party had gone right through the pros and cons of ancient, "redbrick" and modern. These in turn were weighed against the Services: Dartmouth, Cranwell, Sandhurst. Soft drinks and beer were served after dinner, plus a brandy for the Prime Minister, who urged Mountbatten to speak his mind. "Trinity College, like his grandfather," said Charles's great-uncle Dickie, "Dartmouth like his father and grand-father, and then to sea in the Royal Navy, ending up with a command of his own." The traditional pattern, thought Charles's parents, seemed hard to resist.

But there would again be innovations. If he were to go to university, Charles was intent on living in college – like Edward VIII at Oxford, but unlike Edward VII and George VI at Cambridge, both of whom had lived in large town houses, their tutors travelling to them. None of the three had stayed at university the full three years, nor had any taken a degree. This remained a matter of vexed debate between Charles and his parents, who for now postponed a decision. The Prince himself at first favoured a multi-disciplinary course of study, perhaps including a dabble in medicine and other such curiosities – which would have made a final examination impossible. But a thoughtful Prince Philip kept his son's options open for him: "I don't think his course should be constrained by the absolute need to take a degree." Wary advisers whole-heartedly agreed, telling his parents: "For God's sake, don't let him risk exams."

Prince Charles himself opted for Cambridge, always preferring the old to the new wherever possible, and valu-ing his family's links with the university. Edward VIII had been the only Prince of Wales to choose Oxford, where he had won a reputation as a none-too-studious devotee of the high life. The more academically minded Charles had no such aspiration; he wanted, as far as he could tell, to seize the chance for some peace and quiet, to devote his last years free from royal duties to the kind of studies for which he would never again have time. Besides, Cambridge was closer to Sandringham, where he now had his own home in the shape of Wood Farm, the ideal weekend retreat.

The obvious choice of college was Trinity. Commissioned by the Queen to recommend one, the Dean of Windsor placed it at the top of his shortlist – not just because it was his own college, nor because of the welcome fact that his elder son Robert (whom the Prince knew) was already an undergraduate there, and his younger son Edward would be a contemporaneous freshman. Trinity was also the college of the Queen's father, King George VI, and of his brother the Duke of Gloucester, of King Edward VII and his ill-fated son Eddy, Duke of Clarence, quite apart from Bacon and Dryden, Marvell and Thackeray, Byron and Tennyson, Newton and Rutherford, Balfour and Baldwin, Melbourne, Grey and Campbell-Bannerman.

Its newly installed Master, moreover, was another senior politician, a valued and trusted friend to Charles's parents: R.A. Butler, the Conservative Chancellor, Foreign Secretary and Home Secretary, often described as "the greatest Prime Minister we never had." "Rab," it was universally agreed, would be the perfect figure to shoulder *in loco parentis* responsibilities which bore an unusually lofty resonance.

Butlers's genial independence of mind was to cause some problems over the next few years. He began at once, over tea with Charles at the Palace in December 1966, earning the wrath of some courtiers when he urged the Prince not to bother as yet with any specific study of the British constitution. There would be plenty of time later, he argued, for all that. This was a chance to study something in which Charles was genuinely interested; archaeology and anthropology, as the Prince himself was tentatively suggesting, sounded fine. It was also a time to develop some understanding of the structure of British society, perhaps even of the ritual adulation offered a monarchy by its people. Butler's young protégé agreed enthusiastically. In words which would return to haunt him, Charles relished the prospect of "three years when you are not bound by anything, and not married, and haven't got any particular job."

He duly arrived in Cambridge in October 1967, to embark on the Part One Tripos course in "ark and anth" under the supervision of Trinity's senior tutor, Dr Denis Marrian, who agreed to leave future options open. The only overt privilege to set the Prince apart from other freshmen, on Butler's recommendation, was the telephone on his study desk. Workmen from Sandringham had already furnished his first-floor "set" of rooms, number six on Staircase E of New Court, while the college found itself obliged to protest that the new kitchen installed during the summer vacation had been scheduled long before the Prince's arrival.

The chance to cook for himself was to prove a boon when Charles's hopes of dining with his fellow-undergraduates in the college hall soon fell foul of a new version of an old problem. As at Cheam and Gordonstoun people tended to hang back, even to avoid him; at Cambridge, moreover, this was the year of 1968 and all that, and it was not always fashionable to be seen in the company of princes. On one occasion Charles found himself locked out of the college late at night, along with another nervous young freshman; together they had to ring the porter to let them in. It was the kind of modest adventure which sometimes sparks undergraduate friendships. Next night in Hall, however, as Charles wandered down the aisle looking for someone to sit with, he saw the face of his co-conspirator turn away in acute embarrassment. Nobody wanted to be thought too anxious to become his friend.

To Butler's disappointment, Charles's initial circle of Cambridge friends centred around the polo-playing fraternity (he quickly won his half-Blue) and fellow-public schoolboys from the landed gentry (with whom he founded a hearty, all-male dining club) rather than the grammar-school products who comprised three-quarters of the college's population. One such whom he did befriend, largely because they shared rooms on the same staircase, was a Welsh economics student called Hywel Jones, an impassioned young Socialist destined to become president of Trinity's student union. It was Jones who persuaded Charles that it might broaden his outlook on things to join *all* the university political clubs, including Labour – a notion Butler had to scotch smartly.

The Master had by now introduced a pleasant little ritual which was to prove an important part of Charles's maturing process. Butler set aside half an hour for a private chat before dinner each evening, giving Charles his own key to a side entrance to the Master's Lodge, which led by way of what he liked to call "my secret staircase" directly into the Master's study. He found Charles "talented – which is a different word from clever, and a different word from bright." Though still a plodder academically, the Prince had a relentless curiosity about the ways of the world, which the Master was more than qualified to gratify. "He grew here," said Butler later. "When he arrived he was boyish, rather immature, and perhaps too susceptible to the influence of his family."

But if Butler had to explain patiently to the Prince of Wales why he must not show allegiance to any one political party, he was also shrewd enough to urge Charles to continue his exploration of socialist ideas with Hywel Jones, behind closed doors. Both Prince and republican now believe they moderate each other's views; and in later years, when he became a pin-striped member of one of Britain's leading economic think-tanks, Jones remained a regular dinner guest of the Prince as he sought to deepen his understanding of matters economic, both macro and micro.

Those evening chats with Butler, over Charles's three years at Trinity, made perhaps the most important single contribution in his young life so far to broadening his experience and understanding of his fellowman. As the Prince entered his twenties, the Grand Old Man of the Tory Party was quite as much a personal "guru" to the young Charles as was Dickie Mountbatten or, in later years, Laurens van der Post. But it is disappointingly characteristic of the older Charles to have disavowed Butler's influence when it was detailed in the author's earlier volume, *Charles, Prince of Wales*. This may be partly because of the excitement caused by Butler's revelation that he had encouraged a liaison between the virgin Prince and his research assistant on his memoirs, Lucia Santa Cruz, daughter of the then Chilean Ambassador to London, who has subsequently gone down in history as the Prince of Wales's first "real" girlfriend. But it also shows an ungrateful streak in Charles, a man quite as prepared to disown specific influences as to cultivate them. All too aware that he is easily led – but meanwhile wishing to project himself to the world, not without some justification, as his own man – he is increasingly capable of such virulent bouts of *amour propre*.

His immaturity at the time was another ghost the Prince did not particularly care to see returning to haunt him. Did he really think, for instance, that a false beard and spectacles would enable him to escape recognition while watching a student demonstration – "to see what they're like"? It is commendably in character that he was keen to take a look, and a sad comment on his plight that he felt unable to go disguised as himself. But it is no surprise, for all his hours of conversation with Hywel Jones, that the natural conservatism of his upbringing prevailed. "I do try and understand what they're getting at," said the first-year Prince as the Sorbonne students" siege of Paris sparked similar protests on campuses all over the world, including Cambridge, "but I can't help feeling that a lot of it is purely for the sake of change, which from my point of view is pointless."

In studious mood, Charles was otherwise little in evidence around Cambridge that first summer. "He writes useful and thoughtful essays, although sometimes they are a little rushed," reported his director of studies, Dr John Coles, to Dr Marrian. "He is interested in discussion and likes to draw parallels between the people we study and ourselves." It was a victory for dogged effort over natural ability when the summer vacation brought the news the he had won a place in Division I of Class II in the first-year Tripos Exams. An above-average result, it gave him the self-confidence to spurn Butler's advice, switch to a course in history and embark on an overt study of the British constitution.

"But why?" asked Butler.

"Because," the Master recalled Charles replying (though he himself has subsequently denied it), "I'm probably going to be King."

His second year is remembered more for the future King's performance in student cabaret than in his history tutorials with Dr Anil Seal, his engaging new director of studies. Charles's somewhat arch sense of humour – typified by his love of *The Goon Show* a long-running, anarchic British radio programme – was very much at home in undergraduate revue, where funny voices and painful puns tend to be the prime index of wit. Though the Cambridge Footlights have produced several generations of Britain's most talented recent comedians, the attempts of individual colleges to emulate them have always limped several light years behind. The best remembered image of the Prince of Wales's second year at Cambridge is that of him sitting onstage in a dustbin – a lasting icon of how easy it can be to set the nation on a roar. By the time his younger brother Edward aped these antics on national television in 1987 – roping in his siblings to enact his own version of undergraduate humour for charity – the Prince of Wales himself was high on the list of the embarrassed and unamused. Only narrowly did he dissuade his wife from joining in.

At Cambridge, meanwhile, the unequal struggle to keep the real world at bay was also, alas, beginning to fail. Perhaps it had always been a pipedream to expect the student Prince's parents to leave him in peace to enjoy university life, whether getting on with his studies or cavorting onstage. But Butler found himself increasingly annoyed by the number of "balcony jobs," as he scathingly called state occasions, for which Charles was "needlessly" summoned back to London. Then, in November 1967, came an announcement which caused Butler as much rage as it did Charles dismay. To the English historian A.J.P. Taylor, it was "a sordid plot to exploit Prince Charles . . . made for political reasons, and what is worse, for reasons of party . . . Mr. Wilson is imposing on Prince Charles a sacrifice he would not dream of imposing on his own son." Welsh Nationalists too were outraged by the news that Charles would be spending the summer term of 1969, immediately prior to his investiture as Prince of Wales at Caernarvon, studying Welsh at the University College of Wales, Aberystwyth.

Since the death of Llewelyn-ap-Gruffydd in 1282, at the hands of the English invader, Edward I, Welsh Nationalists have always had some difficulty taking English Princes of Wales to their hearts. Edward's installation of his son two years later started a line of *de haut en bas* English princes whom this vociferous minority of Welshmen still cannot abide 700 years later. By the time Charles arrived at Aberystwyth he has passed his twenty-first birthday, delivered his first public speech, attended his first royal garden party and given his first interview (to Checketts's old friend Jack de Manio, of BBC Radio's *Today* programme) – all part of the increasing momentum of the Heseltine – Checketts "launch" package. In the process he had begun to square up to the demands arbitrarily imposed upon him by an unforgiving destiny. But nothing had prepared him for overt hostility ranging from crude student abuse to bomb attacks, hunger strikes and even assassination threats.

The timing proved, to say the least, unfortunate: 1969 was the last year of the second Wilson government, a period of deeply resented public austerity, which boosted the resurgence of a fierce strain of nationalism around the principality. As a spate of bomb attacks was mounted on public buildings, a Special Branch security squad was assigned to mount a twenty-four-hour watch over the Prince. The men of violence were universally denounced, but there was widespread English sympathy for Welsh resentment of this "token" term learning a half-dead language at, ironically enough, this most English of Welsh universities. Even the English-born president of the Aberystwyth student union declared the forthcoming investiture "a cheap, shoddy political gesture.... If I were Welsh, I would feel incensed." On the day of Charles's arrival, students tried (in vain) to saw the head off a statue of the last Prince of Wales, Charles's great-uncle, on the town's promenade.

All Charles could do was confess to "misgivings" and make the best of a bad job – burying himself, with only eight weeks before a major speech in Welsh at an Eisteddfod, in the university's language laboratory. It was an anxious and lonely period – "I haven't made many friends, there haven't been many parties" – but the fact that even his tutor, Edward Millward, was a Welsh Nationalist helped his understanding of Welsh grievances and aspirations. "If I've learnt anything in the last eight weeks," he said as term ended, "it's been about Wales and its problems." Mindful of the Papuans who had caused him such concern while at Timbertop, he had discovered that the Welsh were "depressed about what might happen if they don't try and preserve their language and culture, which is unique and special to Wales. And if something is unique and special, I think it's well worth preserving."

Slowly, Charles's new subjects warmed to him. By the time he had spoken his first few public words of reasonably elegant Welsh, they were beginning to call him "Carlo bach" – a term of endearment as significant in Wales as "Pommy bastard" had been in Australia. His display of resolution in the face of ugly threats had led to a modest personal triumph, much admired by his father – "He came, saw and conquered the Welsh," his proud father confided to a friend – and a source of great relief to David Checketts, whose pride in his young master was fast growing. As Checketts prepared for the next phase of the "unveiling" process, he realized that he had an unexpected ace up his sleeve: by hitherto protecting the Prince as far as possible from direct personal publicity, he had also concealed the fact that this young man was fast showing himself equal to the tasks ahead of him. He was alert, shrewd and solemnly aware of his role. All of which would come as something of a surprise to the great English public, who in the Palace's view could have been forgiven for thinking – after the Cherry Brandy Incident, the Goonish theatricals and the initial inability to handle Welsh protest – that this Prince was just another upper-class half-wit.

Charles may have defused Aberystwyth, but he had as yet won only half the battle. He now knew enough local history to appreciate the significance to the Welsh of Caernarvon Castle, captured by the English invader in 1282. It was there that King Edward I, after killing Llewelyn-ap-Gruffydd (and hanging, beheading, disembowelling and quartering his brother), had declared his infant son the first English Prince of Wales. And it was there, nearly 700 years later, that Charles himself was now to be invested as the twenty-first.

There were times when the Queen had regretted the commitment she had made in 1958, just as she had regretted creating Charles Prince of Wales so young. The decline of the British economy, the rise of Welsh nationalism and the advent of an era of violent protest all conspired to make such a ceremony seem at best a political blunder, at worst a danger to its protagonist's life. There was no historical obligation for such a ritual; the legend that Edward I displayed his infant son from the battlements had long been declared apocryphal, and the only precedent for a public investiture in six centuries was that less than six decades before of the last Prince of Wales, the future King Edward VIII and Duke of Windsor, who had found himself the unhappy victim of some unashamed political chicanery by David Lloyd George, then Chancellor of the Exchequer.

For more then 650 years, well aware that Caernarvon Castle remained a symbol of English usurpation of Welsh sovereignty, most monarchs had been content to invest their sons in Parliament, palaces or safely English county towns. In 1911, however, during the painful disestablishment of the Welsh Church, Lloyd George had talked King George V into a ceremony supposedly designed as a demonstration of Anglo-Welsh unity, but more likely in fact to enhance his own political prestige and appease the opponents of his regular assaults on inherited privilege. The King was duly persuaded that the "mini-coronation" of his seventeen-year-old son would be an apt climax to his own coronation tour of Britain; and the ceremony went ahead over the Prince's strenuous protests that the "preposterous rig" he was required to wear would make him a laughing-stock among his friends in the navy. The episode was a momentous political triumph for Lloyd George, who stands to this day in aggressive bronze splendour in the Castle Square, his back turned on the battlements – "the alternative, I suppose," as Charles himself gloomily pointed out in 1969, "to turning his back on the people."

As Lord Snowdon, Constable of the Castle, made elaborately artistic preparations for the world's first major outside broadcast in colour, the political protests mounted. Emrys Hughes MP launched a sustained Commons campaign against a ceremony to be held "in a castle built by Welsh slave labour under the orders of the intruder, the conqueror," and led better-supported protests against the mounting costs – a cunning ploy, he believed, to facilitate an increase in the Civil List. Plaid Cymru, the Welsh Nationalist Party, dissociated itself from this "piece of English trickery," while the more extreme Welsh Language Society daubed revolutionary slogans in Welsh over roads, bridges and traffic signs throughout the country. Both groups disavowed the sterner forms of protest which began on 17 November, when a time-bomb exploded in the unhappily named Temple of Peace in Cardiff, just as Snowdon and the Secretary of State for Wales, George Thomas, were arriving for a planning meeting with 450 Welsh delegates. It was the first in a succession of fifteen bomb attacks on government and military buildings, post offices and pipelines which moved the Chief Constable of Cardiff to declare: "If this doesn't stop, someone is going to get killed." He was to be proved right on the morning of the investiture itself.

Its imminence was giving a new lease of life to a thin red line of anarchists calling itself the Free Welsh Army – who claimed close relations with the Provisional IRA, then a year into its renewed campaign of violence in Northern Ireland, but were mercifully less well organized. As Plaid Cymru voted to boycott the ceremony, and a poll found that forty-four per cent of the Welsh thought the ceremony "a waste of money," Charles himself sought to pour princely balm on what he recognized as "a friction-point" for many people: "I don't blame people demonstrating. They've never seen me before. They don't know what I'm like. I've hardly been to Wales, and you can't expect people to be over-zealous about the fact of having a so-called English prince come amongst them and be frightfully excited about it." Echoing his great-uncle, he said that he would be "glad when it was over."

Not until a decade after the ceremony did George Thomas (by then Speaker of the House, later Viscount Tonypandy) reveal to the author how near the investiture committee had come to calling it all off. By early 1969, six months before the appointed date, the atmosphere had grown so ugly – and the threats on the Prince's life so realistic – that an emergency meeting was called at the Welsh Office to discuss postponement. Thomas himself, his Welsh eloquence adding an extra edge to his political cunning, argued that postponement would in truth mean cancellation. No part of the United Kingdom, he said, should be allowed to become a no-go area for the royal family. "It will require great moral courage from that young man, but he has already displayed it in considerable quantities." Over the months of preparation Thomas had become a close and avuncular figure to Charles. When he passed on the Prince's own wish that the ceremony should go ahead, the meeting was finally swayed – and officially declared never to have taken place.

It was only three weeks before the investiture, at the dreaded post-Aberystwyth speech, that Charles himself transformed the atmosphere. Three hundred well-pronounced, unfluffed words of Welsh to Urdd Gobaith Cymru, the Welsh League of Youth, were enough to still the noise of protesters. A respectful reference to Llewelyn-ap-Gruffydd, and a promise to work for the preservation of the language, then proceeded to reduce hardened nationalists to tears. "If anyone lays a finger on that lad," one was heard to announce in an Aberystwyth pub that night, "they'll swing from the nearest tree." Plaid Cymru called for an end to the graffiti protest campaign and voted to rethink its boycott. Suddenly, after all the bluster, the open-hearted Welsh people saw what an impossible position Charles had been placed in, and what a decorous exit he had managed to make. "I'm not a royalist. I'm a socialist," declared one mid-Wales trades union official. "But I tell you this: that boy has already done more for Wales than we could dream of." It fell, however, to the Mayor of Caernarvon, Ifor Bowen Griffiths, to scale the true heights of authentic Welsh hyperbole as he declared Charles "the ace in our pack. . . . When he stood up at the Eisteddfod and started to speak in Welsh, he wasn't just a boy. He was a prince. You could have put a suit of armour on that lad and sent him off to Agincourt."

On investiture eve, however, the Queen's progress north with her family in the royal train was delayed for an hour outside Chester, as bomb disposal experts dealt with a sinister cardboard box found beneath the bridge which was to carry them over the River Dee. It turned out to be a hoax. But only hours later, around dawn on 1 July itself, a real bomb exploded in Abergele, thirty miles from Caernarvon, killing the two men who were attempting to position it against the wall of government office. In London the previous afternoon, unknown to the Prince of Wales, Jack de Manio, Denis Marrian and others had foregathered in a BBC television studio to record personal tributes to Charles, to be broadcast in the event of his assassination.

The atmosphere in the coach which carried the Prince, Checketts and Thomas through the crowds to the Castle that morning was decidedly tense. "What was that?" Charles asked Thomas, after a loud bang in the distance, which both recognized as the sound of another bomb. "Oh, a royal salute, Sir," replied Thomas. "Peculiar sort of royal salute," said Charles uneasily. "Peculiar sort of people up here," replied the southern Welshman of his northern compatriots. As they passed the harbour they could see two minesweepers grimly patrolling the entrance, where Charles had hoped for the royal yacht *Britannia* to hover regally. Above them helicopters scrutinized the crowd, relaying the watching faces to a police control centre. A banana skin was thrown under the hooves of the horses pulling the Queen's carriage, and even Princess Margaret was asked for proof of her identity.

Once inside the Castle, according to both Charles and Thomas, everyone felt safer and began to relax. A couple of hours later it was at last all over, as Charles solemnly declared to his mother, before a worldwide television audience of 200 million: "I, Charles, Prince of Wales, do become your liege man of life and limb and of earthly worship, and faith and truth I will bear unto you to live and die against all manner of folks."

At the same moment, across the world, three men were preparing to land on the moon. But this archaic ritual in a coastal corner of Wales – watched with mixed emotions by the aged Duke of Windsor in his Paris home – had a greater contemporary significance than was immediately apparent. The previous evening Heseltine's "humanizing" backdrop, the television film *Royal Family*, had at last been shown, giving the British people an unprecedented peek into the private life of their royals. The majestic hands now raising Charles to his feet had last been seen wielding a barbecue fork; Prince Philip, watching solemnly in his Field Marshal's uniform, had been rowing a protesting Prince Andrew into the Balmoral sunset; Her Majesty's liege man of life and limb had reduced his brother Edward to tears by accidentally snapping a cello string in his face.

Through that film, and a television interview with David Frost, Charles had been discovered in every British home to be every mother's ideal son. The royals may not quite be a family like any other, but they were a family, who at least some of the time did relatively normal things in relatively normal ways. For once, the pomp and circumstance of royalty in full-blown public ceremonial took second place, in the minds of those watching, to the sight of the private family cracking jokes around the breakfast table.

Paradoxically, the antique ritual crystallized a new era of family monarchy that day, to reach its climax in the Queen's silver jubilee eight years later, and to be at the heart of the national outpourings over the Prince of Wales's wedding in 1981. But Heseltine's brainchild would soon grow into something of a Frankenstein's Monster, creating a public demand for private royal titbits far in excess of supply. In time it would grow so insatiable that cynical invention would become the only way many national newspapers could continue to capitalize on its contribution to their profits. And the main victim, in his own eyes, would be the young man for whom the whole master-plan had been invented.

But popular misconceptions about himself, his character and his role were only part of the burden an increasingly unhappy Charles now shouldered as he was thrust, with some reluctance, out into the arms of a rapaciously waiting world.

NINE

Enter Diana

> "I think an awful lot of people have got the
> wrong idea of what marriage is all about. It
> is rather more than just falling madly in
> love with somebody and having a love affair
> for the rest of your married life."

O N HIS thirtieth birthday in 1978, after ritual celebrations in Buckingham Palace and around the land, the Prince of Wales told his staff that he had three priorities for the decade ahead: to learn more about the nation over which he would one day reign, to step up his work overseas as an unofficial salesman for British industry – and, most urgently, to find the nation and the Commonwealth its future Queen.

It was not just politics which had cheated Charles of his most cherished recent ambition. The absence of a bride, to act as his hostess, had been as powerful an argument as any constitutional embarrassments against his becoming Governor-General of his beloved Australia. The notion had been discussed several times throughout the 1970s – at the suggestion, ironically enough, of Gough Whitlam, the Labour Prime Minister who had abolished the National Anthem, and whose dismissal in 1975 by the then Governor-General, Sir John Kerr, brought the office too close to politics for princely comfort. Whitlam's successor, the

Conservative Malcolm Fraser, was already hinting on the royal grapevine that he might be able to "fix" things (thus, *en passant*, shoring up his own political security with a sizable proportion of the Australian electorate). Fraser's own political fragility, and the upsurge in Australian republicanism, were in time to make these promises hollow – but in 1978 they were anyway conditional upon the Prince of Wales finding himself a princess.

Apart from his immediate predecessor, whose eventual choice of bride led him to renounce the throne, Charles was the first Prince of Wales to have reached the age of thirty unmarried since James Stuart, the Old Pretender, in 1718 (and he took a wife the following year). Of those Princes of Wales who became Kings of England, only Henry v and Charles ii were unmarried at thirty. But each remained so only two more years; and each, already on the throne, had had a singularly busy youth.

Prince Charles, soon to become the oldest unmarried Prince of Wales in history had had no Agincourt, no exile from a republican government, to occupy his twenties. The decade had proved a long, often troubled period of slow drift. After his baptism of fire at Caernarvon he had returned to Trinity to win himself an average BA honours degree, Class II Division ii, despite the distractions of more student theatricals, and had then embarked upon a six-year stint in Her Majesty's Services.

From the moment of his arrival at Cranwell, the RAF training college, the Prince displayed a natural talent for flying; besides, he much welcomed the unwonted sense of freedom afforded by the solitude of the cockpit. He won his wings effortlessly before moving on, again in his father's footsteps, to the Royal Naval College, Dartmouth – the springboard to five years service as an officer aboard Her Majesty's wardships *Norfolk, Minerva, Jupiter* and *Hermes*. Again, life out at sea with the navy was as "normal" as it would ever be – no press, no sightseers, no red boxes, not even a private detective – and Charles relished his rare chance to become "one of the lads." For a while he even felt relaxed enough to sport a beard, which lent him a striking resemblance to his great-grandfather, King George V (though it had to come off, on the Queen's orders, before his next state occasion). Typically, alas, the Prince had begun most to savour the bravado of Service life just as it was ending, with a chance to combine his love of both air and sea in the airborne arm of the Royal Navy.

To his mother's occasional dismay, he funked none of the more hazardous aspects of training – from underwater escape practice in a 100-foot training tank to royalty's first-ever parachute jump (a "somewhat hairy" experience, as his feet got caught in the rigging). So he was not best pleased to learn that two Mark V Jet Provosts set aside for his personal use had been specially modified, or to be told that Buccaneer strike aircraft and Sea King anti-submarine helicopters were too dangerous for him to fly. "I'm stupid enough to like trying things," he said at the time, "though perhaps I do push myself too hard." There were shudders between the Palace and Whitehall when the heir to the throne's training course in Wessex V helicopters involved him in a rapid succession of three emergency landings, due respectively to computer failure, engine failure and a broken fragment of metal lodging in his engine. But he survived – and finished his navy days in style with a proud command of his own, aboard one of the smallest ships in the British fleet, the wooden-hulled minehunter HMS *Bronington*.

Amid recurrent suggestions that a military training was no longer appropriate for the throne, the Prince remained mindful of the dictum of Lord Mountbatten's father, Prince Louis of Battenberg, to the future King George V: "There is no more fitting preparation for a king than to have been trained in the navy." The criticism, said Charles, was "pointless and ill-informed." The Services attracted "a large number of duty-conscious people"; military service was "a worthwhile occupation which I am convinced will stand me in good stead for the rest of my

life." These swashbucking years may have provided him
with some of his most down-to-earth moments yet, amid
the hearty camaraderie of Service life, but their always
temporary status had also accentuated his sense of pur-
poselessness. Charles's twenties were to end on a high
note, with his chairmanship of the Queen's Silver Jubilee
Appeal in 1977. But this particular decade – for most
other mortals one of the most vividly enjoyable of their
lives – proved for the earnest young Prince of Wales a
period of increasingly agonised introspection.

He launched, in embryonic shape, his first charity, the
Prince's Trust, and took over from Lord Mountbatten as
president of the United World Colleges. By his thirtieth
birthday Charles was president or patron of some 200
charities, clubs, committees and learned organizations.
But there was no cohesive purpose to his public activities,
nor indeed to his private life. With few friends beyond the
small circle he could trust, mostly his staff and the back-
slapping polo brigade, he remained a very solitary and
rather confused figure. Few Englishmen of thirty, after all,
still live at home with their parents. Unable to go out on a
whim, moreover, Charles was as often as not spending his
evenings alone, eating a solitary meal off a tray with a
glass of milk, with the television as his only companion.
Even he began to see that, for personal as much as constitutional reasons, he needed a wife.

As yet, however, he had simply not met the right girl at
the right time. A late developer sexually as in other ways,
again because of the artificiality of his upbringing, Charles
was still rather clumsy with women. Beyond the obvious
pulling-power of his station in life, the Prince's gentle and
caring nature was his main appeal to the opposite sex; but
he was a gauche and rather awkward beau, often disappearing without explanation from his girlfriends" lives as
abruptly as he had entered them. It did not help that his
sense of propriety obliged all his escorts to call him "Sir,"
even in moments of intimacy; nor that his detective had
to remain with him everywhere he went, playing goose-

berry in the back of the Prince's Aston-Martin. As many a girlfriend came and went, Charles grew more and more depressed, almost desperate. For a while his parents even grew concerned that their oldest son might "go the way of the Duke of Windsor." When Thames TV's series *Edward and Mrs Simpson* was screened in 1978, Charles's thirtieth year, the Royal Household were very struck by the degree of sympathy he showed for his great-uncle's plight. Were all the liberal reforms of his upbringing, in the end, to prove Charles's undoing?

The reasons the Prince hesitated so long over his choice of a bride, disappointing matrons and tantalizing maidens the world over, were many and various: personal and public, domestic and constitutional. For no other man in the world was his quest for a life-partner so complex, so fraught with potential pitfalls, so hedged around with restrictions. Anxious to recreate the happy family atmosphere of his own childhood, Charles considered himself in need of a paragon among women – prepared to be privately loving, supportive and long-suffering, the sole confidante of a man with many confidences to share, as well as publicly conscientious. And yet there were so many restrictions on his choice.

Under the 1689 Bill of Rights – enshrined in the 1701 Act of Settlement, by which his family's claim to the throne is legally established – he was forbidden to marry a Catholic. Under the Royal Marriages Act of 1772, he was barred from marrying without the consent of his mother or both Houses of Parliament. As the future Supreme Governor of the Church of England, he could not marry a divorcee, or indeed any girl with what the British like to euphemize a "as past" – which, in the permissive 1970s, narrowed the field considerably. The Queen, as custodian of the royal blood line, was keen for her son and heir to marry a princess; but eligible, let alone desirable, non-Catholic European princesses without a past were in somewhat short supply.

As a private British citizen, the Prince could of course

marry whomsoever he chose. But a match with an ineligible or even unsuitable girl would have obliged him to renounce his right to the throne, a course which militated against every instinct bred in him. Constitutional niceties take little note of social change, and a late-twentieth-century Prince was quite simply and forlornly stuck with a set of rules devised for his eighteenth- and nineteenth-century ancestors. There were times when his mother considered repeal of the ancient laws governing royal marriages, but in time her own deep-dyed conservatism prevailed.

Only recently Charles's cousin, Prince Michael of Kent, had been obliged to surrender his place in the line of succession to marry a Catholic divorcee, Baroness Marie-Christine von Reibnitz. Elizabeth II's reign had otherwise seen the monarchy catch up to some extent with the social mores of the times. In 1953, for instance, the new Queen Elizabeth II had felt obliged to talk her younger sister out of marrying a divorcee, Group-Captain Peter Townsend; twenty-five years later, she permitted her to divorce the man she had married instead. It was the closest divorce had come to the throne since the profligate reign of King Henry VIII.

But Margaret was way down the line of succession, and the Queen feels very differently about her own children, both as their mother and their monarch. There would be no such relaxation of the royal rules for the Prince of Wales or his siblings. When in later years Princess Anne thought her Aunt Margaret's divorce might smooth her own passage towards a separation, she was firmly told otherwise. Prince Philip himself was the offspring of a broken marriage; but there was no way that Charles could contemplate marrying a divorcee, or making anything other than a lifetime commitment to whomever he did finally choose.

These private agonies were only worsened by the remorseless public pressure. Throughout his twenties, Britain's tabloid press heard wedding bells every time the Prince was seen out and about with any member of the opposite sex. But British newspapers had been marrying Charles off since he was three. In 1952, upon his mother's accession to the throne, the Sunday newspapers were already printing the first of countless lists of suitable brides for a Prince who, mercifully enough, could not yet even read. Twenty years later they were still publishing regular photomontages of literally hundreds of glamorous, pouting candidates, from titled daughters of English stately homes to less comely, often ineligible, obscure foreign royalty. In June 1977 the *Daily Express* even managed exclusively and "officially" to announce the Prince of Wales's betrothal to Princess Marie-Astrid of Luxembourg – "the formal engagement will be announced from Buckingham Palace on Monday" – offering various bland solutions to the minor inconvenience that she happened to be a Roman Catholic. By now the Palace's ever more exasperated denials had become cries in a sceptical wilderness.

The Prince's quest for a bride became an uncomfortable obsession. "Married, aren't you?" he would ask people. "Fun, is it?" The seemingly perennial bachelor forlornly told a friend: "Whenever I invite people to a dinner party these days, they *all* seem to have got married." To his small circle of intimates, he talked of little else. When twenty-seven he had told an interviewer that he thought thirty was "about the right age to marry"; now that remark returned to haunt him with a vengeance. His parents had long tried to remain understanding, but his father began to grow characteristically impatient. "You'd better get on with it, Charles," said Philip, with some justice, "or there won't be anyone left."

By his own account the Prince had "fallen in love countless times"; he had openly enjoyed the company of several racy public figures, such as the film star Susan George, as well as innumerable blue-blooded English roses. But many girls once seen on his arm had long since given up on their indecisive Prince to marry others and start families of their own. Several genuine romances had crumbled under the pressure of pursuit by paparazzi, who were not above pitching round-the-clock camp on the doorstep of their current favourite. A despairing Charles was forced at times to use decoys – such as Penelope East-wood, then the girlfriend (now the wife) of his friend Norton Knatchbull, Lord Romsey – to distract attention from some authentic passing fancy.

Other overtly true loves, such as the beautiful but star-crossed Davina Sheffield, fell by the wayside when jealous former lovers revealed all to the gossip columns. Blonde, dramatically attractive Davina, the soldier's daughter, was one of the few girlfriends with whom Charles was so besot-ted as to allow himself to be photographed arm-in-arm. He had met her at a time of tragedy, in 1976, when Davina was brought home from refugee work in Vietnam by the brutal murder of her mother by raiders at their Oxfordshire home. Of all the Prince's girlfriends, she was the one whose loss he eventually felt most dearly; but Davina became a non-starter from the moment a former boyfriend revealed that they had once lived together.

For years the bookies' favourite was Lady Jane Welles-ley, daughter of the Duke of Wellington, a childhood friend who had grown into a beautiful and talented woman more than equal to the task of becoming Britain's next Queen. But Charles's puppy-love for Jane came early in his twenties, when he was still immature enough to treat women as mere playthings, teasing her *ad nauseam*, and using a secret holiday on her father's Spanish estate to pelt the poor girl with melons. Jane was, besides, a deter-mined career girl with bright prospects in television, who was far from ready to surrender her professional opportu-nities for a life of comfortable incarceration at court. For perhaps the first time in British history, the prospect of a proposal from the Prince of Wales was dodged by a more than suitable young woman who simply did not want to be Queen.

Other authentic loves included the "ice maiden" Anna Wallace, a fiery character who stalked out of the Queen

Mother's eightieth birthday party, Lily Langtry-like, railing that Charles had been ignoring her. At thirty, he still carried a torch for the worldly girl-about-town Sabrina Guinness, although marriage into "the Irish beerage" had always been out of the question. But for solace and companionship he turned more and more to two married girlfriends, Camilla Parker-Bowles and Dale, Lady Tryon, who eventually became his chief advisers on the potential brides on offer. Australian-born Dale, whom the Prince affectionately nicknamed "Kanga," is the wife of lord (Anthony) Tryon, the banker son of the Queen's late treasurer; Camilla, a niece of the Cubitt building family millionaire, Lord Ashcombe, is married to Andrew Parker-Bowles, a career officer in the Household Cavalry.

Like his great-uncle the Duke of Windsor, when he was Prince of Wales, Charles found a unique security in the close friendship of married women; he could be seen with them, for one thing, without any danger of starting more wearisome marriage rumours. They were able to offer advice and friendship without either party having to worry about declarations of interest. Charles is godfather to both their eldest children – though neither woman, understandably, was to find much favour with the bride he did eventually choose.

On the domestic front, many young people suffering for love find it easier to confide in their grandparents than their parents. Charles was no exception. His chief confidants on matters of the heart were the Queen Mother and his "honorary grandfather," Lord Mountbatten. It did not much help that Mountbatten developed a penchant for going public with his enthusiasm for Charles to sow some wild oats; gleefully, if anonymously, he revealed to *Time* magazine that this Prince of Wales, like so many of his predecessors, enjoyed "popping in and out of bed with girls." Something of a Pander by inclination, and a man of devout dynastic ambitions, Mountbatten was secretly anxious for his young protégé to marry his own granddaughter, Amanda Knatchbull. Optimistically he packed

them off on several holidays together – strictly, for protocol's sake, *en famille* – at the Knatchbull retreat on the
Caribbean island of Eleuthera. But their friendship was
never to blossom into love.

The forces of Queen Elizabeth the Queen Mother,
meanwhile, ranged in amorous opposition to those of
Mountbatten, were keeping a dark filly up their sleeves in
the shape of the demure, long-legged, teenage grand-
daughter of the Queen Mother's lady-in-waiting and lifelong friend, Ruth, Lady Fermoy. She was the younger
sister of Charles's other long-term girlfriend, Lady Sarah
Spencer, once herself a potential bride, now merely a
warm friend. Sarah was even forgiven the only indiscretion made by all Charles's long roll-call of escorts, when
press innuendo about the number of rooms in their skiing
chalet moved her to bare her heart to a journalist. "I am
not in love with him," she said, insisting that their relationship was platonic. "And I wouldn't marry anyone I
didn't love, whether it was the dustman or the King of
England. If he asked me, I would turn him down."
Charles, contrary to reports at the time, was more hurt
than annoyed. But Sarah was soon back among his weekend guests at Balmoral.

Over a decade of innumerable romances, Charles had
searched for a genuine love-match with a girl prepared to
endure the loss of privacy, spontaneity and independence
which goes with becoming royal. He did not want, like so
many Princes of Wales before him, to watch a marriage of
convenience slide into one of arrangement, in which his
princess turned a blind eye as he exercised his office's
traditional *droit de seigneur* over other men's wives.
Unlike many of his predecessors, Charles is not by nature
a libertine. "I think an awful lot of people have got the
wrong idea of what marriage is all about," he said before
he embarked on it. "It is rather more than just falling
madly in love with somebody and having a love affair for
the rest of your married life. Much more. It's basically a
very strong friendship. . . . I think you are very lucky if

you find the person attractive in the physical *and* the mental sense. . . . "

So it took ten years and more of heartache, speculation and intrigue before he at last chanced upon the apparently perfect candidate in the girl – for once, literally – next door, born on the royal estate at Sandringham. The sight of blushful young Diana Spencer amid the muddied hunting pinks at Althorp, her father's ancestral home in the Northamptonshire countryside, was manna from heaven. She was strikingly beautiful, poised for her age and seemed to possess a quality close to his heart: a sense of humour.

Charles had known Sarah Spencer's baby sister since she was in nappies. Their parents were lifelong friends. But his younger brothers" childhood playmate had never crossed his mind as a potential bride until this momentous meeting in a ploughed field, on a part of the Althorp estate known as Nobottle Wood, in the November 1977. At sixteen Diana still seemed very young; it took two more years of casual acquaintance, as she blossomed into young womanhood, before he began overtly to woo her. But the autumn of 1980 saw the thirty-one-year-old Prince of Wales confirmed in his original view that this sprightly if slightly chubby nineteen year old was "really rather stunning." Once a journalist had caught them embracing beside the River Dee at Balmoral, the world had a chance to think so too.

The Spencer family, on close investigation, proved to be much more English – and almost as aristocratic – as his own. Diana could boast direct descent from the Stuart Kings of England, five times over from King Charles II (all of them, alas, on "the wrong side of the blanket") and once from King James II. Her ancestors included Dukes of Bedford, Richmond, Abercorn, Marlborough and Grafton, and such illustrious English names as the Churchills, the Cumberlands, the Hertfords, the Waldegraves and – latterly more notorious – the Binghams, alias the Lucans. Her father had been an equerry to the late King George

VI, and later to his daughter Elizabeth II, whom he accompanied on her coronation tour of Australia in 1954. Her mother was a lady-in-waiting to Queen Elizabeth the Queen Mother and the daughter of one of her oldest friends. Althorp, the ancestral home in which Diana grew up, is bigger than any of the royal residences except Buckingham Palace itself – and that belongs to the nation.

The Prince of Wales was twelve when he first met his future wife, who was herself only a few days old. The polite young Prince was among the local gentry who went to pay their respects after Diana Frances Spencer was born on the Queen's estate at Sandringham on I July 1961. If not quite *de haut en bas*, it was virtually a landlord – tenant visit; before inheriting Althorp with his father's title, Diana's father rented Park House, a rambling country residence in the royal back garden, from the Queen.

Sixteen years later Diana was light-heartedly paired off by playful relatives with Prince Andrew, whose picture she kept pinned over her bed in her school dormitory. But she had cherished, all these years, a more ambitious dream. From the moment she set eyes on Charles at Althorp, Sarah Spencer's younger sister saw that it had a chance of coming true. That day in Nobottle Wood her prince had come; the following week, back at school, she had become as determined as any Canadian Mountie to get her man. The fluttering eyelashes which were to become public property, those demure, oh-so-shy looks from beneath her fringe and, later, the wide brims of her hats revealed another of Diana's predominant characteristics: feminine guile. That shyness, as one female observer later put it, was "not the bashfulness of youth, but the statement of her whole style of operating."

As they began to meet regularly in 1980 – Charles would telephone her London flat under a variety of false names – Diana's suitability was duly discussed by the unofficial vetting committee headed by Dale Tryon and Camilla Parker-Bowles. It is tempting to believe, on all the evidence, that only an innocent nineteen year old, much less

worldly-wise than this daunting duo, could have met with
their approval as supreme rival for the Prince's time and
attention. And so it came to pass, just before Christmas,
that it was behind the Parker-Bowles's Gloucestershire
farmhouse, standing in the cabbage patch, that Prince
Charles first raised the subject of marriage with Lady
Diana Spencer. It was not, as yet, a formal proposal –
more an "If I were to ask you, do you think it might be
possible?" – but it amounted to the beginnings of a commitment, sanctioned in advance by his hostess and her
husband. Diana, she told friends, "just giggled." But her
answer was never in doubt, for all the Prince's fears that
the continued attentions of Europe's paparazzi might prematurely dull her enthusiasm.

But still, past his thirty-second birthday, Charles dith-
ered. As speculation reached fever pitch, Diana gamely
earned her royal spurs by handling the intrusions of the
press with charm and aplomb; she even managed more
than once to give the hard-boiled royal-watchers the slip.
But the situation, as Charles departed on a prolonged trip
to India, was becoming intolerable for all concerned.
"Even I don't know what's going on," complained the
Queen rather testily, when asked by intimates about her
son and heir's latest romance. In England the shy young
kindergarten teacher was still being pursued night and day
by rampant media; across the world Charles slipped away
from his hosts, his public and his press for a few days
trekking in the foothills of the Himalayas, in as much
isolation as he could ever find.

It had been a pretty gruelling trip so far, even by royal
standards, with several protest demonstrations, a few
political incidents, even some deaths among the uncontrollable crowds fighting for a glimpse of him. To those
around him, who knew him well, the Prince had seemed
unusually on edge. When he descended from his weekend
in the mountains, however, the rest of the royal party
noticed a marked change in him: a sudden calm and
confidence which seemed to go beyond the mere rigours

of a turbulent tour. "It was as if," said one, "some huge burden had been lifted from his shoulders." It was as if, agreed others in retrospect, he had been wrestling with some major problem and had at last resolved it. And so he had.

Charles said nothing to anyone, including his closest advisers, and was not even ready to share his thoughts with his parents. When he arrived back at the Palace, late at night, he was told that the Queen was anxious to see him early the next morning. There could be only one thing she wanted to see him about. He got up just a few hours later, at dawn, despite his jet lag, and drove down to Highgrove to spend the day with the local hunt. His mother, when she woke to the news, was not best pleased.

Ten days later, the royal family foregathered as usual for its annual Christmas house party at Windsor. Of all their several and seasonal homes, Windsor is the one least vulnerable to the prying eyes and ears of the press. To the Queen, who spent the wartime years of her childhood there, it is the most private of her residences, the one she most likes to call home. So it was at Windsor, seizing this psychological advantage, that Prince Charles told his parents he was seriously thinking of asking Diana Spencer to marry him. Had he finally made up his mind? No, not quite: he was sure of his own feelings, but not yet totally of hers. He needed a few more quiet moments with her, of the kind so hard to arrange with discretion. Would his mother invite Diana to Sandringham to join them for New Year? Of course, she said, but this time he must not linger too long over his decision. "The idea of this romance going on for another year is intolerable for all concerned."

At Sandringham it soon became clear what she meant. The world's press was there in force, taking advantage of the public right-of-way which crosses the royal estate, hounding the royals' every outdoor excursion. What Charles later called "a military operation" went into action, to spirit Diana in and out of the place without the mob overwhelming her. It was not altogether successful. The Queen, who does not entirely share the popular view that she and her family are public property at all times, grew increasingly angry. For all her proven *savoir faire* at public relations, she still believed that photographers had no right to pitch camp on her privacy. Stung by a pre-Christmas report that Charles and Diana had enjoyed a secret "love-tryst" on the royal train, and subsequently by the newspaper's refusal to retract its story, she demanded that Fleet Street's editors call off their dogs. Not this time, Ma'am, editorialized the daily papers: we've got a job to do and we're staying. In a remarkable flash of public temper, unprecedented in her three decades on the throne, Elizabeth II one day rounded angrily on the royal press corps and shouted: "Oh, I do wish you people would go away!"

Charles himself caught the royal mood and added what was for him a most uncharacteristic message to the people whose faces he had come to know so well. "A Happy New Year to you," he shouted to those journalists known to themselves as Charles-watchers, "but a particularly nasty one to your editors." Fleet Street next day waxed indignant, while the royal family continued to fume. One reporter claimed that her car had been peppered by royal gunshot. Whatever the rights and wrongs of the episode, it scarcely created an atmosphere conducive to royal romance.

Throughout January, Diana went through the ultimate in testings for membership of the royal family. Each day she braved, with dignity and discretion, an ordeal by camera and notebook as she travelled to her job in Pimlico. Despite it all, she and Charles managed several secret meetings – at a house he owned in Central London, at Highgrove and at the Queen Mother's home in Scotland, Birkhall. Sensing that Charles was still not quite ready to commit himself, Diana forced the pace a little by telling him that she planned to flee for a while to Australia, to her mother's ranch, for a much-needed break from all the attention. She had made arrangements to travel early in February. Charles, who would be away skiing in the meantime, invited her to dine alone with him at Buckingham Palace on 4 February, a couple of evenings before she was due to leave.

And there, at last, he proposed. Diana accepted at once, but a still cautious Charles urged her to "think the whole thing over" in Australia, lest on mature reflection it prove "too awful" a prospect. With her mother at her side, Diana never wavered. Three years before, she had thought she might one day see her elder sister crowned Charles's Queen. Now it was all offered to her: the tedium, the loneliness, the frustrations, the lack of privacy – all of which Charles had been at pains to point out – as much as the pomp, the privilege, the wealth and the adulation. It was, she decided, what she wanted. "It is," she corrected herself, "what I want."

On Saturday 21 February, at a secret dinner party at Windsor Castle, Lady Diana Spencer was the Queen's guest of honour at a table crammed with contemporary British royalty, gathered to toast the happy couple. By now Charles had gone through the proper motions of asking the permission of the bride's father, Earl Spencer, and it was decided that the announcement should be delayed no longer. For Charles's affectionate family, it was the climax to what seemed like a lifetime of waiting, accentuated by these last twelve months of hesitancy.

Still, that evening, Charles seemed anxious and somehow bowed down by it all. Diana herself, by contrast, told the assembled company that she had never had a moment's doubt.

TEN

A Modern Marriage

"A woman not only marries a man. She
marries into a way of life – a job."

AT 11 A.M. on 24 February 1981, the Lord Chamberlain stepped forward unexpectedly at the beginning of an otherwise routine investiture at Buckingham Palace. The Queen blushed with pleasure as Lord Maclean told the august throng that Her Majesty had commanded him to read "an announcement that is being made at this moment":

> It is with the greatest pleasure that the Queen and the
> Duke of Edinburgh announce the betrothal of their beloved
> son, the Prince of Wales, to Lady Diana Spencer, daughter of
> the Earl Spencer and the Hon. Mrs. Shand-Kydd.

Within minutes the news had prompted a sharp rise in the stock-market value of such companies as Wedgwood, Royal Worcester, Royal Doulton and Royal Crown Derby, manufacturers of upmarket china and porcelain souvenirs for all royal occasions. There were smiles that day in the board-rooms of firms making anything from tea-towels and biscuit tins via coins and commemorative medallions to posters, marquees and flags. Hotel chains, the British, Tourist Authority and Moss Bros, purveyors of temporary morning-dress to the mighty, were not unmoved. Publishers of Bibles quickly organized special editions, and brewers licked their lips. Only Readicut International, whose production lines were primed for the mass manufacture of Charles-and-Di rugs, faced disappointment; although the Lord Chamberlain's office had temporarily lifted the usual restrictions on the use of royal features and insignia for commercial gain, it was deemed unacceptable to encourage the British people to wipe their feet on the princely face.

Over the next few months many a forest was felled to accommodate the gushing newspaper verbiage which would dog the happy couple all the way to the altar of St Paul's Cathedral that July, for the first wedding of a Prince of Wales in well over a century. Charles had chosen St Paul's not because it could seat more guests than Westminster Abbey, the traditional (and somewhat miffed) venue for royal weddings, but because there was more room for musicians; when told that the processional route was much longer, and that the need for more troops to line it would escalate costs, he said simply: "Tell them to stand further apart."

"A princely marriage," wrote Walter Bagehot, "is the brilliant edition of a universal fact, and as such it rivets mankind." The Prince of Wales's wedding to Lady Diana Spencer on 29 July 1981 was the biggest media event the world had ever seen. Seven hundred million people watched worldwide as Diana endearingly muddled her husband's forenames, while he made the not insignificant nervous error of endowing her with her own worldly goods rather than his. As the gloriously sunny day went off without any worse hitches, ending with the first royal kiss ever seen on the balcony of Buckingham Palace, they were universally deemed a fairy-tale couple, openly in love.

When a son, William, was born less than a year later – relieving Charles of another monstrous burden, ensuring the succession – the fairy tale was complete. The thoroughly modern Prince was even present at the birth in a London hospital, another royal first, as indeed he was when a second son, Harry, arrived two years later – providing the royal couple with the proverbial "heir and spare."

In the summer of 1982, as he left the hospital with his first son in his arms, his radiant wife at his side, Charles seemed at last to have found the happiness and fulfilment he had sought so long. The reason, gushed the royal commentators, was that his was the first "unarranged" marriage of a Prince of Wales in British history. But *was* it? In the succeeding six years, as the marriage has all too publicly developed its problems, there has been growing dissent from his view. "In many ways," said Harold Brooks-Baker, editor of *Burke's Peerage*, "it was an arranged marriage. He needed a lovely wife, and she fitted the bill. Diana was an infatuated nineteen year old only too eager to marry him."

Given all the restrictions on his choice, in other words, Charles had enjoyed less freedom than most men in finding himself the right bride. Before their engagement, moreover, the couple had scarcely time or opportunity to get to know each other as well as do most people before pledging to spend the rest of their lives together. By virtue of the Prince's position, their courtship had consisted of snatched moments in the homes – or indeed the cabbage patches – of discreet friends. Were they in love? The question was duly put by the television interviewers, handpicked for their blandness. "Yes – whatever love means," replied Charles with painful candour. "Of course," added his bride-to-be, shooting him a rather anxious glance.

Unlike her fiancé, Diana knew from painful personal experience how marriages can go wrong. The royal couple's respective parents, indeed, provide remarkable contrasts in the art of modern matrimony, some of it ammunition for the school of thought that parental difficulties plant the seeds of trouble for the next generation.

Princess Elizabeth, heiress to the throne since her uncle's abdication only three years before, fell in love with the first man she ever met. Elizabeth was only thirteen when she first set eyes on the dashing Prince Philip of Greece and Denmark on a day-trip to the Royal Naval College, Dartmouth, with her father, King George VI. After a long courtship, interrupted only by war, they overcame some parental opposition to marry in 1947. By 1956, when Elizabeth had already become Queen, Buckingham Palace was denying rumours of a "rift" in the marriage; Philip was away, on his own, strikingly often, and unseemly gossip had surfaced about his relationship with Hélène Cordet, a television presenter who had been a childhood friend. There had been other such gossip in the subsequent three decades, but the Palace has long since risen above bothering to deny it. For the deeper truth is that the Queen's marriage to Prince Philip, always a very private one, has overall been very happy. The stable family atmosphere in which Charles grew up was very different to that of his less lucky future bride.

Diana was the third born to Viscount "Johnny" Althorp, heir to the seventh Earl Spencer, and his wife Frances Ruth Burke Roche, younger daughter of the fourth Baron Fermoy. The birth of another girl frankly dismayed her father, who had been hoping for a son and heir to guarantee the direct survival of the title in his charge. One son had already died in childhood, and it would be three more years before the Althorps at last had another to ensure the Spencer succession. They proudly named him Charles, after their distinguished young neighbour.

By then, however, their marriage had gone steadily downhill. Diana was only six when one day her mother simply disappeared. That morning in 1967, as one family servant put it, Lady Althorp "just wasn't there any more." Weary of her marriage to Johnny, whom she subsequently sued for divorce on the grounds of cruelty, Frances had run away with a wallpaper heir namer Peter Shand-Kydd. The Spencer wedding in 1954 had been one of the high society events of the year, graced by the young new Queen and her husband. Thirteen years later, Frances was prepared to surrender not only her title, but her children, to escape from it.

As Diana was smartly sent away to a fashionable private boarding-school, she had to endure the knowing looks of her classmates as an ugly and very public custody fight ensued, during which Johnny Spencer mobilized enough witnesses from the British aristocracy to make France's cruelty suit hopeless. She finally let him counter-sue for adultery and lost her custody of her children in the process. The experience was so painful that to this day she will not speak of it.

But Diana, who soon began the shuttle so familiar to the children of divorcees, managed to remain very close to her mother. Both her parents were soon remarried: Frances to Shand-Kydd (from whom she was to separate in 1988), Johnny to the formidable Raine, Countess of Dartmouth, daughter of the rose-tinted novelist Barbara Cartland. While formally living with her father, however, Diana remained very much her mother's daughter. Holidays were spent at Frances's Scottish retreat and the Shand-Kydd ranch in Australia. The bond between mother and daughter was most evident during Diana's trial-by-press before her wedding. It was her mother who sheltered her, writing to *The Times* to plead for some privacy, while her father joined the gleeful crowds celebrating the news of the engagement outside Buckingham Palace.

Within months of their marriage, it became clear that Diana was rapidly changing her husband in a number of ways. After persuading him to give up shooting and steeplechasing – if not, to her chagrin, polo – she smartened up his suits, put some colour into his socks and ties, got his hair under the blow-dryer, bought him some boxer shorts and helped him grow more in touch with the values of his own generation. "You're only as young as you think you are," said a grateful Charles, prematurely middle-aged for many years already. "Diana will keep me young." Even more significantly, she liberated him sufficiently from his royal strait-jacket to investigate with more vigour and freedom the alternative "back-to-nature" values and pursuits close to his heart.

Soon Charles had all but turned vegetarian ("Oh, do grow up," said the Queen when he told her). Under the tutelage of a leading exponent, Patrick Pietroni, he explored and championed holistic medicine. Miriam Rothschild helped him design a wild-flower garden at Highgrove, about which he became obsessive; at its heart he designed and built himself a bower in which to meditate and relax. He began to practise organic farming on his Duchy of Cornwall estates, and took to regular stints living the life of a Cornwall dairy farmer or a Hebrides crofter. "A-loon again," sniggered Rupert Murdoch's *Sun*.

The press mockery was grossly unfair, but persistent enough to inspire public concern, much of it satirical. Was our future King becoming a bit of a crank? Among those who thought so was his less romantic, ruthlessly down-to-earth father, who had never had much time for matters of the spirit, and now worried that married life with Diana was turning his eldest son "soft." The word "wimp" was even heard on Prince Philip's lips; visitors to his office in Buckingham Palace noticed two photographs of his daughter on display, but none at all of his other children. When Charles cut down on his public engagements, retreating even further into himself, Philip went so far as to make his displeasure public by refusing for six weeks to visit his newborn grandchild, Prince Harry, with the rest of the family. By that time Diana had also made an enemy of Princess Anne, who might have expected to be one of Harry's godmothers; rather than attend her nephew's christening, Anne chose to spend the day at home shooting rabbits.

The Queen smoothed things over between father and son, but Philip remains deeply suspicious of Diana's influence on an heir he thought he had programmed to emulate his own no-nonsense, shoot-from-the-hip persona. Even today, a forty-year-old father-of-two, Charles can still be reduced to tears by his father's criticism.

In his youth the Prince had been adventurous enough to earn himself the nickname of "Royal Action Man"; for all his protests at the time, he rather enjoyed his reputation as the playboy Prince, always out parachuting, playing polo, windsurfing and skiing. But the price of emulating his father was that he became more conservative in his attitudes, both public and private. Now, at last, with his new-found liberation from Philip's shadow, Charles was becoming able to take intellectual risks as well as physical ones. Marriage to Diana had finally freed him – rather later than most young men – from life at home under the powerful sway of his parents, amid the values of their generation. The thoughtful, even somewhat eccentric Prince whom his future subjects now saw for the first time was the real one, his natural self – locked, perhaps, in a perpetual version of the adolescence he had never had, but able and anxious to pursue the natural inclinations of his inquiring mind.

Britons warmed to his attacks on modern architecture, his fact-finding tours of industry and his overt concern for the urban deprived, which saw him out in the middle of the night chatting up the homeless street dwellers of London. But they worried about the spiritualism. Had Charles *really* been trying to talk to his much-missed Uncle "Dickie," Lord Mountbatten, via mediums and even ouija boards? Though it was true that he had explored his interest in spiritualism with the medium Winifred Rushworth, the short answer is no. The ouija board was shamelessly invented in a Fleet Street wine bar, by a British journalist on orders from an American scandal sheet to come up with a front-page lead overnight. When the British popular press gleefully picked up the story, and the cartoonists had their fun with it, its widespread acceptance did the Prince untold harm. But the simple truth is that Charles, when he first heard about it, did not even know what an ouija board was.

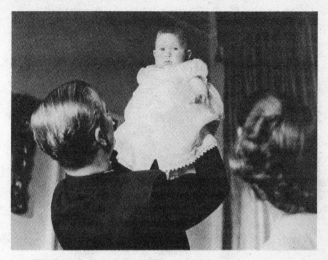

The Prince's birth thrills his parents and the world

(*opposite*) Cecil Beaton
captures the young Prince
with his baby sister and
his grandmother

Bored by his mother's
coronation (*above*), he is
all too soon the first heir
to the throne ever to go to
school (*right*)

An eighth-birthday portrait by Tony Armstrong-Jones, the future
Lord Snowdon, in a Buckingham Palace doorway

(*opposite*) The Cheam schoolboy moves on to Gordonstoun

Cambridge: the unhappy student Prince cheers up for an undergraduate revue (*inset*)

The Services: from the passing-out parade at Dartmouth (*above*) to bearded commander of HMS *Bronington*

(*over page*) Invested as Prince of Wales at Caernarvon, and launched upon public life

The bachelor Prince lets his hair down in Rio de Janeiro

(*opposite*) The world's most eligible bachelor with three girls he loved: Davina Sheffield (*above left*), Lady Jane Wellesley (*above right*) and (*below*) Lady Sarah Spencer

Enter a new girlfriend (*above*), to whom he is soon engaged

26 July 1981: offstage moments photographed by Patrick Lichfield

Lichfield's portrait of the fairly-tale couple, who pioneer the art of the balcony kiss

On honeymoon, on the bridge of *Britannia;* and (*left*) a radiantly happy beginning to life together

A pregnant Princess with
a Princess-to-be, shortly
before the birth of Prince
William (*below*)

(*over page*) The Prince of
Wales and his family in
the garden of Highgrove

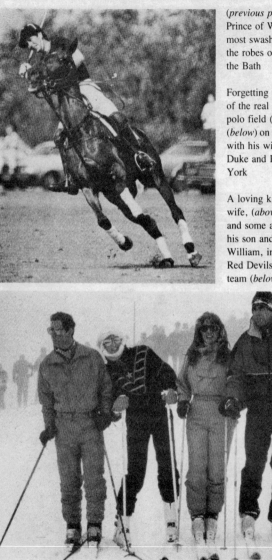

(*previous page*) The Prince of Wales at his most swashbuckling in the robes of the Order of the Bath

Forgetting the problems of the real world on the polo field (*left*) and (*below*) on the ski slopes, with his wife and the Duke and Duchess of York

A loving kiss from his wife, (*above opposite*) and some assistance from his son and heir, Prince William, in greeting the Red Devils aerobatics team (*below opposite*)

(*opposite*) A Downing Street
meeting with the Prime Minister
and a White House conversation
with President Reagan

A courtly greeting to his mother;
with his father at the funeral of
Lord Mountbatten and with his
grandmother at the Derby

Relaxing in the garden of Highgrove and (*below*) sketching water-colours in Japan

Three Princes and a piano

(*over page*) In contemplative mood, in the wild-flower garden at
Highgrove

The crusading Prince inspects 'intolerable' housing in East London

A planning meeting with his private secretary, Sir John Riddell.
Below: Learning about community architecture with John
Thompson at Lea View (*left*) and Rod Hackney in Macclesfield

(*opposite*) 'Two-thirds of the Prince of Wale's income comes out
of the udder of a cow': Charles lives the life of a Duchy of Cornwall
farmer

Marital problems force the Prince to interrupt his seclusion at
Balmoral (*above*) with a disastrous flying visit to Wales (*below*)

(*opposite*) Seeking solace from his friend 'Kanga', Lady Tryon,
(*bottom left*) as the tabloids go on the rampage

33 DAYS

That is how long since we last saw the drifting royals in public together

THE STAR

BRITAIN'S LIVELIEST DAILY   MONDAY, APRIL 27, 1987   20p (21p Cas)

World Exclusive Interview

CHARLES IN CRISIS

* * * *   NEWS OF THE WORLD, SUNDAY 15, 1987

Exclusive: Fight to save Royal marriage

CHARLES AND DIANA ARE NOT SPEAKING

⚜ **WHY** he is sad and lonely . . .

⚜ **HOW** he is drifting away from his Diana

THE SUN, Wednesday, August 13, 1986

Age gap is beginning to cause tension

ARE CHARLES AND DI MOVING APART?

WHEN Prince Charles flew home alone yesterday, leaving his wife in Majorca, few people close to the Royal couple were surprised.

Special pact to save troubled Royal marriage

CHARLES AND DIANA — he likes spend for the nights in bed

Enjoys

Cold

N * * *

CHARLES ⚜ DIANA: THE UNTHINKABLE QUES

Will it end in divorc

Returning home from the
tragedy in Klosters

In Australia, in January 1988, all seems to be marital bliss, until Diana takes to the piano to upstage Charles' return to the cello

At this favourite sanctuary, Balmoral, the Prince can always rely
on the companionship of his labrador and his fishing-rod

The Prince of Wales had, however, retreated far enough from his own familiar public profile for the nation to grow concerned. When the American millionaire Armand Hammer went to lunch at Highgrove, he emerged with the news that it had consisted entirely of organically produced vegetables: Charles boasted that he had grown them himself and apparently talked of little else. The Prince's public appearances grew intermittent and were little publicized. At first delighted to be relieved by Diana of the unremitting spotlight he had endured all his life, he had grown weary of – and somewhat irritated by – the open disappointment of crowds if he arrived without her. The Queen, the Prince and their staffs, and indeed the Princess herself, all believed that the insatiable appetite for Di-dolatry would ebb after, at most, a couple of years. They were all taken by surprise when it continued to grow to uncontrollable proportions and to manifest itself, inevitably enough, in less pleasant ways.

It did not take long for the rumours of trouble to surface. First Diana had become anorexic. Then she was spending all his money in wild shopping sprees, often with her mother, along Knightsbridge. Then she was grumbling about the royal way of life, dragging Charles back from the annual holiday at Balmoral, shutting herself away from the claustrophobia of royal life behind the headphones of her gold-plated Sony Walkman. Though exaggerated at the time, the rumours were ominous. Diana does worry constantly about her weight, and had in the immediate aftermath of pregnancy grown painfully thin, as she warmed to her new role as international fashion model. She does enjoy shopping, especially for expensive clothes, to the compulsive point where it becomes known as "retail therapy." She does prefer the sunshine of Majorca, where King Juan Carlos keeps stylish open house, to the grey summer weather of the Scottish Highlands and a schedule of hearty outdoor pursuits by day, charades by night, with the world's most formidable, least escapable in-laws. The first time she left Balmoral, famously leaving Charles behind her, it was with just two words: "Boring. Raining."

Diana's boredom with the less glamorous aspects of her new life became publicly apparent as early as the autumn of 1982, when she turned up five minutes late – after the Queen, an unforgivable breach of protocol – at the annual Festival of Remembrance for Britain's war dead at the Royal Albert Hall. The story of that evening's events gradually began to emerge. Diana, struggling to lose weight after William's birth, had at first told Charles that she felt unwell and would stay home. A violent argument ensued, as Charles reminded her of the significance of the occasion. "My duty," he was heard to say before stalking out, "lies above my loyalty to you." Within minutes of his departure, Diana had a change of heart. Despite pleas from her staff that it was too late, she dried her eyes, adjusted her make-up and set off after Charles to the Albert Hall. By the time she arrived in the royal box, her chair had been removed. Once it had been recovered, she duly took her seat at her husband's side. The row which followed was so impassioned that Prince Philip felt obliged to move, to screen them from the eyes of horrified onlookers.

As the twelve-year age gap between them began to tell, it also became clear that Diana did not get on with her husband's friends, and vice versa. For all the increasing dignity of most of her public appearances, the private Princess remained very young even for her age, as gauche as she was glamorous, as light-headed and fun-loving as Charles was sober and austere. Diana found Charles's contemporaries boring – she would sit in morose silence throughout dinner parties, out of her depth with the worldly conversation – while he found hers, notably her former flatmates, very naïve. There followed a series of tragic vignettes illustrating the difference in their interests and enthusiasms – most vividly the sight of a bored Charles in a suit and tie at Bob Geldof's Live Aid concert, thinking wistfully of Berlioz as Diana's feet tapped to the same beat as the rest of world youth. After only an hour he dragged her away to watch a polo game, telling his chums she had hijacked him to "some rock music jamboree."

Diana became all the more determined to banish as many as possible of Charles's pre-marital friends, a process which she had begun soon after the honeymoon. Out went the hearty polo-playing set, hard on the heels of his handful of close female friends, notably the two married women to whom he had been especially close, Camilla Parker-Bowles and Dale Tryon (who was by now designing and selling clothes as "Kanga"). David and Elizabeth Emanuel, who had designed Diana's wedding dress, were exiled for supposedly trading too much on their royal connection; it was to be some years before Diana, for designers the world's most coveted clothes-horse, relaxed enough to commission the Emanuels again, let alone to patronize the Beauchamp Place salon run by "Kanga."

In her first few years as a princess, Diana had been swept away by her own publicity. Never before in the history of personality cults had someone become so famous and adored simply by existing. Diana was one of the world's best-known and best-loved women before she had uttered even a hundred words in public; a voracious reader of her own cuttings, the Princess had soon fallen into the old trap of beginning to believe them. As they turned sour, however, so did she, spurning the journalists she had hitherto cultivated. Charles attempted to be protective, but there are always limits to what even he can do. The couple held a series of private lunches at Kensington Palace for newspaper editors, for instance, in an attempt to safeguard the privacy of their children; but one tabloid editor so honoured still printed a paparazzi pram photograph on his front page the very next day.

As it took her a long time to understand the workings of the press, so Diana had difficulty with various apparently stuffy royal traditions. Boldly she rebelled by taking Prince William on a royal tour of Australia and travelling by air to Scotland with both the children aboard; but even she soon began to see the practical sense as much as the protocol behind royal custom and practice. Gradually Diana grew into a more conventional royal, while at the same time cleverly preserving her own individuality. It was the natural Diana, for instance, who excitedly rushed across a room to greet the pop singer Boy George, despite the awkward detail that he was facing drugs charges, as opposed to the ever more regal Princess who greeted older and wiser figures with a photogenic smile and a confident handshake. Soon she was adding to the embryonic list of charities and public organizations to benefit from her support. A visit to Britain's first AIDS ward, in which she conspicuously refused to wear gloves when shaking hands with virus victims, did more to dispel public fear and misunderstanding than the pleas of a thousand disc jockeys.

Already her devotees had forgotten that she came from a home bigger than all the royal residences outside London. She fired little of the jealousy which might have been expected, because of her unspoilt, girl-next-door innocence, strictly in the you-too-can-be-a-princess tradition. But Diana did not remain that kind of princess for long. Even before the emergence of a potential rival in the shape of "Fergie," Duchess of York, she had carefully transformed herself – by her expensive taste in clothes, if nothing else – into a pedestal princess, the fantasy kind who live in Walt Disney castles and are too fragile to be touched by human hand. It was a neat twist to the public relations juggling act. Still only twenty-six, Diana had swiftly metamorphosed from ingénue lead into potential Queen.

Part of the process were other equally stern measures, needed to bolster Diana's self-confidence, flagging in the face of her husband's growing self-absorption. Feeling she had arrived in an alien world, Diana began to make it her own. The cleansing of the Wales stables, begun with the friends, now continued with the staff. One by one, a trail of Charles's most loyal retainers felt obliged to leave: Stephen Barry, his valet and friend (who subsequently died of AIDS); Michael Colbourne, a navy chum who had become the indispensable major-domo of his private office; Alan Fisher, the butler they inherited from Bing Crosby; Lieutenant-Colonel Philip Creasy, comptroller (financial controller) of the Prince's Household; Oliver Everett, a Foreign Office secondee especially close to Charles, who had reluctantly stayed on to midwife Diana's arrival in the royal family, and now departed to become the Queen's librarian; and Edward Adeane, their private secretary, scion of a family in senior royal service for over a century. Even Charles's faithful, long-serving detectives, Chief Inspector Paul Officer and Superintendent John Maclean, took their leave as Diana – in the words of her brother Charles, Viscount Althorp – "got rid of all the hangers-on who surrounded Charles." By the end of 1985, eighteen months before the children's nanny, Barbara Barnes, also left the royal employ, no fewer than forty members of the Royal Household had chosen to quit, from dressers and cooks to chauffeurs and cleaners, many of them blaming the Princess and her petulant ways. Charles appeared to have surrendered both purse-strings and apron-strings. "The debonair Prince of Wales," wrote the journalist Tina Brown, "is pussy-whipped from here to eternity."

Diana was taking charge. Her staying power as a world superstar was giving her the self-confidence she had hitherto lacked. As she mastered the art of the royal public appearance, she began to take an almost sadistic pleasure in upstaging her husband at every occasion, private and public. For every new speech he made, she would wear a different hairstyle or hat; the photographers, she knew, were much more interested in her than him – as, still, were the crowds, who continued to groan if Charles rather than Di headed in their direction. Charles's increasing distress, however, sprang from more than merely an understandably bruised royal ego. The insatiable appetite for details of the Princess of Wales's hair, her clothes, her hats, her tiniest asides, drowned out anything he might do or say. For a man desperate to be taken seriously, the tidal wave of trivia became desperately irritating.

As his preoccupations grew ever more earnest, so hers grew more frivolous. While Charles denounced the architecture of the modern London skyline, Diana frequented fashion shows and discos. Whenever Charles toured Britain's blighted inner cities, on a social campaign fast becoming his central mission in life, his Princess was rarely at his side. Hers, she had long since realized, was a passive power, both over her public and her husband. It was best preserved by opening her mouth as little as possible, and best explained by telling delighted bystanders: "I'm as thick as a plank." This subsequently celebrated remark proved just how savvy and street-wise Diana really was, while reinforcing the empty-headedness of which her meditative husband increasingly despaired. Inspecting the sumptuous garden of a friend's country home, he complimented his foreign hostess on her excellent English. "My father believed in educating girls," she explained. "I wish," muttered Charles, "that had been the philosophy in my wife's family."

For her part, Diana seems to have underestimated the many hours of boredom which offset the perks of life as a princess in gilded cage. She married a man much more mature than herself, whose interests – philosophy, painting, politics, – she did not share. All too soon she began to feel isolated and bored, and took little trouble to hide it. To this day, it is only when by herself, on public or private appearances, that she really comes to life. Back in 1985, the guests of her favourite fashion designer, Bruce Oldfield, were astonished by her extravagant behaviour at a fund-raising ball, one of the first such events she attended conspicuously alone, leaving a moody Charles behind at Highgrove. Any doubts about recent rumours that she had been out partying alone, dancing the night away without her husband, were staunched when the

Princess stayed on after the appointed witching-hour of midnight – on and on, until the French musician Jean-Michel Jarre, handsome husband of the actress Charlotte Rampling, asked her to dance. Diana, said one witness, "positively lit up. . . . Everyone within twenty yards got the fallout from Diana's mood that night. She was suddenly aware of everything she'd been missing."

At first Charles and Diana were just like any other young couple with problems, albeit deep ones. Asked if they had anything at all in common, one of Diana's closest friends, her former flatmate Carolyn Pride, had to cast around for some moments before replying: "The children?" All too soon the couple had reached a practical accommodation, recognizing their different interests and enthusiasms, and giving each other the freedom to pursue them. When added to a gruelling royal schedule, however, the most rational of *laissez-faire* arrangements can become corrosive. A royal couple get little enough time alone together, without choosing to spend it apart – particularly at the expense of their puzzled young offspring. Charles had for so long been portrayed as a softhearted, doting father; this sudden, apparent neglect was another problem the years were not to heal. In his own youth he had written a children's story, *The Old Man of Lochnagar*, for his baby brother Edward. It was published, even converted into a stage musical. But there were no signs of such efforts for his own children. Charles was apparently happy for them to accept their detectives, in his absence, as father-figures. Was the Prince of Wales, after all, the kind of man who cannot muster much interest in his children until they are old enough to kick a football? Was he, in fact, a chip off the royal block typified by King George V?

From the first, post-honeymoon teething troubles, Charles and Diana's unique difficulty was that they were obliged to sort them out in the public spotlight, while continuing to grit their teeth and grin their way through a remorseless schedule of joint public engagements. Amid the claustrophobia of life at court, such private problems were squared: the price of life in the royal goldfish bowl. If Charles's sister Anne also had her problems with her husband, Mark Phillips, from whom she was now leading a virtually separate life, their position on the periphery of the royal soap opera made it easier to keep their troubles to themselves and to maintain some appearance of public dignity.

Diana's childhood unhappiness, she has said, made her all the more determined to create a stable and lasting marriage for herself. Her choice of partner, in fact, made permanence a *sine qua non*: whatever its ups and downs, the match she had fought to win was one from which she could never, like her mother, simply "disappear." But Charles was no longer the man Diana had married. When first she had fallen in love with him, her Prince had been a stylish James Bond-style contemporary hero, the world's most eligible bachelor with the looks and lifestyle to match. Diana's effect on him, by the cruellest of ironies, had been to expose that identity as a self-deluding sham. She had liberated Charles to be himself: a tortured, self-doubting, almost monkish introvert, a man of ever more furrowed brow, bowed down by the accident of his birth, born in a century which he increasingly mistrusted. A very nineteenth-century figure, he increasingly wanted out of the modern world. All Diana's James Bond wanted now was to be an organic farmer.

He, for his part, had been crushed by the realization that his wife could not function as a soulmate. They still shared a great joy in their children, but little else. A man overloaded with sombre preoccupations and grave responsibilities, the Prince had been hoping for so much more. As his depression worsened, the Queen became his only real spiritual companion within the family. "Off to see your mother again, I suppose?" Diana was astonishingly heard to cry after him at Sandringham. Not only did she lack the emotional depth to help him, she was fast becoming the major source of his problems.

"A woman not only marries a man," Charles once said. "She marries into a way of life – a job." That, coming from him, was right royal understatement. A self-proclaimed opponent of feminism, the Prince had expected his wife's identity to merge into his own. A royal upbringing tends to breed such expectations. Diana, being almost half his age when she married him, seemed unlikely to put up much of a struggle. Now she was not only a passive disappointment but she was an active source of constant difficulty, petulantly stamping her foot when required on royal parade, insisting on pastimes unbecoming the private Charles's wife, let alone the public Charles's princess.

It was not long before they were taking separate holidays. Diana's thinly disguised boredom, for instance, while sightseeing on an official visit to Italy, led Charles to return there alone for a private week painting watercolours, the first of many such solo trips. Even the children, it had become painfully clear, were no longer a strong enough bond to keep them together in their rare moments off duty. For a professional couple with more freedom than most to dovetail their schedules, they were now spending a revealing amount of time apart. By the autumn of 1987, the rift in their marriage was to become embarrassingly public.

PART THREE

"Something Must Be Done"

"The best reason why Monarchy is a strong
government is that it is an intelligible
government. The mass of mankind
understand it, and they hardly anywhere in
the world understand any other. . . . "

Walter Bagehot,
The English Constitution

ELEVEN

Into the Inner Cities

"This is not acceptable ... there is a great
deal to be done. ... "

NINETEEN eighty-one, in retrospect, was to prove an
annus mirabilis for the Prince of Wales.

In stark contrast to the holiday atmosphere of his wedding that July, Britain's long hot summer also saw a series of alarming civil disruptions all over the country. Large-scale rioting and ugly street violence, looting and arson erupted from Brixton in South London to the Toxteth area of Liverpool, from the St Paul's district of Bristol to Handsworth in Birmingham and Moss Side in Manchester. As the physical damage was counted in tens of millions of pounds, the social cost was evaluated by a growing coalition of experts anxious to identify causes and seek solutions. By the time trouble erupted again four years later, on the Broadwater Farm estate in Tottenham, North London, Prince Charles was deeply involved in attempts to improve the social conditions at the root of the disturbances. In the summer of 1981 he had at last found himself not only, for better or worse, a bride; he had also, if as yet unconsciously, been offered the sharp focus he had so long been seeking for his public role.

For years the Prince had been stung by constant, ill-informed taunts that it was time he got "a proper job."

For more than a decade his work for the Prince's Trust and countless other personal initiatives had involved him in long, hard hours of committee meetings, paperwork and speech writing, travelling the length and breadth of the country to encourage the beneficiaries of his various self-help schemes. To him, and to any informed observer, it was certainly a proper job – one he had fashioned for himself out of the awkward, restrictive job-description which came with his birth – and a very demanding one too. To the British press and broadcasting media, however, it was worthy but dull stuff, scarcely worth sending a reporter to cover. The real trouble was that it was so piecemeal; the Prince's efforts were scattered around a bewildering array of trusts and charities launched in his name, in a profusion which blurred his attempts to develop a central philosophy.

After his marriage, moreover, it did not help, when he was trying to promote one of his pet causes, that the attendant press were fed pieces of paper giving fashion-page details on the Princess of Wales's outfit and accoutrements. Few Britons were aware of, let alone understood, the nature and scale of the Prince's work. At times he became depressed enough to wonder if it were all worthwhile.

He was above all haunted by a remark attributed to his great-uncle, the last Prince of Wales, when visiting the unemployed steel workers of the Welsh valleys during the great depression of the 1930s. Having heard them sing a hymn against the backdrop of the idle Bessemer steel plant, Edward said: "These works brought all these people here. Something must be done to find them work." His subsequently celebrated choice of phrase – "Something must be done" – has gone down in recent history as an index of the kind of reforming, crusading King so compassionate a Prince of Wales might have made. It is, in fact, a dangerously inaccurate impression. Edward was not Prince of Wales when he made the remark; he was already King Edward VIII, privately aware that abdication was likely within a few weeks. So his words were deeply hypocritical. But they were also unconstitutional; Edward showed how little he understood this fifteen years later, when as Duke of Windsor he looked back on the parliamentary fuss which ensued:

> The episode is important only in that it reveals the unfathomable complications that the economic issues of the twentieth century have introduced into the technique of Kingship, rendering it almost impossible for a Monarch to continue to play the role of the Good King, free to move unhindered among his subjects and speak what is in his mind.

No modern British monarch, nor indeed any Prince of Wales, can make so overtly political a remark without breeching the fundamental tenets of the constitutional monarchy. A Prince of Wales can, however, help to *get* things done. He can act as a searchlight for social and economic problems, and a focus for efforts to solve them. King Edward VII, as Prince of Wales, prefigured his great-great-grandson by touring the slums of East London in disguise, as a member of a House of Lords inquiry into poor housing conditions. Prince Albert anticipated Prince Philip by getting involved in the housing reform movements of his day. But such royal concern for social conditions have in recent history been little more than well-meaning, *en passant* gestures. Charles was by now determined to make it his life's work.

Fifty years on, he relished a chance to put his great-uncle's apparent principles into practice. In the riots of the early 1980s he was to find a spur to his endeavours; and in the words of Lord Scarman, the eminent lawyer who conducted a public inquiry into the Brixton disturbances, he was to find the makings of a creed:

> Local communities should be more fully involved in the decisions which affect them. A "top-down" approach to regeneration does not seem to have worked. Local communi-

ties must be fully and effectively involved in planning, in the provision of local services, and in the managing and financing of specific projects . . . Inner-city areas are not human deserts. They possess a wealth of voluntary effort and goodwill. It would be wise to put this human capital to good use. It is essential that people are encouraged to secure a stake in, feel a pride in, and have a sense of responsibility for their own area.

It was to take Margaret Thatcher six more years, and severe Conservative losses at the 1987 general election, publicly to acknowledge that any problem worth her government's attention existed around Britain's inner cities. But there were a number of captains of industry, otherwise her staunchest supporters, who felt at the time that the disastrous decline of the nation's once prosperous industrial conurbations had been badly exacerbated by her government's policies. It was, they believed, the increasingly grim conditions of life around urban Britain, above all mass unemployment, which had led to growing discontent, violence and crime among minority groups on the poverty line, especially blacks.

The events of 1981 thus saw a small, somewhat maverick group of businessmen form an innovative aid organization called Business in the Community (BiC). The contemporary counterparts, perhaps, of those enlightened British industrialists of the nineteenth century, they hoped to persuade major companies to donate sums of money, personnel or resources to be invested in community trusts, projects and, above all, local enterprise agencies. BiC would serve as a catalyst for local action, inspiring partnership projects rather than managing them; it would act as honest broker – or, in the vogue word, "enabler" – between the companies and the communities they served, creating mutual goodwill as much as mutual advantage. Clearly, it was in any company's interests to be seen playing what could pass for a philanthropic role in the run-down, disadvantaged areas of a country whose big business was growing all too conspicuously prosperous. It was also, even more clearly, in those companies" interests to create more jobs, train people to fill them and thus invest in their own continuing growth.

The notion of BiC had grown out of the 1980 Anglo-American Conference on Community Involvement, chaired by Tom King, then local government minister, at which British tycoons had heard of American success during the 1970s in persuading big business to help finance the regeneration of decaying, post-industrial cities. A working group had been formed under Sir Alastair Pilkington, whose Lancashire glassmaking firm had long enjoyed a fine record as an enlightened employer. The result was Business in the Community, which got off to an uncertain start amid dissent from an influential chorus decrying "industrial philanthropy." It was industry's business, they argued, to maximize profits, provide jobs and pay taxes; creating the right conditions in the community was the government's job.

The Toxteth riots changed all that. Given special responsibility for the area, the then Environment Minister, Michael Heseltine, took a busload of leading industrialists to see the bleak post-riot landscape for themselves. Only by partnership, Heseltine argued, could a thriving community arise from these ashes with any effective speed. Urban development corporations would be set up around the country; tax incentives would be offered in the hope that the private sector would quadruple government contributions. Chairmen and chief executives returned to their offices that day intent on getting their companies involved with the existing local government enterprise agencies, which soon became much more numerous and dramatically more effective.

BiC's founding fathers had placed a special emphasis on the creation of new black businesses, albeit small ones, and training programmes for unemployed black youth. Late in 1984 its new chief executive, Stephen O'Brien, was casting about for ways to regalvanize an initiative called

Project Fullemploy, specifically created ten years before to alleviate the high unemployment rate among black youth. An active Christian who in 1983 had given up a flourishing business career to promote BiC's ideals and ensure efficient use of its resources – he lists "causes" among his recreations in *Who's Who* – O'Brien knew of Charles's work in the field via the Prince's Trust. He approached him for support and was invited round to the Palace.

The two men warmed to each other immediately, discovering a mutual depth of knowledge and concern about Britain's black community which stirred them both. He himself, the Prince said, was looking for new ideas, even a new direction. He would throw his weight behind anything reasonable O'Brien might suggest. Thus was born one of the unlikeliest events in the recent history of both industrial and race relations in Britain, subsequently known as the Windsor Conference.

Between them Charles and O'Brien cooked up the apparently preposterous notion of shutting away together over a weekend some of Britain's most prosperous industrialists and a group of angry, articulate blacks. Most of BiC's corporate members would have stayed firmly away, were it not for the allure of a weekend behind closed doors with the Prince of Wales. At a hotel in Windsor, quite privately and without publicity, this extraordinary event duly took place at the end of 1984.

For two days and one night the chairmen of sixty major British companies talked, ate and drank with as many bright, motivated, persuasive young blacks. Charles made a keynote speech, stressing that racism was a problem of the white rather than the black community, and arguing that it was as senseless as it was inhuman to make so little practical use of the black community's talent and potential. Chastened white businessmen – bankers, for instance, unused to being laughed at when they protested that they did not discriminate in their employment policies – listened intently as the young blacks seized their rare chance with a vengeance. By the end of the conference it was his fellow-bankers who raised a storm of protest when the Bank of England representative conceded that its Youth Training Scheme required a minimum of five "O" levels. "They still talk about it today," says O'Brien. "Leading businessmen said they had no idea there was such talent among the leadership of the black community, and the blacks themselves said that they had not expected such understanding of their problems from big business."

The Windsor Conference, of which word quickly spread through the business community, amounted to a major advance in race relations in modern industrial Britain. O'Brien well knew that without the Prince's involvement he could never have convened it; he had also been mightily impressed by Charles's understanding of, and rapport with, the young blacks, as well as his tact and skill in stewarding this most unlikely of dialogues. As a result of Windsor, O'Brien realized how much BiC would benefit if Charles could be persuaded to accept some formal role at its helm. The same idea had occurred to Sir Charles Villiers, former chairman of the British Steel Corporation, who had worked with the Prince on BSC's enterprise schemes. Villiers undertook to make informal approaches, which lasted through most of 1985. By September the Prince of Wales had agreed, for an initial five-year term, to become president of BiC.

It was to be the making of him. The previous year had seen Charles at his most frustrated and despondent, depressed both by the decay in his marriage and by the apparent failure of all his continuing, piecemeal good works to achieve anything concrete. A demanding tour of the USA, to promote British exports, had seen him uneasily trapped into a $5,000-a-plate dinner, at which he had been obliged to cut the world's largest cake, complete with its maker's logo writ large for the cameras. The commercialization of the monarchy was not unfamiliar in the United Kingdom; it was uncomfortable, but worth it if the results were tangible.

On his return home, however, Charles was dismayed to

learn that the Confederation of British Industry had done nothing to capitalize on his efforts, and furious to be told that they had no plans to. By the time the BiC invitation arrived, his rage had turned to dejection. Again the sense of resentment and failure began to become almost palpable. Family and friends grew worried that Charles seemed on the verge of "giving up" and devoting himself to farming and polo. "What's the point?" he was quoted as saying. "I'm no good at anything. It's all a waste of time."

Stephen O'Brien was to prove a crucial figure in the royal renaissance. It was with uncanny timing that he arrived in Charles's life just as John Higgs so abruptly and tragically left it, for O'Brien was to prove a warm and like-minded new friend for the Prince, very much in Higgs's mould. But BiC itself was also to be the single most important contributor to the revival of Charles's self-esteem and self-confidence. It was staffed and supported by vibrant young optimists, brimming with enthusiasm about the movement's ideals and what could be achieved. More important, its highly professional management contrasted sharply with the enlightened amateurism of the rest of Charles's bewildering array of trusts, charities and committees. BiC would provide the central focus so badly needed by the disparate array of worthy organizations under the ever wider umbrella of the Prince's Trust, and a cohesive philosophy for the man at the heart of it all. For the first time in his life, Charles had the makings of a clear central purpose to his public work.

It was thirteen years since he had first conceived the notion of the Prince's Trust, almost a decade since it was launched. Sir Harold Haywood, who supervised its alliance with the Royal Jubilee Trusts, had seen his empire expand enormously before his retirement in March 1988. "It is the fighting arm of the Prince's concern," he says. "And the Prince really has a 'hands-on' approach to the things he cares about." Behind the elegant facade of No. 8 Bedford Row – now under the command of Tom Shebbeare, a dynamic Eurocrat the Prince's own age – lies a

bee-hive of worthy organizations so labyrinthine that
Charles had been accused of "spreading himself too thin."
If there was more tactical truth than justice in the gibe, it
was certainly true that Charles's involvement with "social
work" on the grand scale had gone largely unpublicized. It
was little noticed and less understood.

A brief Consumer's Guide to the operations of Bedford
Row when Charles teamed up with BiC illustrates the
problem:

THE PRINCE'S TRUST
Established in 1976 "to help disadvantaged young people
to help themselves." It provides small one-off grants to
young people who (a) produce their own proposals aimed
at setting up self-help activities which contribute to their
welfare or personal development, or enable them to help
others; (b) make the application themselves, either individually or as a spontaneous group but not as an existing
organization; (c) are socially, economically or environ-
mentally disadvantaged, or physically handicapped; and
(d) would not anticipate further funding from the Trust
after the initial grant. Age range: fourteen to twenty-five.
Annual grants total around £250,000, to a maximum of
£300 per person or £500 per group.

THE ROYAL JUBILEE TRUSTS, a merger of THE QUEEN'S
SILVER JUBILEE TRUST and KING GEORGE'S JUBILEE TRUST
Established in 1977 "to help young people to help others
of any age in the community," the Queen's Silver Jubilee
Trust puts resources directly into the hands of young
volunteers to enable them to carry out practical projects
which will benefit others in need in the community at
large, in the UK and the Commonwealth. Grants, to individuals or groups, are given for tools, materials, travel (not
overseas), training of young volunteers, volunteers"
expenses, but specifically *not* for staff salaries, foreign
travel, professional building work, educational grants and
bursaries or medical treatment, equipment or research.

Age range: twenty-five and under. Annual grants total around £1 million.

Established in 1935 "to assist the physical, mental and spiritual development of young people," King George's Jubilee Trust provides financial support for voluntary youth projects in specific areas of priority in the UK only, particularly those involving the young unemployed, ethnic minorities, young people on housing estates or in rural areas, with special emphasis on creative, artistic and outdoor pursuits. Grants, to ad hoc groups or voluntary organizations, are specifically *not* given for general appeals, overseas travel, sports and social clubs, educational grants and bursaries, or medical equipment, treatment or research. Age range: eight to twenty-five, inclusive. Annual grants total around £500,000, in a range of £50 to £500.

THE PRINCE OF WALES'S ADVISORY GROUP ON DISABILITY
Established after the Prince was Patron of the Year of the Disabled in 1981. He has since chaired a group of experts in the field, many of them themselves disabled, who lobby new building developments as well as existing housing estates, places of work, education, recreation, etc., to make provision for the needs of disabled people.

THE PRINCE OF WALES'S COMMUNITY VENTURE
A separate organization, working under the umbrella of the Prince's Trust, which provides young people with a chance to offer an array of services to their local communities for a year – a concept which might become compulsory, to take the place of National Service, if the Prince had his way.

THE YOUTH BUSINESS INITIATIVE, merged in 1986 into THE PRINCE'S YOUTH BUSINESS TRUST
Established in 1986 "to educate, advise and support young unemployed people with a view to setting up small businesses of their own." Training and work experience may

be arranged. The Trust provides bursaries and ongoing tutorial help to selected individuals and group applicants. Grants are usually given for tools and equipment, transport, fees, insurance, instruction and training; they are *not* given for working capital. Applicants are required to provide a realistic business plan, help with which can be arranged, and accept the advice of two tutors. Age range: eighteen to twenty-five and unemployed. Maximum grants are £1,000 to individuals and £3,000 to groups.

Early in his presidency of BiC, the Prince began to see the advantage in establishing close links between its City Road headquarters and Bedford Row. Stephen O'Brien joined the council of the Prince's Trust and the Royal Jubilee Trusts, blowing some of the dust off their rather creaky administrative machinery. There were many BiC projects, moreover, in which the legion of Bedford Row beneficiaries could put their grants to use in a broader cause. Charles now had a dynamic centre to his charitable spider's web.

With the Prince at its head, meanwhile, BiC and its works expanded with remarkable rapidity. The list of corporate sponsors grew to more than 200 of Britain's major companies. Some 3,000 more were involved in BiC's work around the national network of enterprise agencies, which had grown from just twenty-three in 1981 to over 350 by 1987. O'Brien estimated that BiC was now creating more than 70,000 jobs a year.

Hitherto, BiC had been regarded by the Thatcher government as somewhat "wet," even "pink," in its "One Nation" Tory advocacy of joint state-private enterprise initiatives. The politician who had done most to promote it, Michael Heseltine, had long since quit the government, and the Prime Minister herself still placed a far greater emphasis on private sector enterprise than on partnership. But the end of 1986 saw a further development which finally won the organization – and thus, by implication, the Prince's work – formal government approval.

Just before Christmas, at No. 10 Downing Street, the Prime Minister and the Prince of Wales jointly hosted a reception to launch the Per Cent Club – an offshoot of BiC modelled on a Minnesota group of businesses called the Five Per Cent club, who had pledged five per cent of their annual pre-tax profits to community training programmes. The British version rather more modestly required members to contribute no less than half a per cent of their pre-tax (UK) profits, or one per cent of their gross dividends, "to the community." Companies could donate to local economic development or job creation schemes, to inner-city regeneration programmes, to charities, education or the arts. The potential yield, given recent tax changes, was some £300 million a year. But donations did not have to take the shape of hard cash; equally acceptable was the offer of office space, equipment, personnel or even the cost of the chairman's time making the occasional speech on corporate responsibility. Particularly welcome was the secondment of talented staff to work with the enterprise agencies.

Founder members of the Per Cent Club included high street banks, major insurance companies, IBM and British Nuclear Fuels. As its philosophy took shape, the high philanthropic ground was occupied by such grandees as Robert Reid, the chairman of Shell UK, who summed up its aspirations in terms of the obligations of large companies "to take on societal responsibilities beyond those areas directly relevant to their business activities." Others argued, more honestly, that their goals were not entirely idealistic. It suited major companies to develop the communities in which they had a stake, as was plainly stated by James Robinson, the chief executive of American Express: "Call it enlightened self-interest, call it altruism. I call it common sense. However you look at it, it's good business to be a community player." At the Downing Street launch, the Prince of Wales diplomatically merged both themes when he described BiC's new partner as an initiative "with charitable and with business motives in mind."

At his side as he spoke was the industrialist Sir Hector Laing, chairman of United Biscuits, a close friend and adviser of the Prime Minister, who now became chairman of both groups. With the advent of the Per Cent Club, BiC was swinging more and more squarely into the Prime Minister's orbit. Its working parties now reported directly to No. 10, and its staff helped to write the inner-city and employment-policy sections of Mrs Thatcher's post-election victory speech to the 1987 Conservative Party Conference. If some were uneasy about this new closeness to government, given the movement's original spur, others simply counted the benefits: "With Mrs Thatcher's interest," said one BiC official, "BiC's credibility increased. It is all suddenly quite in vogue. Unlike years ago, BiC is now a great club to belong to." Sir Hector Laing, for all his reputation as the Prime Minister's "industrial guru," meanwhile insisted that BiC remained "non-political, a-political and unpolitical." His own personal creed, as spelt out to the Per Cent Club's annual general meeting, was to foment "a revolution centred on the recognition that in a developed economy, no government can provide all the answers to all the problems. ... The surest way to generate greater wealth, and therefore employment and a rising standard of living for all the people, is through constructive, private sector-led co-operation."

But the government was already making ambiguous noises about renewing its original grants to the network of regional enterprise agencies through which BiC's activities are channelled. Clearly Sir Hector's role, as the Prime Minister's emissary, was to ensure via BiC, the Per Cent Club and their offshoots that the private sector relieved central government of most, if not all, of that financial obligation. Laing told the 1987 BiC annual general meeting:

> The major public challenge of today is the regeneration of
> our deprived urban areas. The Prime Minister has declared
> the government's intention to mount a campaign to meet
> this challenge, and has called on the private sector for sup-
> port and co-operation. We must respond, and I am calling
> on you – the private sector – to support a comprehensive
> package of long-term programmes to address the problems of
> the inner cities.

Though walking a narrower political tightrope than
ever, the Prince of Wales managed as yet to remain
immune from accusations of party political involvement.
The support he could give BiC was dramatically illustrated in July 1987, when his visit to the Spitalfields area
of London's East End attracted enormous publicity.
Charles was visibly close to tears as he toured a slum
district colonized by Indian immigrants. He was appalled,
he said, by the rotting stairwells, the peeling wallpaper, the
dingy, ill-lit one-room flats. Conditions were "unacceptable," no better than those the Indians had left behind in
Bengal. "There is a great deal," he said, "to be done."

It was not quite "Something must be done," but it had
much more effect. Spitalfields is a particularly delicate
case for treatment. The advent of huge office blocks on its
borders, to create more secure and lasting employment,
must be balanced against the largely immigrant community's traditional way of life – often living and working in
the same building – if they are not to suffer economically.
BiC's task is to ensure a sympathetic and gradual
approach to providing buildings fit for the area's legion of
small business entrepreneurs – a delicate task with which
their project manager, Stephen Lord, had already been
grappling in Finsbury Park, North London.

Three months later, under the auspices of the London
Education Business Partnership, Prince Charles was back
in East London, almost in the shadow of the City, helping
on its way yet another BiC initiative in the London bor-
oughs of Hackney and Tower Hamlets. The pilot scheme

which launched London Compact – another idea borrowed from the United States – united four schools and eighteen local businesses in securing jobs for 300 schoolleavers who would otherwise certainly have joined the area's already lengthy dole queues. Service industries (such as the Post Office and British Telecom) were joining forces with financial institutions (Kleinwort, Benson, major clearing banks), retailers (Asda, Tesco) and heavy industry (John Laing Construction, Whitbread, Canary Wharf Development Company) in a partnership project designed as a model for the rest of London, ultimately the entire country. By achieving pre-set targets under such headings as punctuality, personal skills and academic achievement, sixth-form pupils were automatically entitled to a job with one of the companies participating in the scheme.

Throughout 1987 – 8, Prince Charles visited some seventy-five different BiC projects around Britain and was pleased to conclude that "it seems as though we have really begun the process of listening to those who live and work in local communities, and are learning how to reinforce their aspirations, rather than wading in to impose solutions from the outside." Typical projects under way at the end of 1987 were summarized by Robert Davies, deputy chief executive of BiC, as follows: Warburgs, Kleinwort, Benson and Lloyd's of London had each launched enterprise loan funds to assist the development of new businesses in the East End of London, with professional advice from enterprise agencies; British Telecom had converted redundant premises in Islington, North London, into workshops for enterprise training and small business start-ups; the Bank of England, Citibank and Stewart Wrightson were refining techniques for inner-city recruitment with bodies such as Project Full-employ and offering management training opportunities to ethnic minorities; and the London Enterprise Agency and the Inner London Education Authority had launched the London Education Business Partnership, through which companies such as John Laing and Whitbread were working to improve job opportunities for inner-city school-leavers. Outside London, Peat Marwick McLintock had launched an enterprise initiative to channel £250,000 worth of marketing and financial consultancy into new enterprises throughout the country; both Girobank and Barclays were sponsoring inner-city loan funds in the northwest of England; and the Midland Bank had committed over £500,000 to support economic development and training initiatives in Birmingham, where it was founded 150 years before.

Charles's close personal interest in each and every one of these myriad enterprises began to dominate his public time-table. But the climax came in December 1986, when he personally launched BiC's most ambitious project yet – a "demonstration partnership" designed to regenerate an entire, 140-square mile district borough of Yorkshire: Calderdale, population 192,000, centred on Halifax, commanding a strategic location at the heart of Northern England. When announcing the experiment – based on the very similar regeneration of the Massachusetts town of Lowell, near Boston – the Prince expressed the fervent hope that it would pioneer more such schemes around other depressed areas of Britain's post-industrial landscape.

The Calderdale district was typical of north country regions suffering from industrial decline, since the collapse of the Halifax carpet industry; but with unemployment below the national average at thirteen per cent, it did not qualify for regional assistance from the government. It had one proud example in the work of an enlightened local musician-turned-property developer, Ernest Hall, who had stewarded the conversion of disused textile mills into elegantly renovated breeding-grounds for a legion of eager new small businesses. What next?

BiC's project team under Richard Wade and Paul Greetham – acting, again, as "enablers" – began sponsoring co-operative links between the community, its local politicians and businessmen. Soon a plethora of plans were afoot for new businesses, both big and small, leisure centres, recreational parks, even a children's museum called Eureka!, of which the Prince and Princess of Wales agreed to be patrons. Between Charles's first visit to Calderdale at the beginning of 1987, and a follow-up visit at the end of the year, enormous progress was made, laying plans to bring thousands of jobs to the area. Projects under way included the development of industrial, shopping, hotel and conference facilities; improvements to transport links, both road and rail, even water; provision for new education, arts and youth centres; environmental improvement programmes; and the development of leisure and tourist facilities. At the heart of all these plans was the principle of preserving the area's cultural past: renovating its disused industrial plants for more contemporary purposes, for instance, rather than demolishing them; adapting the Rochdale Canal into a water-sports centre, complete with marina; converting disused army camps and derelict factories into community centres and sports halls. The direct involvement of the local community gave them their own substantial role in the rebirth of the area, inspiring them to take due civic pride in the results.

Everywhere he went, the Prince of Wales sang the praises of the Calderdale experiment: in speeches to business leaders at the Per Cent Club, to City stalwarts at the Stock Exchange, even to American architects in Pittsburgh. He "dragged" numerous captains of industry to the area, to enlist their financial support; kept up his own frequent visits, occasionally escorted by his wife; and took enormous pride in his own role as a co-ordinating focus for the ever-growing range of schemes – a legion of piecemeal efforts which would surely have foundered, as the history of British post-industrial development showed time and again, without such lofty inspiration.

Calderdale, to the Prince, was becoming the first tangible evidence of what his leadership could achieve in terms of rejuvenating entire communities. Within the next few years the Yorkshire towns of Halifax, Elland and Brighouse, Todmorden, Sowerby Bridge and Hebden Bridge were set to become living proof that the ideas which he now espoused and championed could work in practice – and that he could use his office to effect real, practical improvements in the quality of thousands of British lives. In the Calderdale experiment as elsewhere, he had meanwhile divined an umbilical link between his concern for Britain's disadvantaged urban areas an his other, much more publicized recent passion: the state of modern British architecture.

TWELVE

Glass Stumps And Monstrous Carbuncles

"I rather like to stir things up. . . . "

A T 8.45 A.M. on the sunny Wednesday morning of 26 March 1986, in the forecourt of Kensington Palace, a disparate group of nine men and one woman boarded a battered orange minibus. Rented for £20 from the Limehouse Transport Co-operative, a left-wing East London community service group, the bus had quietly arrived at the Palace the previous afternoon to be checked over by security and explosives experts, who had secretly scrutinized its proposed route two days before.

The day's outing had been organized by Nicholas Falk, an urban planner and environmentalist. With him came two architects, John Thompson and Richard McCormac; Nick Wates, an architectural journalist and campaigner; David Couttie, inner-city specialist of the Halifax Building society; Alice Coleman, an academic sociologist, specializing in the relationship between high-rise buildings and social ills such as urban crime – plus two detectives assigned to protect members of the royal family, one private secretary and the Prince of Wales.

Charles sat in the front – formally dressed in suit and tie, amid the blue-jeans and corduroys of his travelling companions – as the bus anonymously headed south-east, across the Thames, making for one of the most notorious

housing estates in South London. Even in the hard-
pressed London Borough of Southwark, the Aylesbury
estate is one of the worst examples of a hybrid nexus of
council housing, both low-rise and tower-block, where
vandalism, crime and ill-health run riot. Here, at the
group's first port of call, the Prince took a quiet look
around and dropped in for a chat with the caretaker.

The six experts on board then took turns to give
Charles a running commentary on some of London's
most run-down districts, as the minibus headed east, back
across the river, towards the Limehouse Basin and the
crumbling tenements of the St Vincent's Estate – where
Wates had arranged for a cross-section of the local community, including Chinese and Asian immigrants, to be
waiting. Little did they know that the royal minibus had
been rented in the name of the Limehouse Development
Group, a volunteer lobby organization openly opposing
the £70 million development plan for the area proposed
by the British Waterways Board and the property group
Hunting Gate – and thus awkward company for the
Prince to be keeping. Charles led a forty-minute discussion of their woes before reboarding the bus and heading
further north, through more desolate urban landscapes, to
the London Borough of Hackney – where, according to
that day's Court Circular, his first official engagement of
the morning was to inspect Lea View House, a showpiece
among newly refurbished council estates. The minibus
stopped in a side street around the corner from Lea View,
where a Jaguar from the Royal Mews was waiting. The
Prince got out, thanked his companions, told them he
would like to make more such trips in future and asked
them for contributions to his forthcoming speeches on
architecture and inner-city problems. Then he boarded
the official car, rounded the corner and arrived to be
greeted by sundry local dignitaries bang on time at 11.30
a.m.

Four years before to the month, unknown to the Prince
of Wales or countless millions of his fellow Britons, build-

ing workers from Hackney Council's direct labour organization had arrived on this grim, forbidding East London estate to begin the £6.5 million renovation of its five-storey block of 300 council flats. The residents of Lea View greeted them with a giant "Welcome!" sign and a breakfast party. This kind of start to a local authority project was unheard-of in the murky history of council-tenant relations in Britain. But the story behind it was also to prove a landmark in post-war British architecture, and in the Prince of Wales's long quest for a creative role in the society which would one day be his kingdom. Here he was to find a new dimension to his work in the inner cities, his study of Jung and Schumacher – all his beliefs about the rights of the individual to have a say in, and thus take a pride in, the conditions in which he lives and works. The princely jigsaw was about to fall into place.

The Lea View estate had hitherto typified the social, political and environmental problems which beset so much inner-city council housing throughout the United Kingdom. It was a hard-to-fill, multi-racial, "sink" estate hated by those who lived in it. The buildings were vandalized and strewn with litter; muggings and thefts were commonplace; the occupants' health was poor. "They only moved there if they had no other choice," wrote Nick Wates and Charles Knevitt in their book *Community Architecture* (which was to become a Bible to Charles). "Existing tenants felt trapped and helpless, resigned to a life of misery from which there was no escape." As many as ninety per cent had told the council they wanted alternative accommodation.

In the autumn of 1980, after constant pressure from the tenants, Hackney council had finally brought in a firm of architects – Hunt Thompson Associates, a go-ahead but thoughtful practice who proceeded to take the bold step of setting up their project office, with four full-time staff, in an unoccupied flat on the estate. "The architects are using Flat No. 3," warned the wary tenants' newsletter, "so beware!" But Flat No. 3, as its new occupants had hoped, quickly became the social focus of the estate. A "creative dialogue" soon began between architects and tenants, who were delighted to find themselves invited to become involved in the redevelopment planning to an extent which they had not believed possible.

John Thompson, one of the Prince's companions on the minibus, was now among his hosts on the royal tour of Lea View. As he had begun work five years before, he told Charles, this growing mutual trust with the residents had led him to realize that the greatest resource available to him was the tenant community itself, "available at first hand and with detailed and highly critical knowledge and opinions about every single aspect of their own environment." In a report subsequently published by the Royal Institute of British Architects, Thompson expanded this argument:

> If this knowledge could be tapped and the real nature of [the tenants'] problems understood, then the architects could start to apply their own skills as designers to see if these daunting, overpowering, prison-like buildings could be transformed into a humane environment in which the tenants could once again live their lives with dignity and with a sense of pride in their own homes.

By applying the fundamental principle of "community architecture" – that people should be involved in the design and construction of the buildings in which they live and/or work – architects and tenants were between them to turn Lea View into "Heaven-in-Hackney." Hunt Thompson gathered information both scientifically, by means of a social survey, and "intuitively, over cups of tea." Thus, said Thompson, the architects began to perceive "the inextricable relationship that existed between the physical design of the original estate and the true extent of the social and physical deprivation of the community." Above all, they also realized that merely making physical improvement to the flats, although it would satisfy the tenants" original demands, would not be enough.

It would be money wasted, for "it was the underlying organization of the estate that was now the major factor in creating an unsatisfactory environment for people to live in."

So the entire rehabilitation concept was broadened, to include rearranging the basic layout of the flats, to restore an individual identity to each home and improve access to it; redefining public and private areas, to improve management of communal space and corporate pride in it; introducing insulation and solar heating systems to reduce fuel bills; and customizing flats for tenants with special needs, especially the elderly and the disabled.

As these plans developed, the architects expanded the project team to include representatives of the building workforce, officials and elected members from the council's housing department, and of course the tenants themselves. Hunt Thompson took Lea View residents to look at other similar schemes, so that they could assess the options on offer. Tenants soon found themselves, to their delighted surprise, involved in every aspect of the planning and design of the new estate, right down to the choice of their own internal decoration. While temporarily rehoused by the council, they visited the site as work proceeded and were invited to make any reasonable last-minute adjustments to their new homes. Their children were encouraged to take part in the tree-planting and landscaping programme. By Christmas tenants, builders and architects were working so well together that they laid on a joint party to raise money for local charities. Where once ninety per cent of tenants had wanted to leave, now ninety per cent wanted to stay.

"Through participating," said Peter Kahn, deputy leader of Hackney council, "we helped Lea View to become a community, to get people to live together, to work together, to communicate together. The direct relationship that exists between the workforce and the tenants had produced a very high level of motivation on the site, and the standard of workmanship has been excellent."

The end result, in the view of Wates and Knevitt, was "an estate which works well and looks good." Crime and vandalism have today been virtually eliminated. Communal areas are litter-free, the residents" general standard of health has improved, and there is a new-found community spirit. "We take so much pride in it," said one tenant, "that we won't allow anybody to come around and destroy it or disturb it." Said another, Dolly Pritchard:

> It seems like your own little bit of creation. . . . I just walk around and admire my place, I'm so chuffed with it. It's been worth every meeting, every protest. Before, we hardly knew anybody. Now everybody is mixing, and we are beginning to get a really good community again. Once people fought to leave Lea View, now they're all wanting to get in. . . .

Reopening the Lea View estate in July 1983, Hackney council's leader, Anthony Kendall, described it as "a model example for us all to learn from, a pioneering scheme that shows the way forward as to how we should modernize our estates in the future, concentrating on quality rather than quantity." The architect, John Thompson, summed up:

> The process of regeneration of the estate has also regenerated the community spirit. People now know their neighbours can respect each other's territory. Once you can reestablish pride, you can solve all the other problems which flow from loss of pride, loss of dignity and loss of selfrespect.

The lesson "for all architects, and probably for all other professionals," he said, was "to get out of our ivory towers, get away from our institutes, get away from our offices, and to go out take real people as the client, to work with real people and to genuinely serve the people." Lea View became a living symbol of what could be achieved by community architecture – an ideal which had recently become a growing movement within the profession, as yet regarded with suspicion by Britain's best-known and most powerful architects, and by the potentates of the RIBA itself. The John Thompsons of British architecture were very much a minority, who regarded themselves as voices crying in a wilderness of entrenched, reactionary professionals, greedy property developers and vested interests.

Largely through historical accident, they were now to find a crucial new ally. Thompson and his partner Bernard Hunt had been Cambridge contemporaries and partners in practice of Charles's cousin and close friend, Richard, Duke of Gloucester – the only architect in the royal family until his elder brother's death in a plane crash had forced him, on inheriting their father's title, to abandon full-time practice for more royal duties. Charles's neighbour in Kensington Palace, Prince Richard had for some time been pleased to foster his cousin's growing interest in architecture, a subject which fused the Prince's artistic and reformist inclinations, a topic about which he was always happy to talk over public dinner tables otherwise creaking with ineffable boredom.

A traditionalist in matters of design as in so much else, Charles had recently found himself deploring many of the new buildings sprouting around the London horizon. But he had hitherto thought this a matter of personal taste, another grudge which he must reluctantly keep to himself, rather than realizing that it might be a policy issue on which he could speak out, which might even provide the missing link towards the cause for which he had been looking for so long. The turning-point came in May 1984 when the Prince of Wales was invited to speak at a dinner celebrating the RIBA's 150th anniversary and to present its annual gold medal.

A few weeks earlier Charles had attended a Royal Academy dinner at the invitation of its president, Sir Hugh Casson, a long-standing friend who had also fostered his early interest in architecture. When the conversation turned towards the principles and achievements of community architecture, Charles surprised his companions with the intensity of his interest. He asked for more information. Over the following days, writers and journalists specializing in the subject were asked to send articles and cuttings round to Kensington Palace, specifically on the theme of community architecture. Charles, meanwhile, took up the subject with Prince Richard, who told him the story of his erstwhile partners' achievement at Lea View and of a similarly successful project in Black Road, Macclesfield – the work of a brash young Northern architect called Rod Hackney, who even lived in the place. Thus was born the Prince of Wales's enthusiasm for community architecture.

He chose the big RIBA speech to proclaim it – along with a wholesale denunciation of contemporary architects who did not espouse its *modus operandi* and a colourful assault on one proposed building in particular. At Hampton Court Palace, that most splendid of all the royal residences, there was a heady, celebratory atmosphere that May evening among all but a select few of the RIBA leadership, who had discovered – by accident, only that afternoon – what the Prince intended to say. Sensing the scale of the controversy he was about to cause, Charles had "leaked" an advance copy of his speech to his friend Charles Douglas-Home, editor of *The Times* – and also, to avoid accusations of favouritism, to Peter Preston, editor of the *Guardian*. Douglas-Home, as requested, had kept it to himself, sharing its contents with his own architecture correspondent only when *en route* to Hampton Court. Preston, as is the way of more conventional editors, had passed it on his staff. When a *Guardian* reporter sought the response of the RIBA president, Michael Manser, only a few hours before the speech was due to be delivered, he was so thunderstruck that he considered boycotting the evening. Manser's inquiries to Buckingham Palace revealed total confusion: the press office had never heard of the RIBA gold medal and Edward Adeane had to confess that his boss had not shown him the final version of his speech.

For days the Prince's own staff, especially Edward Adeane, had been trying to talk him out of the assault he proposed to make, as had others of his advisers and friends. Its strength and passion, apart from appearing an unseemly abuse of hospitality, would incur the enmity of a British professional institute under royal patronage; it would involve him in an already heated public debate, in an area which was wholly new ground to him. To Adeane, the speech had become a resignation issue.

The night before, Charles himself had become sufficiently concerned about his speech to lose sleep over it. As he tossed and turned, a particular phrase occurred to him which inspired renewed confidence. While drafting the most striking phrase in the entire tirade, he had been thinking in terms of "warts" or "pimples." Now the word "carbuncle" – used by his step-mother-in-law, Raine Spencer, in a recent book on British spas – swam into the royal psyche and helped it at last find rest. Next morning, as Adeane still urged caution, the Prince of Wales was adamant. He had found a cause about which he cared; he was convinced he was in the right and he was determined to speak his mind.

Lit by celebratory candlelight, graced by the first masque commissioned since the eighteenth century, it was the biggest party ever held at Hampton Court. The 700 British architects present anticipated a predictable string of princely platitudes, a royal celebration of their 150 years of glorious service to the community. As their guest of honour rose to speak, however, the evening suddenly turned utterly sour as the Prince proceeded to tear his hosts limb from limb:

> For far too long, it seems to me, some planners and archi-
> tects have consistently ignored the feelings and wishes of the
> mass of ordinary people in this country. . . . To be concerned
> about the way people live, about the environment they in-
> habit and the kind of community created by that environ-

ment should surely be one of the prime requirements of a really good architect.

Too many architects, declared the Prince, tended to design houses "for the approval of their fellow-architects and critics – not for the tenants." He went on to praise community architecture by name, citing its effects in the housing co-operatives of Liverpool, "where the tenants are able to work with an architect of their own who listens to their comments and their ideas, and tries to design the kind of environment they want, rather than the kind which tends to be imposed upon them without any degree of choice."

Community architecture, in short, had shown "ordinary" people that their views are worth having; that architects and planners do not necessarily have the monopoly of knowing best about taste, style and planning; that they need not be made to feel guilty or ignorant if their natural preference is for the more "traditional" designs – for a small garden, for courtyards, arches and porches – and that there was "a growing number of architects prepared to listen and to offer imaginative ideas."

The Prince proceeded – most unusually – to single out two such architects, Rod Hackney and Edward Cullinan, for personal praise by name. They were, he said, men after his own heart, men who strongly believed that architects "must produce something which is visually beautiful as well as socially useful." He then proceeded, in the most outspoken moment of his public life so far, to denounce the proposed extension to the National Gallery in Trafalgar Square in terms as emotional as they have since proved memorable:

> Instead of designing an extension to the elegant facade of the National Gallery which complements it, and continues the concept of columns and domes, it looks as if we may be presented with a kind of vast municipal fire station – complete with the sort of tower that contains the siren. I would better understand this type of "high-tech" approach if you

demolished the whole of Trafalgar Square and started again with a single architect responsible for the entire layout. But what is proposed is like a monstrous carbuncle on the face of a much-loved and elegant friend.

As for the Mies van der Rohe building which a consortium headed by Peter Palumbo proposed to erect in Mansion House Square: it was a "giant glass stump, better suited to downtown Chicago than to the City of London." In a theme to which he would in time return even more provocatively (with his so-called "Luftwaffe speech" in December 1987, see pages 255-63), Charles asked:

> What have we done to our capital city? What have we done to it since the bombing of the last war? Why can't we have those curves and arches that express *feeling* in design? It would be a tragedy if the character and skyline of our capital city were to be further ruined. . . . Those who recall [prewar London] say that the affinity between the buildings and the earth, in spite of the city's great size, was so close and organic that the houses looked almost as if they had grown out of the earth and not been imposed upon it – grown, moreover, in such a way that as few trees as possible were thrust out of the way.

Far from praising the achievement of British architects, the Prince had been thoroughly damning, ending with an "earnest hope" that "the next 150 years will see a new harmony between imagination and taste and in the relationship between the architects and the people of this country." As Charles presented RIBA's gold medal to the Indian architect Charles Correa, whose outstanding work for the Third World homeless he had completely ignored, the British architects present were severely shaken. Some gave the Prince points for having the courage to play "Daniel in the lions' den," but most remain highly critical of his remarks to this day. Manser, his reluctant host for the evening, bit his tongue long enough to declare that "members of the royal family are entitled to their point of view," adding that he hoped the Prince of Wales would "think more about modern architecture, because it is here to stay." It was "deeply unsatisfactory," Manser later argued, "that the debate had become locked into the argument of new versus old. What we need to discuss is good or bad." The Prince's remarks, though they had sparked a considerable debate, had caused "more harm than good."

Peter Ahrends, whose National Gallery extension was doomed from that moment, did not mince words. The Prince's remarks were

> offensive, reactionary and ill-considered.... He seems to have a rather nostalgic view of buildings, as if they grow out of the Earth – a view of life no longer with us. He seems to be looking backwards rather than forwards.... If he holds such strong views, I am surprised he did not take the opportunity offered by the public inquiry to express them.

Prince Charles, said Ahrends, had "done nothing to further the debate on modern architecture." His views were "out of step with those of the country as a whole." But the huge response next day seemed to prove him wrong. Buckingham Palace was deluged in letters of support, and the Prince sensed that he had touched a raw nerve of enormous future potential. Anxious to keep his institute and its royal patron on speaking terms, Manser persuaded the Prince to host a private dinner party for architects at Kensington Palace, attended, among others, by Rod Hackney. While handling the protests of outraged orthodoxy with civility, Charles quietly asked Hackney to organize a further series of meetings with community architects of like mind, to explore other aspects of the movement such as public education and development finance.

Although the "monstrous carbuncle" controversy rages to this day, it has never before clearly emerged that Charles's denunciation of Ahrends's building that night was less than fair and its consequences wholly disproportionate. A closer look at the long and tortured saga of the

National Gallery extension shows that the design so reviled by the Prince was a compromise between the authorities and the architect, about which Ahrends himself was less than happy.

The saga began in 1981, when the National Gallery's trustees, chaired by Lord Annan, secured government approval in principle for a composite extension of gallery and offices. (As a Crown property within the purview of the Property Services Agency, the Gallery did not need listed-building consent for amendments to the old, existing building; it did, however, need planning permission for an extension, direct from the Secretary of State for the Environment rather than Westminster council.) Seven teams of developers and architects were invited to submit proposals, the winner to be chosen by a panel of expert judges including Lord Annan and the Gallery's director, Sir Michael Levey.

In December 1982 the judges announced that they could not agree; the Gallery representatives favoured the scheme of an American firm, Skidmore, Owings and Merrill, but their aesthetic advisers considered the proposed building "architecturally undistinguished." A typically British and, as it proved, disastrous compromise was then reached with the commission of revised designs from the architects Ahrends, Burton and Koralek, whose financial partners were the development company Trafalgar House. This consortium was not to be regarded as winners of the competition; it was more that the scheme proposed by this particular partnership offered "the best prospects of a wholly satisfactory result" – but only if Ahrends would agree to make fundamental amendments to his original design in collaboration with the Gallery, who sought an ideal combination of office space as well as gallery space to help finance the building.

When Charles, therefore, criticized the sacrifice of gallery space to office space, he was in effect criticizing the aspirations of the National Gallery's trustees, rather than those of the architect. There were even suggestions that

Charles had got the wrong building, that his remarks were directed against the plans submitted by Richard Rodgers – which did indeed, to some, resemble a fire station. When the then RIBA president Owen Luder had first seen the models, he had sown the seeds of the Prince's resentment by declaring to Rodgers's proposal: "That's the one I'd go for! It says "Sod you" to the public!" But the truth is that the Prince was attacking a hybrid design with which the architect himself was, at that stage, far from pleased. Like most less than satisfactory end-products, the proposed National Gallery extension had, in fact, been designed by a committee.

The whole question of a new building on a site of such national prominence as Trafalgar Square was always going to attract controversy and the personal involvement of the Secretary of State. So a public inquiry inspector, David Woolley QC, had been appointed as early as January 1982, though his work had been postponed for two years during the Trustees" deliberations. Arguments still raged about the status of the site and the buildings, quite apart from its functional effectiveness and aesthetic merits. The inspector finally made his report on 8 June 1984, a week after the Prince's tirade; and three months later the Secretary of State refused planning permission. Charles's remarks, on all the evidence, had clinched the decision to scrap the Ahrends – Trafalgar House plan. Even as the Prince sat down at Hampton Court, the then Secretary of State for the Environment, Patrick Jenkin, had whispered to a neighbour: "Well, that's another decision I don't have to make!"

Three years later, Ahrends was described by sympathetic fellow-architects as "a broken man," "a tragic figure" who had "every right to feel very aggrieved." By his own account his practice would take years to recover; since becoming jocularly known as "the carbuncle architects," Ahrends, Burton and Koralek had lost millions in commissions. (Sensing that he had chosen the wrong occasion for his tirade, and that he had misjudged the effect of his remarks, Charles later agreed to Manser's suggestion of a "peacemaking" lunch with Ahrends, who has since refused to comment publicly on the episode.)

For the National Gallery, meanwhile, it was back to the drawingboard. Sir John Sainsbury of supermarket wealth, along with his brothers Simon and Timothy, now stepped in with an offer to underwrite the extension, on condition that a new competition was held – eventually won by the American architect Robert Venturi, of the Philadelphia practice Venturi, Rauch and Scott. Prince Charles had by now been made a trustee of the National Gallery in a Macchiavellian attempt to pre-empt further trouble. When he laid the foundation-stone of the National Gallery's Sainsbury Wing on 30 March 1988, it seemed highly significant that he kept his mouth firmly shut.

Back in 1984, the immediate effect of the "carbuncle" row was to drown out the main theme of Charles's speech: his attempt to champion the "community" approach to architecture. Undeterred, the Prince asked Hackney to set up a series of private visits to community schemes, especially Lea View House. Over the next two years he also inspected Limehouse Basin, near Lea View in East London; the Zenzele self-build housing co-operative in Bristol; riot-torn Lozells Road in Birmingham; the Community Design Service in Cardiff; and Edward Cullinan's Lambeth Community Care Center. Among Hackney's own projects on the royal agenda were Black Road in Macclesfield and the Liverpool housing co-ops mentioned in the Prince's RIBA speech, as well as the Weavers Triangle scheme in Burnley, Lancashire, and the Colquhoun Street project in Stirling, Scotland.

More major speeches on the subject were soon to follow, but the Prince immediately lent symbolic support to the cause by commissioning work from avowed community architects around his own properties and estates. Culllinan was asked to design some new gates for Kensington Palace (which Charles, ironically enough, eventually rejected), while two members of the RIBA's Community Architecture Group, Joe Poynton and Ben Derbyshire (also of Hunt Thompson), were awarded Duchy of Cornwall rehabilitation projects in Curry Mallet, Somerset, and Kennington.

Nine months after the RIBA speech, in February 1985, Prince Charles returned to his new theme in a major address to the annual conference of the Institute of Directors at the Royal Albert Hall. To the captains of British industry the Prince of Wales conjured up "a trail of devastation throughout the country, particularly in the north of England." He spoke of the "desperate" plight of inner-city areas, the "inhuman conditions" in which people were forced to live and "the cycle of economic decline leading to physical deterioration and countless social problems." Whole communities were "shattered," forced to live from day to day in a "hostile environment." Clearly, this was a direct and emotional appeal to British industry – especially its banks, insurance companies and pension funds – to invest in the inner cities. But Charles also seized the chance to relaunch his attack on the architects, embarking upon a theme which has since become a constant of all his speeches on the subject. More than just a heartfelt plea, it amounts to the nearest a Prince of Wales can get to the vexed and complex argument about the influences of market forces on architectural design: "Money by itself is not necessarily the answer, as demonstrated by most postwar redevelopment schemes."

So what *was* the answer?

> The real answer, I would contend, lies in the enormous human potential and resource waiting to be given the incentive and encouragement to play a fuller part in contributing to the common good; waiting to be released from the over-numerous shackles of bureaucracy and the all-pervading atmosphere of "the professionals" knowing what is best for you.

He spoke at some length of his visits to community architecture projects, introducing another now familiar theme – the notion of architects as "enablers," or catalysts within communities to help individuals learn how to help themselves. In such a forum it was only appropriate to outline community architects" work in the commercial and industrial field as much as housing schemes, and to encourage more co-operation between the public and private sector. But he also warned against "the "them-and-us" syndrome which leads to mutual distrust taking the place of mutual understanding," and predicted that it could turn Britain into "a fourth-rate nation." As is his wont, however, the Prince concluded on an upbeat note: "The possibilities in the field of regeneration are immense, the challenge is awesome, but the rewards, I feel sure, will be nothing less than a *Great* Britain once again."

Community architecture had never enjoyed so high a profile. Prince Charles seemed to have started something of a revolution within the profession, exciting considerable resentment among the older hands at the RIBA, who dubbed him a "reactionary" with "Ruritanian" aspirations. In other areas of his life, during this same period, he was also beginning to earn himself a label as something of an eccentric, pursuing "natural" and "alternative" approaches to, for instance, medicine and farming – because, in the words of one wag, "his own life has been so unnatural that he *needs* to look for alternatives." As he began to build a bridge between his architectural hobbyhorse and his growing concern about the inner cities, there were those who saw the Prince of Wales on a collision course with the entrenched government of Mrs Thatcher, then riding high in its sixth year of office.

Among the great beneficiaries of the publicity generated by the Prince's outspoken support, meanwhile, was Rod Hackney, who had never met Charles before his Hampton Court speech and had been astonished to hear himself singled out for princely praise. He earned, in his own words, "a thousand enemies" that night as he was "summoned" backstage to meet the Prince. Eighteen months on, by October 1985, Hackney was one of Charles's closest advisers and friends.

Hackney's rise to prominence had been remarkably swift and was almost entirely due to his increasingly publicized role at the Prince's shoulder. Born in Toxteth, Liverpool, in 1942, the son of an army chef, he had studied architecture at Manchester University before building monorail stations at Expo 67 in Montreal, Canada, for the Ottawa practice of Hart Massey, and joining the Danish master Arne Jacobsen (on whom he wrote his PhD thesis) in the design of the gold-roofed National Bank of Kuwait. Like Prince Charles, Hackney then stumbled upon the notion of community architecture almost by mistake.

Having returned from Denmark with £1,000 in savings, he bought himself what he thought a doomed house in Black Road, Macclesfield, despite the expectation that it would be demolished within two years, on the principle that it would be cheaper than renting. Hackney soon discovered that the other residents of Black Road were less prepared than him to move on. As "the only educated man on the block," he was drafted in as leader of the movement to fight the bulldozers, and thus began to discern the advantages of concerted communal action. Under Hackney's energetic leadership, Black Road became one of the early models of "self-help" community architecture, which he then proceeded to put into practice elsewhere around the north-west of England. An entrepreneur as much as an architect, he soon expanded his practice into such ancillary areas as plant hire and project management, even estate agency and photography. By 1986 Rod Hackney Associates did not only employ thirty full-time community architects but some 200 other staff in a variety of related disciplines; the annual turnover of his corporate parent company, Castward, had reached some £5 million; and Hackney himself was well on his way to being a millionaire, the proud owner of a custom-built six-wheel Range Rover, remembered for having a telephone in his old Citroen long before they became commonplace.

Already his conspicuous success was giving pause to those who felt it was somehow wrong for community architects to become rich.

But Hackney's tireless gift of the gab, allied with an informed confidence in his beliefs, entranced the Prince of Wales – a man who easily falls under the spell of like-minded idealists who talk to him straight. Unlike previous members of the Prince's "junior court," let alone his "kitchen cabinet," Hackney seemed to have been permitted to exploit his royal connection without incurring banishment, even displeasure – until, that is, the notorious night of 20 October 1985, when a confessional conversation with the Prince proved too much for Hackney to keep to himself.

On a tour of his Duchy of Cornwall estates in the West Country, Charles was spending the night aboard the royal train in a Somerset railway siding, where Hackney joined him for dinner. As a routine discussion of current and future projects expanded into a global discussion of the inner cities and their problems, the Prince felt he knew the architect well enough to speak candidly. Any member of his inner circle, after all, well knew that discretion was part of the price of admission.

But when Peter Sharples, an enterprising reporter from the *Manchester Evening News*, interviewed Hackney by telephone two days later, his breezy self-confidence led him to go too far. To be fair to Hackney, he has always disputed the way the journalist used what he said. Across the front page of next day's *Evening News*, however, soon to be trumpeted from every page in the land, was a picture of Hackney and the Prince touring riot-ravaged Toxteth, and a banner proclaiming:

"EXCLUSIVE – PRINCE CHARLES: MY FEARS FOR THE FUTURE." "The biggest fear of Prince Charles," read Sharples's story, "is that he will inherit the throne of a divided Britain. The Prince is prepared to force his way through parliamentary red tape to ensure that his country is not split into factions of "haves" and "haves-nots." " Hackney was quoted as saying: "He is very worried that when he becomes king there will be "no-go" areas in the inner cities, and that the [racial] minorities will be alienated from the rest of the country. He does not want to become king in an atmosphere like that."

By now, Charles had left for a tour of Australia. After hectic consultations on antipodean telephone lines, Buckingham Palace issued a forthright statement confirming that Hackney had been aboard the royal train that night and had indeed dined with the Prince: "We have no idea what was discussed, but obviously the Prince is extremely concerned about the plight of the inner cities and is doing everything he can to find a solution to the problem." To suggestions that it might have been a deliberate leak, a Palace spokesman responded testily: "If the Prince wishes to say something, he is perfectly capable of doing it for himself." To further reports that the Queen was enraged and had been rebuking her son down secure long-distance telephone lines, the same velvet-voiced courtier added: "The provenance of that story was very dubious indeed."

Besieged by reporters, both at the RIBA in London and at his new home in the Peak District, Hackney at first denied the remarks attributed to him, then went on to express views strikingly similar to those ascribed to him in the article. "They were my views I gave to that journalist," he insisted, "not the Prince's." In Australia, meanwhile, Charles was visibly hurt by the episode. At an off-the-record party for the travelling press, then a regular item on the agenda of such tours, he told reporters in confidence that he had been "betrayed" by someone he had thought to be his friend. It was not the first time this had happened, nor would it be the last, but the particular breach of royal etiquette had particularly wounded Charles. He valued Hackney's advice and thus his friendship; this was scant reward for all the work he had done to promote community architecture; and there was the nagging feeling that now this passionate new cause, so close to his heart, could turn sour, even rebound on him.

The Prince of Wales's morale was not helped by an angry phone call from the Prime Minister in the United States, asking him what he thought he was "up to." In Washington for talks with President Reagan, Mrs Thatcher had received with horror reports of the political fall-out in the House of Commons. Waving a copy of a newspaper trumpeting Charles's Doomsday predictions, the Labour opposition's Shadow Home Secretary, Gerald Kaufman, had seized the chance for a wholesale political offensive:

> Is this Government determined to preside over the destruction of the Queen's realm? Does this Government lack the will or the compassion or patriotism to insist on including the whole of our society and all people in a national commonwealth? Is it resigned to presiding over a Britain in which, as Lord Scarman has warned, disorder will become a disease endemic in our society?

Kaufman's opposite number, Douglas Hurd, could muster only appeasing platitudes as the Labour leader, Neil Kinnock, then entered the lists, closely followed by dissident Tory backbenchers and the ever outspoken Enoch Powell, in his cherished role as guardian of the British constitution.

In their desperate search for new leads, to preserve the momentum of a thumping good story, the press soon came up with the startling revelation that "the caring Prince" had even been out at night, incognito, visiting the dossers sleeping rough on the benches of London railway stations and the bleak concrete landscape of the Thames Embankment. As lofty columnists were then wheeled on to pronounce their verdicts – supportive, without exception, of the Prince and his supposed concerns – it soon became clear that the entire fuss was proving far from counterproductive. Community architecture was on the map as never before, hallmarked as a forthright Prince Charles's solution to a contemporary malaise universally acknowledged to be a cause for growing concern.

Despite the spate of riots, the Thatcher government had not as yet publicly conceded any notion of a common problem around Britain's inner cities, as opposed to a specific one in Liverpool. But royal patronage, if by unorthodox methods, had now placed the problem – and the community approach to a solution – squarely on the national agenda. Both protagonists were so delighted that any estrangement between Charles and Hackney was soon forgotten, though a six-month period of public "distancing" was deemed appropriate, lest the breach of protocol be seen to go unpunished. Their work together would go on and would soon achieve even more striking results.

Another eloquent supporter of community architecture was the journalist Charles Knevitt, a close friend of Hackney, and architecture correspondent of the *Sunday Telegraph* until he had moved in 1984 to *The Times*. Within a year Knevitt had persuaded the Prince, the RIBA and his employers to lend their names to an annual series of awards for projects best demonstrating the ideals of community development. The scheme's first chairman would be Rod Hackney. By the time Prince Charles presented the first *The Times*/RIBA Community Enterprise Awards in June 1986, entries were received from no fewer than 184 ventures throughout the United Kingdom – the accolade going to the Inner City Trust of Derry, Northern Ireland, whose "ambitious, regenerative self-help project" had created 500 jobs in the city, making it second only to Du Pont Chemicals among local employers.

The Prince seized the occasion to re-emphasize what was fast becoming the central theme of his working life, as well as a passionately held personal philosophy:

> The crucial issue today is how to give people more pride in their environment, involvement in their housing and more control over their lives, all this leading to increased

confidence and hope, a development of new organizational skills and a consequent flourishing of new enterprise. We are talking about the regeneration of thousands of local communities, and this is really the essential point about the whole thing. How can we achieve such an aim while ensuring that it isn't pie in the sky? The fundamental point to stress is the urgent need for partnership between the public and private sector, between local politicians, community groups and non-public sources of finances. To restore hope we must have a vision and source of inspiration. We must sink our differences and cut great swathes through the cat's cradle of red tape which chokes this country from end to end.

This rapid breakthrough in public recognition of community architecture, almost entirely due to the Prince's promotion of the movement and its ideals, was still taking place against a background of internecine warfare at the RIBA. By now, however, support within the profession had grown too strong for the leadership to succeed in its attempts either to emasculate the Community Architecture Group or, as Knevitt darkly revealed, "to wrest control of the Community Enterprise Awards scheme from *The Times*." At a furious secret meeting, only hours before the presentation of the first awards, senior Institute officials had argued that Hackney was an "unacceptable" chairman; *The Times*'s managing editor blithely told them that the newspaper, which had arranged the royal patronage, stood by its choice. The Prince's new private secretary, Sir John Riddell, sat through the meeting in circumspect silence.

Now came the counter-punch. Only two months before the Institute presidential elections – expected to be an unopposed victory for the "Establishment" candidate, RIBA's senior vice-president, Raymond Andrews – Hackney announced that he too would be running. He would not stand simply as the "community" candidate; in a "man of action" manifesto, Hackney shrewdly promised the membership overdue reforms of their professional code of practice and in the central bureaucracy of the Institute itself. Given the high profile which he could bring the profession, thanks to his association with the Prince of Wales, Hackney's surprise candidacy appeared to pose a real threat to the in-house favourite.

In the week before the election, in late November 1986, Hackney hosted a gathering at the Astoria Theatre, London, under the title of the Building Communities Conference. More than a thousand delegates were attracted from all over the world by the "community" twang of the title – the conference was summed up by one delegate as "the greening of architecture" – and the promise of a keynote address by the Prince of Wales.

Charles did not bat an eyelid when introduced by Hackney as "the champion of the community architecture movement, our patron and friend." He began by saying that he knew he was about to "invite a barrage of criticism." But it would not, he also knew, be coming from inside the hall. So it was with confidence of a warm reception that he went on: "I am here because, frankly, what is known as the community architecture approach makes a great deal of sense to me, and I would like to see more people become aware of what it actually means." Amid thunderous applause from the converted, he went on to build in some chunks of his other, longer-term preoccupations:

> One of the main reasons I believe that the community architecture approach makes sense is because I believe in the individual uniqueness of every human being. I believe that every individual has a contribution to make and a potential to achieve, if it can be brought out. . . . Individuals tend to operate best within a community of other individuals, within an environment that is based on human scale and which is designed to create a sense of belonging rather than alienation and anonymity. . . . The rebuilding of communities is, I know, a very difficult process and requires extraordinarily patient, dedicated professionals to make it happen. . . . [But] so

much more can be achieved by creating partnerships. Community groups can often contribute vital elements, such as local knowledge, care and maintenance, and, above all, sheer unadulterated enthusiasm.

Charles could not resist the chance for yet another swipe at the modern stylists of the architectural profession. Now the audience grew noticably restrained, for he was again confusing method with taste as he went on: "I think it is time to resurrect the principles by which classical Greece operated . . . to restore harmony to architecture. Rhythm, balance and equilibrium have been missing too long." Quoting Ruskin and Betjeman, he concluded:

> Can't we try and make mankind feel grand? Can't we raise
> the spirits by restoring a sense of harmony; by re-establishing
> human scale in street patterns and heights of buildings; by
> redesigning those huge areas of what is euphemistically
> known as "public open space" between tower blocks, which
> lie derelict, festering and anonymous? Can't we restore peo-
> ple's pride; bring back self-confidence; develop the potential
> and very real skills of individual people in this island? How
> can any country survive unless it has an aim and an inspira-
> tion?

The Prince chose the occasion to announce the setting up of another new national initiative: Inner City Aid, "a Band Aid for the Inner Cities" – the Prince of Wales's own answer to Bob Geldof's Live Aid, which had by now spawned several such offspring. Its ambitious goal – under the chairmanship, again, of Rod Hackney – was to raise £10 million in its first year alone to provide grant aid, in cash and kind, for development and rehabilitation projects initiated by community self-help groups. Inner City Aid, the conference was told, would teach new skills, create long-term jobs and big reinvestment in decayed inner cities "from the bottom-up," by funding grass-roots projects around the community. There would be a special emphasis on housing, aiming "to improve the built envi-

ronment – particularly by stimulating community housing – through community enterprise and initiative, in
partnership with the public and private sectors and other
voluntary and charitable agencies."

"This is about regenerating Britain's inner cities," trumpeted Hackney at the launch. Benefactors, he declared,
would be investing in "the renaissance of the United
Kingdom from the inner city outwards." Only eight hours
later, at a Mansion House dinner, Charles also launched
the Prince's Youth Business Trust, which he described as
"a scheme for job-makers rather than job-seekers . . . in
catering for some of the harder hit youngsters in the UK,
it sets an example to others." A merger of the existing
Fairbridge Youth Enterprise Scheme and the Youth Business Initiative, the Trust's charter was to offer "bursaries"
(grants) and free professional advice to help "disadvantaged" young people between the ages of eighteen and
twenty-five start their own businesses. PYBT would offer
grants up to £1,000 per person, or £3,000 per company,
and so-called "easy-term loans" on condition that successful applicants took compulsory counselling from two professionals. To the heady conference delegates that night,
the Prince of Wales was lending not merely words to the
cause of community architecture in Britain's troubled
inner cities and elsewhere; he was, with the conspicuous
support of Rod Hackney, promising action.

Two days after the Astoria convention, Hackney was
elected the new president of the RIBA. David, as one
Sunday newspaper put it, had triumphed over Goliath. In
a record poll, the most publicized and controversial in the
Institute's history, he had beaten the internal candidate by
a surprisingly high margin. A few weeks later, Hackney's
stature and influence were soon enhanced even further
when he was also elected president of the International
Union of Architects – despite another campaign against
him from inside his own Institute. Feelings were riding so
high that Hackney took legal advice about criticism of
him attributed in the *Daily Telegraph* to the then secre-

tary of the RIBA, Patrick Harrison – who did not remain secretary of the RIBA very much longer.

Community architecture had really arrived, and a sea-change seemed in prospect within the very heart of the British profession. Characteristically, Hackney got to work immediately; even before he took office the following July, RIBA was hosting the British launch of the United Nations" International Year for the Homeless. As internal reforms of the Institute's creaky administrative machinery began to follow, its new president was soon in demand in the highest councils of the land. Apart from his still fre-quent visits to Kensington Palace, Hackney's name was quietly vetted by Downing Street, as a potential adviser on the inner-city crisis. "Community architecture has come of age," said Hackney. "We're no longer fighting the corner. We've got the corner. Governments, having tried their approach and found that it failed miserably, are saying they need help."

Three years after the Prince of Wales's Hampton Court tirade – still remembered, misleadingly, as the "carbuncle" speech – the Prince's tireless promotion of a minority cause was fundamentally challenging the philosophy of one of Britain's most entrenched professions and raising its new goals, against mighty odds, into a major issue at the top of the nation's political agenda.

Something, in other words, *was* being done.

THIRTEEN

1987: A Bad Year

> "If they'd rather I did nothing,
> I'll go off somewhere else."

NINETEEN eighty-seven was the year in which everything began to unravel again. It began badly on the professional front, with an infuriating gaffe by the Prince's private staff, and grew much worse on the domestic. In spring and summer Charles was again being lampooned as a loony; by the autumn the breach in his marriage had become agonisingly public. After he and Diana had spent their sixth wedding anniversary apart, clearly by choice rather than necessity, he retreated on his own to Balmoral for a month, publicly snubbing his Princess and his children. No longer could the gossip be dismissed as tabloid hysteria; Charles's own self-conduct had become the prime cause of national concern, as he appeared content to let an ever more damaging sequence of events spiral out of control.

The bad start could so easily have been avoided. Even he should have foreseen the damage that would be done by launching Inner City Aid and the Prince's Youth Business Trust on the same day. By February, less than three months after that heady reception at the Astoria, it had become clear that they could not co-exist. As Jim

Gardner, the new chairman of the Prince's Trust, put it: "We were all fishing in the same pond."

Thanks to its deliberate echo of Bob Geldof, Inner City Aid was attracting much more publicity than the less glamorous PYBT, which already seemed doomed as both chased the same sources of institutional cash – already badgered by BiC, the Prince's Trust and all their offspring. Geldof himself helped Inner City Aid by persuading a number of well-known architects to lend their support free of charge, even though several of them fundamentally disagreed with the Prince's so oft expressed views. But it was institutional weight rather than surface glamour which won the day. Lord Boardman, chairman of the National Westminster Bank, who had agreed to chair the PYBT, declared himself "dismayed." On 4 February Charles convened an emergency meeting of the Presidents Committee – the chairmen of the nine main charities to which he lends his name – at which Boardman's forces won the day. It was agreed that the two organizations could not go on fund-raising simultaneously, that the same-day launch had been a momentous disaster and that Inner City Aid would cease fund-raising until two years after its launch.

Now it was Inner City Aid's turn to suffer as PYBT prospered. It had raised only £33,000 of its original £10 million target; only two projects, in Bradford and Lambeth, South London, had even reached the planning stage. "Somebody at Kensington Palace dropped a clanger and now we're paying the price," said a leading member of the group, placing the blame squarely on the Prince's senior staff. "He needs advisers like this like he needs a hole in the head."

By September Inner City Aid's director, Charles Knevitt, had resigned; and even his circumspect successor, Canon Sebastian Charles, was quoted as saying that someone was guilty of "a terrific gaffe that should never have happened. We may be forced to consider whether to get the project going soon, or allow it to die. . . . There is now a clear choice: either it should come fully to life, or be put paid to." Inner City Aid is still, at the time of writing, in limbo; but there are high hopes that it will take off when relaunched on the Prince's fortieth birthday in November 1988. Lord Scarman, one of its trustees, while also conceding that "a great mistake" had been made over the launch, suggested that in the early days, anyway, "enthusiasm had tended to get in the way of sensible planning." The delay was a chance to "define our role more clearly," probably by limiting the charity's role to "fairly modest self-help schemes."

The PYBT, meanwhile, began to flourish. By the end of the year it had helped to set up more than 3,500 new businesses, creating 5,000 jobs, with only a twenty per cent failure rate. After a year in business it was criticized as a "soft touch for con-men," despite the fact that all applicants were vetted by experienced businessmen on secondment from firms such as Marks & Spencer, British Telecom and Yorkshire Television. Private sector contributions to the Trust were matched pound for pound by the government. Its 1987-8 target was to provide £4 million in grants and loans, and develop twenty training and support centres – or "one-stop shops" – around the country over the next two years.

Its inspiring case-histories – symptomatic of Charles's as much as Thatcher's Britain – were legion. David Griffin of Hereford, badly crippled from birth, was eighteen when he received a grant to open a flower stall in Hereford Market; after repaying the loan, he opened his own florists. Kevin Brown, made redundant by a South Wales glass-blowing firm, received a £1,000 grant to start his own glass business; within eighteen months he too had paid off the loan and was totally self-supporting. Will Thompson, a twenty-one-year-old sports enthusiast, received a £2,000 loan to start "European Adventures", a holiday firm organizing educational and sporting summer camps around Europe for young Americans. The Prince took a personal interest in them all.

Heartened by the Trust's success, though Inner City Aid's false start still rankled, Charles felt free by April to fulfil his long-standing, oft-postponed ambition to visit the Kalahari Desert for a few nights under canvas with his elderly companion and mentor Laurens van der Post. For the Prince it was an interesting anthropological exercise – in many ways, though he dislikes this interpretation, the climax of a long voyage of self-discovery. For Britain's popular press, it was further evidence that the heir to the throne was more than halfway round the bend.

Africa had always been a regular stop on the beat of any Prince of Wales – the future head of what was once the Empire, now the Commonwealth – but most of Charles's predecessors had spend their "time off" there happily blasting wild animals into oblivion. The sight of this one spending four nights under canvas with an eighty-year-old Jungian philosopher, communing with the lost world of the Kalahari bushmen, again raised the national eyebrow. It was unfortunate that Charles's meditative retreat coincided with a scare about insanity in the royal genes; while he was away, two of the Queen Mother's nieces were discovered to have been lifelong inhabitants of a mental hospital. The revelation lay uneasily beside the tabloid picture of Charles's venture into the "spirit world" of primitive dances beneath the desert stars, communion with the dead via messages buried in bottles in the sand and soul-searching camp-fire chats with bare-breasted natives. No doubt he would also be having a few words with the local plants.

It was as well that the Prince was not in Britain to read all that the sneering, superficial tabloids threw his way. Even the heavy Sunday papers had trouble wheeling on paperback philosophers to explain the basics: that the world-view of Carl Jung, van der Post's mentor and friend, "amounts to a contemporary code by which many choose to attempt to give some purpose to their lives, or to all in aid when facing difficult decisions. For his followers Jung provides a quasi-religious pattern of guiding principles, a system for interpreting human behaviour, almost a code of practice." In the primitive, unspoilt, "natural" world of the Kalahari bushmen, van der Post had discovered a society ignorant of the civilized world, which unconsciously illustrated Jung's teachings. Van der Post had explained it in memorable television documentaries and a thought-provoking book, *The Lost World of the Kalahari*. For a long time, Charles had been anxious to take a look for himself.

He had known van der Post some twenty years. The South African-born writer and explorer spent the immediate aftermath of the Second World War with the 15th Indian Army Corps in Java, as military-political officer to Lord Mountbatten, through whom Charles first met him while at Cambridge. If Mountbatten was role-model and confidant to the earnest young Prince, van der Post took over from Lord Butler as a less worldly, more spiritual guide, even guru (another word the Prince detests, but it is not inappropriate).

Charles had long since come to terms with the unenviable fate of his birth, but the sheer unfairness of it all had now begun to trouble him again. if any quest into abstract anthropological niceties is also a journey into oneself, the dilemma with which Charles was now struggling was one not unknown to many men approaching forty: given the unique circumstances of his life, how to reconcile them with leading the professionally productive and privately happy life to which all humankind aspires? He had spoken out on some of the causes close to his heart; his quietly busy charities were at work every day for the unemployed and disadvantaged, the handicapped and the deprived; yet still he had a nagging sense, as middle age loomed, that he had not achieved much. A man with a great capacity for self-criticism and self-doubt, the Prince of Wales had come to think himself a failure.

Relieved of other pressures – notably to marry and ensure the succession – he still saw several decades stretching ahead when his public life would continue its familiar cycle of frustration, criticism – even, in his own terms, defeat. But now there was another dimension to worry about. Where he had looked to his married life for consolation and comfort in his continuing distress, he had conspicuously failed to find it.

Whatever brief comfort he gleaned from this desert sojourn with his octogenarian sage, Charles returned with sinking heart to a land again bleak with rumour about his marriage. Why had he and his Princess spent so much time apart this year? She had returned ahead of him from their annual trip to Klosters; now, fresh from the African desert, he did not help his own public relations by disappearing without her for a week painting water-colours in Italy. One Sunday newspaper even "discovered" a putative Italian romance.

It was no longer enough to argue that a royal marriage cannot be conducted like those of others, lived as it is amid an arduous routine of public engagements which see the couple heading in separate directions virtually every day – even, as another Sunday paper chose to reveal, occupying separate bedrooms. It was not enough to explain that many English upper-class marriages are traditionally less than romantic, more about breeding and entertaining than feeling the need to share much beyond a distant interest in the children. It was even inadequate to suggest that "Charles and Di" were, in fact, a thoroughly "modern" professional couple, learning to juggle their individual private lives and interests with their joint public life together.

By that autumn, children or no children, the couple met only once in five weeks. Charles fished moodily beside the trout streams of Balmoral, bemoaning his lot to "Kanga" Tryon, now returned from her temporary "exile"; Diana, meanwhile, stayed in London, where she was seen out on the town with dashing young escorts. All summer Buckingham Palace had resisted increasing pressure for a statement. Charles himself was instrumental in refusing to acknowledge that the appalling publicity was worth a response. Then, after an especially lurid set of Sunday newspapers, he and his wife were talked into an absurd and disastrous publicity stunt.

The night of 15 October 1987 saw Britain devastated by a freak hurricane, the worst for 300 years (of which the television weathermen, notoriously, had given no warning). A week later, as the battered nation was still clearing up, the Prince of Wales flew from Balmoral to visit flood victims in Carmarthen, in the heart of his principality – whither his Princess travelled from Highgrove to join him. Staff at Kensington Palace had been instructed to prepare for them both to return together that night. Yet, after six hours beside each other in Wales, during which they had not one private moment alone, the Prince took himself straight off back to Balmoral and "Kanga," leaving Diana to return to London without him.

It had been their first public appearance together for over six weeks, and only the second time Charles had seen his wife at all – let alone his children – in the month and more since for most other Britons the summer holidays had ended. If the British public reached conclusions he resented, Charles had only himself to blame; if he had not thought it appropriate to issue a statement, presumably saying how blissfully happy his marriage really was, it was now too late. As a public relations stunt, the visit to Wales was an unmitigated disaster. Whatever comfort it brought to the flood victims was drowned out by the fact that it was so obviously and hastily stage-managed; and any salutary effect it might have had was immediately washed out as they once again went their separate ways.

With the Queen and Prince Philip away in Canada, what seemed like heedless indifference to public opinion came at a particularly damaging moment. Earlier in the summer Prince Charles had shown some signs of asserting his leadership role among the younger royals, whose wayward ways were beginning to tarnish the monarchy's otherwise immaculate image. Now he seemed too immersed in his own problems to care.

Quis, went the argument, *custodet custodes*? If the eldest Prince of the new generation was not going to show a lead, though painstakingly raised to be the next custodian of the world's senior monarchy, who was? There was a sense of drift about Britain's young royals, which, if unchecked, could undo all the hard and worthy work of their elders. The previous week had seen the Duke and Duchess of York giggling through the profanities of a new movie, *Beverly Hills Cop II*, in the company of the singer Boy George and the former brothel-keeper Cynthia Payne – good for a laugh, perhaps, but too closely associated with drugs and prostitution to be acceptable regulars at a court royal as opposed to criminal.

Prince Edward, meanwhile, since demeaning the monarchy with *It's a Royal Knockout,* and ill-advisedly insulting the press in the process, had shown little initiative and less gumption. He had been given the benefit of the doubt over his bold decision to quit the Marines, but an undergraduate flair for amateur theatricals was no substitute for finding a useful national role – as opposed to a job with Andrew Lloyd Webber's Really Useful Company. Only Princess Anne, recently honoured by her mother with the title Princess Royal, was displaying consistent dignity and achievement.

Since the departure of Michael Shea, the monarchy's public relations machine seemed to have lost its direction. Little more than a "damage containment" department at the best of times, the Palace press office now seemed more in the business of damage creation. When a mad gunman went on the rampage in the town of Hungerford, Berkshire, for instance, even the loyal *Daily Telegraph* felt constrained to point out that there had been – unthinkably – no telegram of condolence from the Queen to the relatives of the dead. Now the saga of Charles and Diana's marital problems was drawing even fiercer criticism.

"Over the last five years," Reginald Watts, a public relations consultant, told the *Sunday Times,* "the monarchy has really lost direction. It has allowed the glitter to overwhelm the deeper, more mysterious elements. There is a very strong case for the monarchy, and they are totally failing to put it. They have become over-exposed, over-democratized and willing to accept far too many public engagements."

The words of Mr Watts offered an intriguing glimpse of what might happen if Madison Avenue were given the royal account. For he was also, if unconsciously, echoing the seminal warning of Walter Bagehot against letting in "too much daylight" upon the monarchy. Prince Charles, it had become quite clear, was blithely indifferent to the damage being done. Whether his press relations were in the hands of Saatchi & Saatchi or Bagehot & Bagehot, the Prince would defiantly set a higher premium on his own privacy than on public concern. At moments like this, he has a wilful way of forgetting that there are even more fundamental issues at stake.

"I know the people of this country," said the socialist leader J.H. Thomas at the time of King Edward VIII's agony over Wallis Simpson. "I know 'em. They '*ate* 'aving no family life at court." Behind Thomas's misplaced aspirates lies a fundamental truth with which Elizabeth II would be the first to agree. The monarchy has a wide array of semi-mystical roles in Britain national life; the sovereign is head not just of state and Commonwealth, but of the armed forces and the Church of England. Above all, in a secular age, the Queen believes she has a solemn responsibility to offer her people a living symbol of the traditional virtues of Christian family life. Charles's refusal to conceal his increasing distance from his wife was more than just an apparent personal tragedy; it carried grave constitutional implications. By now the prospect of a Wales divorce, satirized with painful accuracy in *Private Eye*'s "Heir of Sorrows," was being discussed in earnest in the *Sunday Times* by the Professor of Modern History at Oxford University, Norman Stone.

October ended with the Princess defying the Queen's wishes by failing to accompany her husband to the wedding of Amanda Knatchbull, Lord Mountbatten's granddaughter, once rumoured to be a potential Princess of Wales. Long scheduled to make an official visit to Germany the following day, the couple chose to use it as another attempt to put on a show of marital bliss. Again, however, it needed more than a sprinkling of affectionate references to Diana in Charles's speeches to reassure an anxious public. Those travelling with the royal party noticed a conspicuous lack of warmth between them; Diana tended to look away in embarrassment, rather than flash her practised shy smile, whenever the Prince lavished loving public praise upon her. Not once during the entire trip, noticed an army of observers, did they publicly look each other in the eye. Back at Westminster, meanwhile, matters had reached the point where a group of senior Conservative Members of Parliament met in emergency session to discuss a two-page document detailing recent damage done to the monarchy by its younger generation. That weekend a MORI poll for the *Sunday Times* showed that twenty-seven per cent of voters thought the royal family "an expensive luxury which Britain cannot afford," while twenty-nine per cent thought that the abolition of the monarchy "would make no difference to the country."

While in Germany the Prince managed to deflect less savoury headlines with a few words of praise for NATO's nuclear defence policy, thus angering Her Majesty's Loyal Opposition at home; then he outraged older Britains with a few innocent words of praise for the German officer corps. On his return, however, he was to find an even better way of banishing the marriage rumours from the front pages. In his latest foray into the world of modern architecture, the heir to the British throne found a few kind words in his heart for the Luftwaffe.

Undeterred by impertinent invasions of his privacy, and determined not to let them drown out his public role, Charles was hell-bent on another controversy of carbuncular proportions. On 1 December 1987 the Prince of Wales was guest speaker at the annual dinner of the Corporation of London's planning and communication committee at London's Mansion House. The Prince's audience were the men and women largely responsible for the sixty-five million square feet of new office space that the City of London now holds. Charles had been made privy to their plans to add to them via the redevelopment of Paternoster Square, the area to the north of St Paul's Cathedral. The commercial demand for sheer square-footage seemed to the Prince to threaten the respect due the noble proportions of Sir Christopher Wren's building, also the spiritual heart of his future kingdom.

To Charles, St Paul's was "without doubt one of the architectural wonders of the world, the equal in architecture to Shakespeare's plays." He had been "deeply depressed" by a sneak preview of the plans. Like the architects at Hampton Court three and a half years before, the planners were about to receive a piece of the Prince's mind, delivered in words of a passion and vigour unprecedented in his hitherto fairly measured crusade. After opening with fewer pleasantries than is his wont, Charles plunged in with: "It is not just *me* who is complaining. Countless people are appalled by what has happened to their capital city, but feel totally powerless to do anything about it."

Then he got straight to the point:

> What *have we done* to St Paul's since the bombing [of 1940]? In the space of a mere fifteen years, in the Sixties and Seventies, and in spite of all sorts of elaborate rules supposedly designed to protect that great view, your predecessors, as the planners, architects and developers of the City, wrecked the London skyline and desecrated the dome of St Paul's. Not only did they wreck the London skyline in general.

They also did their best to lose the great dome in a jostling scrum of office buildings, so mediocre that the only way you ever remember them is by the frustration they induce – like a basketball team standing shoulder-to-shoulder between you and the Mona Lisa. . . .

There was some uneasy laughter as the Prince, after a brief European *tour d'horizon* – "Can you imagine the Italians walling in St Mark's in Venice or St Peter's in Rome?" – reached his memorable climax; "You have, Ladies and Gentlemen, to give this much to the Luftwaffe: when it knocked down our buildings, it didn't replace them with anything more offensive than rubble. *We* did that." Clausewitz, he went on, had called war the continuation of diplomacy by other means. Around St Paul's, planning had turned out to be "the continuation of war by other means."

Lord Holford's redevelopment of Paternoster Square in the 1950s had set the precedent for the subsequent "destruction" of the city centres of Bristol, Newcastle, Birmingham, Worcester and many more. It amounted to no less than "the rape of Britain." Did modern planners and architects ever use their eyes? They everted them now, under the lash of the Prince's tongue, as he protested that "large numbers of us in this country are fed up with being talked down to and dictated to by the existing planning, architectural and development establishment." They must seize this second chance to build something "of real quality, of excellence next to so great a building, in the heart of our capital city" – perhaps even to convert London back into a "city without towers" by the year 2000.

The well-informed power of Charles's remarks that evening emerged from a series of secret meetings over the previous few months with an informal, *ad hoc* group of architectural and planning advisers. Six weeks before the speech, on the afternoon of Friday 18 September, Charles had flown from Balmoral to Highgrove to chair a third and final get-together of a dozen or so architects, conservationists, journalists and other experts under the general heading: "Is architecture too important to be left to the architects?" He had convened this series of meetings after being shown the seven alternative designs for Paternoster Square by its developer, Stuart Lipton of Stanhope Properties, who was working on the scheme with the Mountleigh Group, well known as one of the more enlightened of current development conglomerates. An acquaintance of the Prince's for some time – he had persuaded him to open a development near Heathrow Airport two years before – Lipton had offered to show the Prince the plans in an attempt to defuse potential trouble. When, as he had feared, Charles did not like any of them, Lipton went so far as to ask the Prince for his suggestions. "It was completely crazy," says one observer. "It was like inviting Charles to join the board of Mountleigh." Lipton's colleagues promptly gave him the nickname "Lip-service."

But the group's chairman, Tony Clegg, impatient with the delays, had nevertheless authorized an announcement that one of the seven competing firms, Arup Associates, were to be designated "master-planners" for the area (even though several official assessors had preferred a scheme by Richard Rodgers). The Arup scheme made no attempt to recreate the original mediaeval street plan, as traditionalists such as Charles hoped; instead it used an "inhabited wall" to define a formal, classical space and act as a screen for the densely packed blocks of offices rising high behind it around the Cathedral. Says Lipton:

> Their design was extraordinary interesting. Their respect for the cathedral was clearly shown. . . .
> I'm not sure that we conveyed properly to the Prince that all we were seeking to do at that stage was to choose an architect as master-planner, who would then work on some designs. The Prince said that he did understand this – but I'm not sure, to put it diplomatically, that he was fully aware.

Aware or not, Charles was incensed and became determined upon a dramatic public intervention. The invitation to make the Mansion House speech was seen by *Architects Journal* as "proof that the royal outbursts virtually carry the stamp of official arbiter." Even a City Corporation spokesman conceded: "The fact that he has been invited must give some indication of how seriously the City planner takes the Prince's views." Charles, meanwhile, polished his guns.

Among those at Highgrove on 18 September was Michael Cassidy, chairman of the City's planning committee, who had issued the invitation to make the speech. Others present Jules Lubbock, architecture critic of the socialist weekly *New Statesman*, lecturer at Essex University and perhaps, after Rod Hackney, the most influential of the Prince's advisers on architecture; Dan Cruickshank, features editor of *Architects Journal*, a genial "new Georgian" also influential in the conservation movement; Colin Amery, architectural correspondent of the *Financial Times*, a champion of the trend away from high-tech design to the "neo-classical post-modernism" so beloved of the Prince (and considered "Toytown" architecture by its opponents); Jeremy Benson, president of the Georgian Group; Leon Krier from Luxembourg, a controversial theorist with a penchant for "monumental classicism"; and Alice Coleman, Professor of Geography at King's College, London, and one of the passengers in the Lea View minibus eighteen months before. Hackney arrived by helicopter in time for tea. Another guest, the architect Theo Crosby, later said he recalled the conversation less than the monotonous burr of helicopters and lawnmowers.

Among those present who had also attended an earlier meeting in May was Lady Roisine Wynne-Jones, the colourful chairman of the Londoners" Society, a self-styled "volcano" of schemes for fighting high-rise development, who is in the habit of lobbying the Prince by telephone. "Have you seen what they're doing to St Paul's?" she had said to him. "Don't forget it's where you got married." Lady Wynne-Jones had already got Charles involved in the controversy over the redevelopment of Covent Garden, of whose Royal Opera House he is a passionate trustee; in that instance he said rather less in public, for fear of being on the losing side.

There had been a second Highgrove gathering in July, attended among others by Dan Cruickshank. Charles's deep-dyed sensitivity to criticism now had him shuffling his advisers round, drawing consistently only on a small hard core. Finding talk of a "kitchen cabinet" distasteful, he deliberately called on a changing group so that there could not be any one cabal, or indeed individual, claiming to be the power behind the throne. Today, indeed, most of these advisers live in as much fear of revealing their meetings with the Prince as any courtier bewaring banishment. People in so rarefied a walk of life cannot believe their luck in being regulars at court; and Hackney's object-lesson in the dangers of capitalizing on the royal connection has since concentrated the minds of the less self-assured.

The etiquette of that final September meeting, according to one of those present, was "quite strange," in that people "kept coming and going"; the Prince would talk to them both separately and collectively. There was some tension between the assembled experts and the Prince's staff, who kept counselling caution in the face of the outspoken views being urged upon him. Most guests had, as asked, brought notes which they left for the Prince to draw on when drafting his speech. Hence, for instance, the Lubbock-inspired section on ridding London of its towers and the demand for new height restrictions; hence, from other sources, a long, well-argued section concerned with the technicalities of the planning process, protesting on behalf of the British public that they had no say in the debate, nor even a view of the short-listed proposals, before the planning decision was made (or, in fact, pre-empted by the Prince). Hence also Charles's well-informed coda urging three specific areas in need of reform: new rules to govern proportions, materials and heights – he proposed a maximum of 100 feet – in building proposals for historic urban areas.

Even those advisers who could discern their own hand in the Prince's speech were baffled, however, by his reference to the Luftwaffe. Reluctant though they all were, for fear of exile, to take the credit for anything he had said, all of them were at pains to distance themselves from that particular phrase. The irony, unknown to any of them, was that the Prince had in fact half-remembered it from an article written by Michael Manser – the Leader, as it were, of the Opposition – in the wake of the Hampton Court speech three years before. Making the point that "there never really was a London skyline since the eighteenth century, when it was formed by Wren's churches," Manser argued in the *Sunday Times* that the vista had already been destroyed by the building boom of the nineteenth century – "which destroyed more of eighteenth-century London than ever the Luftwaffe did." Charles, stung at the time by the force of Manser's argument, now had his private revenge by twisting it around to his own needs.

Though the speech was primarily about planning, the Prince could not resist another, more overt side-swipe at the architects. He went so far as to make a bitter attack on one "prominent architect" – not Manser, but another eminent "modernist" all too easily identified by his colleagues – who had "recently confessed, airily and with no apparent sign of shame, that some of his own earlier buildings have ceased to interest even him, now that the thrill of creativity has worn off."

Well, what kind of creativity is that? To put up a building which other people have to live with, and leave them to live with it while you wander off saying you're tired of it, and then to put up another one which you will presumably get tired of too, leaving yet more people to live with the all-too-durable consequences of your passing fancy. There is a terrible fecklessness to all this, when grown men can get whole *towns* in the family way, pay nothing towards maintenance and call it romance.

Returning to the "God-forsaken" area round St Paul's, the Prince wanted to see "a roofscape that gives the impression that St Paul's is floating above it like a great ship on the sea." Did London still have to strive to be "a stunted imitation of Manhattan"? The city of Wren's day was "of such a splendour that the vista Canaletto painted surpassed ancient Rome and even rivalled that of his own native city of Venice." Charles's "personal vision" of the new Paternoster Square would be "a beautiful area on a human scale, built at ground level not on top of a car park square, with small shops and businesses at ground level – above all to cater for the needs of, and to create something special for, the three million tourists who already visit St Paul's each year."

By remarkable coincidence just such a plan was not only on the drawing-board, but in the pages of *The Times* next morning (printed before the Prince rose to speak) and in detail in that week's issue of the *Architects Journal* (which went to press four days before the Prince's speech). Earlier in the year a community architect named John Simpson had been Charles's escort around an exhibition of classical buildings by a new generation of architects, "Real Architecture," at the Building Centre in London. Charles had declared himself particularly impressed by the work of Leon Krier, whom he had subsequently met over dinner *chez* Lady Wynne-Jones, and who had attended the September meeting at Highgrove. Krier had also advised on Simpson's "alternative" scheme for Paternoster Square, very much more in the princely vein, which now became the subject of some none too discreet lobbying. By the summer of 1988, as Arup Associates proceeded tentatively, the London *Evening Standard* was earning princely favour by financing a maverick application for planning permission on behalf of the Simpson alternative. It was eventually included in an exhibition of all the proposals, organized by Arup themselves, in the crypt of St Paul's.

Again, as at Hampton Court, the immediate effect of Charles's speech was not quite what he intended. Although Londoners seemingly backed him to a man – the capital's radio "talk" station, LBC, was inundated with calls of support – other voices quietly question the wisdom of his apparent habit of praising Nazi Germany. Charles's suggestions, said Tony Clegg of Mountleigh, were anyway impertinent: "We don't need a Hitler to help us deal with our mistakes."

Clegg was soon to make a speech which crystallized the legacy of Charles's "Luftwaffe speech": an architectural establishment bitterly divided over the conflicting demands of art, commerce and decent conditions for urban man to live and work in. The *Guardian*, typically, appeared divided against itself. Where once its editorial columns had regarded the Prince's pronouncements on architecture as "simply nostalgic and conservative," it now offered a cautious welcome to his new role as "an increasingly constructive radical critic of British architecture and planning," giving voice to "a widely repressed popular resentment against the bleak, gross and exclusive aspects of modern architecture embodied in so much of the City of London." In the same issue, however, its architecture specialist Martin Pawley declared the Prince's proposals an "impossible" pipe-dream. His audience of planners well knew that "property is not something you put up and tear down at will. They know that all these so-called "obsolete" office blocks have tenants with leases, and that quite a few of the tall ones like the NatWest Tower reach ninety years into the future." When it came to Paternoster Square, they knew that "either the undistinguished modern buildings will have to be replaced with a million square feet of new offices, or redevelopment will not be economical, and the result will be refurbishment – in effect another twenty-five years or so of the Holford plan the Prince so roundly condemned." The Prince was surrounded by advisers who "assure him that his nostalgic dream of a quaint Ruritanian city is perfectly feasible and that only ignorance, silly laws and wicked men stand in its way. . . . "Why should not commerce pay for beauty?" he asks, without ever wondering what borrowed money is – or beauty too for that matter."

It was perhaps no coincidence that Pawley and his paper's leading article were at one – and spoke for a growing section of the architectural community – in deploring the Prince's motley gaggle of advisers. To the *Guardian*'s anonymous leader writer he was allying himself with people who had no time for anything designed after Lutyens and had "yet to come to terms with the motor car" – "aesthetic reactionaries" who were contemptuous towards the Prince's views on other subjects but thought him the ideal person to lead their crusade against the architectural consequences of market forces, "which in every other respect they worship."

Market forces were also at the heart of Tony Clegg's overt riposte a fortnight later. "I thought," said Mountleigh's chairman to an audience of architects, "why not join the ranks of the non-experts and give you my views on architecture?" It was time to respond to "recent suggestions" that "the way forward is backwards, in other words that there is no way forward and that architects should start to recreate the past."

> I shall not bore you with my likes and dislikes, because the fundamentals of buildings are more important than that. Buildings are for people. They are for people to look at and enjoy from the outside, to be sure. But they are also for people to live and work in from the inside. Buildings must be functional. They must move with the times. . . . Modern architects should be encouraged to design modern buildings, using today's materials and catering for today's needs, but at the same time build for the future, and why they should do so without fear of criticism from however on high. . . .

Looking back with nostalgia – to the days when, however beautiful the buildings, conditions were "pretty awful for the vast majority" – was "all right for princes in palaces, but not so hot for the rest." Great architecture, Clegg argued, had always been at its grandest when the country was at its grandest; the Prime Minister was doing her best to put the Great back into Britain, and all "people of influence" should be doing the same. Some of Britain's leading modern architects had done their best work overseas – Norman Foster's Hong Kong and Shanghai Bank, James Stirling's Stuttgart Museum extension, Basil Spence's British Embassy in Rome, Richard Rodgers's Pompidou Centre in Paris. "That we lack the confidence to build them here is something within our power to correct. . . . We must *encourage* architects with vision."

Deyan Sudjic, editor of the architectural magazine *Blueprint*, described the Prince's intervention, short-circuiting normal planning procedures, as "an abuse of the royal prerogative." Even Lipton privately believed that "we can't have whole towns plastered in Georgian architecture; what we want is originals, not reproductions." He hoped that the Prince might make the occasionally encouraging public remark, rather than thrive on a reputation for negativity.

Two weeks later, when he fulfilled a commitment to open the second phase of another Arup design (at London's Broadgate) for Mountleigh, Charles said about three words. Who knows what had been said, meanwhile, even closer to home? For Clegg's indignation seemed to have found distinguished allies beyond the architectural profession, in a quarter of which the Prince was wont to take notice. A few weeks later, in a speech to an urban planning conference in Liverpool, Prince Philip himself appeared to take public issue with his son when he said: "It would be a pity if regeneration created eighteenth-century cities in the twenty-first century."

Charles may relish causing controversy – "throwing," in his own words, "a proverbial royal brick through the inviting plate glass of pompous professional pride" – but the backlash to his St Paul's speech seemed to get under his skin. Although he enjoyed huge public support, the violence of his abuse was reaping its rewards, as his staff had warned; now the Prince of Wales was in the uncomfortable position of trading insults with a major British profession, who had been roused into giving as good as they got. It was not out of character for Charles to wilt under the strain. With a plaintive edge in his voice, he told Brian Redhead of BBC Radio 4's *Today* programme: "There is no need for me to do all this. But I can't just sit around and do nothing. If they'd rather I did nothing, I'll go off somewhere else."

The Prince's sensitivity was beginning to show. Determined to be taken more seriously, he invited to lunch a group of upmarket newspaper editors – Charles Wilson of *The Times*, Peregrine Worsthorne of the *Sunday Telegraph* and Rupert Pennant-Rea of the *Economist*. Why, he asked them, was the royal family depicted as a soap opera? Why was his work in the inner cities drowned out by a tide of interest in his wife's clothes and his marital problems? One of the editors pensively suggested that he had brought it upon himself, by inviting the television cameras of ITN to Kensington Palace and Highgrove, for Sir Alastair Burnet to wax sycophantic while the Prince revealed his *penchant* for talking to his plants. Failing to grasp the journalist's point, and taking it to mean that he should confine himself to purely ceremonial duties, Charles answered "with incandescent rage":

> I've had to fight every inch of my life to escape royal protocol. I've had to fight to go to university. I've had to fight to have any sort of role as Prince of Wales. You're suggesting that I go back and play polo. I wasn't trained to do that. I have been brought up to have an active role. I am determined not to be confined to cutting ribbons.

It was all said, according to one of those present, with "frightening intensity." The Prince was "either going to have a public function or a nervous breakdown." When the episode was leaked, moreover, the Prince was again dismayed. As he approached forty, could he still be quite so innocent of the ways of the world? Did he really expect to entertain a group of journalists to lunch and be surprised when the conversation was passed on? If he wanted to be taken more seriously, moreover, why should he be annoyed that this became more widely known? To many, such "controlled" leaks would seem to be the sole purpose of inviting newspaper editors to lunch – especially to one so experienced in the ways of newspapers, by virtue of his position, which in turn endows the rare privilege of being able to invite leading national newspaper editors to lunch and expect them to accept. And why, come to that, if he was so concerned about tabloid trivialization of his life and work, discuss the matter with the three editors least relevant to the problem?

Charles did not seem to understand that he was caught in a Catch 22 largely of his own making. Any public figure who uses and benefits from the media as much as he does must also learn to live with its slings and arrows. The positive publicity generated for some years by his marriage, for example, was bound to turn sour at some point, especially when his own absenteeism fanned the flames of rumour. It is part of the British way of life, after all, to build up heroes to the point of idolatry and then print diagrams of their feet of clay.

The episode did Charles no good at all, coming as it did in the wake of several such public complaints about his lot. The difficulties of the Prince's life had been widely understood and sympathetically discussed in the responsible media for some years. Now he was labelled "the whining Prince," as his discontent with his life became almost too public – even, to many, his most signal characteristic. It was the Prince's own sense of self-importance, quite as much as the trivial obsessions of the tabloids, which was distracting attention from – and diminishing respect for – his manifestly worthy public work.

By the turn of the year, Charles was at a very low ebb. Another series of blunders by his staff – his own appointees, he was curtly reminded – led to undignified scenes in the councils of Operation Raleigh, an Outward Bound-style adventure course for young mariners in which he had for five years supported his explorer friend John Blashford-Snell. The American oil company Atlantic Richfield (ARCO) were offering sponsorship to save the enterprise, their *quid pro quo* being their own appointee at the head of the organization, in Blashford-Snell's place, and the guarantee of the royal presence at regular promotional occasions. The ensuing row was allowed to reach unseemly proportions in front of the Prince himself, an appalling error by his staff which had Charles beating the table: "Why wasn't I informed of all this?" Three days later, he had to undergo the acute embarrassment of attending an Atlantic Richfield reception in Pittsburgh, Pennsylvania, after the oil company had angrily withdrawn its sponsorship. The amateurism of the royal machinery had again brought its boss to grief.

The Prince was in Pittsburgh for the Remaking Cities Conference, successor to the Astoria Conference which had preceded Rod Hackney's election to the presidency of RIBA. Community architects were everywhere; among Charles's guides through the redevelopment plans for Pittsburgh's abandoned steel mills were John Thompson and Peter Ahrends's community-minded partner Richard Burton. But the Prince's speech, billed in advance on the royal grapevine as a major one, was a rather tired reiteration of his now familiar themes. The past forty years of architecture and urban planning on both sides of the Atlantic had been "pretty disastrous"; what was needed was "an acceptable, liveable, human environment for everyone." The most significant aspect of the speech was that he was unburdening himself of these views, for the first time, in the United States. But for some curious reason – perhaps its editor's desperate attempt to thank the Prince for lunch and apologize for the leaks by taking him more seriously – the *Sunday Telegraph* thought it "an extraordinary insight into his personal feelings" that the Prince said he had been made to feel a "frightful reactionary imbecile" for his views on the architectural scene. For observers of either the Prince or the architectural scene, the remark was by now an all too familiar commonplace.

After heading to Florida for a particularly angry game of polo, Charles looked and felt in need of a rest. After all the disasters of 1987, 1988 had not begun much more promisingly. It looked as if his annual skiing holiday in Klosters – for which his wife and the Duchess of York would be joining him, with the Palmer-Tomkinsons, Catherine Soames and other friends – could not have come at a better time. He saw it as a chance to relax with a vengeance and defuse his worldly angst with some delicious physical risk. But again – this time tragically – it was all to go desperately wrong.

FOURTEEN

Tragedy at Klosters

" . . . The whole mountainside seemed to
hurtle past us into the valley below."

"IT'S NICE to know I would have been missed," Prince
Charles wrote to a friend after he had come within
inches of death in an Alpine avalanche. "I only wish
everyone could have survived. But that's fate, I suppose"

The morning of Thursday, 10 March 1988, the first full
day of their skiing holiday, carried a slight note of anxiety
for the otherwise relaxed and happy royal party. The
Duchess of York – now three months pregnant and criticized at home for taking her third skiing trip of the year –
had suffered a nasty tumble. She and Diana decided to
take the afternoon off. Over lunch in their chalet, meanwhile, the Prince of Wales and several other companions
agreed to spend it tackling the most dangerous skiing
available in Klosters – a descent of one of the steepest "off-
piste" runs in the Alps, the Gotschnawang, locally known
as "the Wang." There had been avalanche warnings
posted that day, but then there always were.

Escorted as always by a Swiss policeman, Prince
Charles set out that afternoon with his perennial hosts and
close friends Charles and Patti Palmer-Tomkinson; thirty-
five-year-old Major Hugh Lindsay, another close friend
since his three years in royal service as an equerry to the

Queen; and one of the most experienced of all Alpine guides, Herr Bruno Sprecher (who had actually been hired to look after the Duchess of York). All were accomplished skiers, who had many times before enjoyed braving what Charles called the "special dimension" of off-piste skiing – and all, by the Prince's own account, were well aware of the scale of the risk they were taking. "We all accepted," he said, "and always have done, that mountains have to be treated with the greatest respect. . . . "

It was a beautiful winter's day, with brilliant blue skies and near-perfect skiing conditions. After their first run, the royal party had just paused for breath when – "with a tremendous roaring," as Charles put it – the avalanche was suddenly upon them. The Prince, his policeman, Palmer-Tomkinson and Sprecher all managed to ski to one side. But Charles could only watch "with horror" as Lindsay and Patti Palmer-Tomkinson were "swept away in a whirling maelstrom as the whole mountainside seemed to hurtle past us into the valley below." It was all over "in a terrifying matter of seconds."

Sprecher immediately took command. Having told the policeman to radio for assistance, he skied to the bottom of the avalanche – where, thanks to the radio detection devices which all the royal party were wearing, he quickly located Patti Palmer-Tomkinson. Charles and her husband skied down after Sprecher, arriving just as he was giving Patti mouth-to-mouth resuscitation. Handing Charles a shovel, the guide told the Prince to dig her out as fast as possible. Charles clawed at the snow with his hands until she was free; then, seeing that she was badly injured, he stayed to comfort her while Sprecher went back in search of Lindsay. Fifteen yards higher up, the guide soon discovered the Major's body. He had been killed instantly by the sheer impact of the speeding wall of snow.

For the next frantic hour, as confused reports of the accident began to seep out to the world, Charles wept openly. "The Prince looked very distressed," said one eyewitness. "He was crying with his arms around somebody else, comforting them." The first reports to reach London were that the Prince had been stretchered to hospital, gravely injured, and that the Princess of Wales and the Duchess of York were missing, unaccounted for. On duty in the Buckingham Palace press office that afternoon, by cruel irony dealing with the first flood of newspaper inquiries, was Hugh Lindsay's wife, Sarah Brennan, six months pregnant with their first child (a daughter born on 14 May). Two particular favourites with the royal family, they had been married only the previous July.

The national soul-searching began even before a grim-faced Charles flew back to Britain the next day in the same aircraft as the Major's body. Clearly, the Prince of Wales had himself been extremely lucky to escape death. Had he been taking a risk improper for the heir to the throne? Had he, in fact, been the one to suggest the off-piste skiing, thus saddling himself with an appalling legacy of private guilt? Could he, wondered the ever faithful tabloids, survive the experience without a nervous break-down?

An official inquiry quickly adjudged that the skiers themselves had precipitated the avalanche, by destabilizing the heavy fall of icy snow above them. But the continuing debate about the off-piste risk was as quickly shown to be irrelevant, when only two days later another avalanche swept down on the Alpine resort of Davos, killing people asleep in their beds. Avalanches, as the Prince himself put it, "are a natural phenomenon of the mountains, and when it comes to avoiding them no one is infallible." All skiers risk the danger of avalanche, even on the nursery slopes.

There was never any constitutional doubt that the Prince is not as other mortals; given the huge public investment in him of time, money and goodwill, he has a clear duty to ensure that he reaches the throne intact. Ramsay MacDonald, when Prime Minister, pleaded with the then Prince of Wales to give up steeplechasing, for fear that he would break his neck; the future King Edward VIII, like his great-nephew Prince Charles, was simply not very good at it. Fifty years on there was no sign of Mrs Thatcher – not herself without experience of wayward sons – intervening with the next Prince of Wales, for whom some cautionary words from his own mother were enough. Far from contemplating a monastic retreat, however, the new, self-possessed Prince Charles was better, to a fault, at spurning advice than taking it. It seemed certain that the following year, as every year, would see him back on the ski slopes of Klosters – though not, perhaps, on the more dangerous off-piste tracks. He would resent this curtailment of his personal freedom, as he does all such constitutional inhibitions on his natural inclinations. But would he also resent it for reasons he might not himself fully perceive? Did the Klosters episode suggest that the Prince, after so miserable a year on both the public and private fronts, might even be harbouring a deep-seated, subconscious deathwish?

A striking urge to take risks has always run deep in him. It is partly compensation – at times, perhaps, over-compensation – for the large amount of his life he must spend wrapped in the cotton-wool of royal protocol. Only recently, via those editor's leaks, he had again complained of his lifelong struggle to break through the constraints of privilege and out into the real world. But Charles has also long felt a need to justify the ex-officio adulation he receives. This Prince of Wales has always wanted desperately to be respected for himself and his achievements, rather than merely the genetic accident which made him who he is. Throughout his youth, as he searched in vain for some purpose to the unenviable, predestined life ahead of him, Charles had shown a tendency to take physical risks at the expense of intellectual ones.

There was always, meanwhile, the shadow of his father – a strong-minded, outspoken *paterfamilias* with great expectations of all his sons. As Charles grew up in a world of older people, most of them female, he had come to hero-worship this often absent parent – a staunch proponent of Juvenal's (and Kurt Hahn's) *mens sana in corpore sano*. As the young Prince followed him to Cheam and Gordonstoun, he found Philip's name engraved on most of the sporting trophies. When his own talents tended more to the academic that the athletic, he determined to make up through sheer effort what he lacked in natural ability. Hence the need to tackle the most dangerous slope available, regardless of avalanche warnings, in Klosters. From his Pittsburgh speech, and an award from President Reagan for his "outstanding leadership" in the rejuvenation of dying urban communities, it seemed a natural progression offstage to a violent game of polo and the toughest skiing on offer.

The "Royal Action Man" image Charles had cultivated throughout his teens and twenties, and enjoyed enough to maintain into his thirties, had already led him into more than his due share of close shaves. As he earned his pilot's wings, the Prince had come perilously close to death in a training aircraft. When he took his first parachute jump – proud to be the first Prince of Wales to do so – his legs had become entangled in the rigging and he was lucky to land intact. More recently he had passed out, and believed himself near death, when playing polo in severe, dehydrating heat in Florida. Polo has also bequeathed a deep scar on his left cheek, alongside the disfigured nose he broke playing rugby at Gordonstoun, not to mention many a damaged limb; to watch the vigour and determination with which he often plays polo, itself one of the most dangerous of sports, is to see an angry man working out his worldly frustrations. In April 1988, a team-mate fell heavily and broke his shoulder after his polo mallet became entangled with the Prince's; as his friend lay writhing in agony at his feet, the suffering in Charles's own face vividly revealed the lingering shadows of Klosters.

Skiing may seem an absurdly remote, and typically privileged, activity to drive home such unwelcome lessons. But it seemed to the sympathetic observer that the newly fulfilled, purposeful Prince now had no further need so crudely to prove himself to anyone – his father, his future subjects or even himself. Now that he was at last taking intellectual and moral risks, and pride in the results, with his work in the inner cities and beyond, the Prince might perhaps be persuaded that physical prowess need be less of a priority. His father might still dissent, but most other men approaching forty were prepared to live with that. The tragic events of Klosters, in short, might prove salutary. There was a finer courage to be displayed around the blighted conurbations of his future kingdom than on the most challenging and hazardous of foreign ski slopes.

As he returned from Klosters in mourning, the emotional terms of Charles's handwritten account of the incident – read by his press secretary to reporters at Zurich Airport – contained a revealing element of special pleading. The Prince was clearly aware that he would be criticized, even blamed, for risking his life. No one could blame him for the death of a friend – except, perhaps, himself. But he was coming home very much on the defensive. A man with a huge capacity for self-criticism, and for remorse, Charles knew that the episode would spell some curtailment of his life "in the fast lane." It was time to slow down a little – as, after all, do most people embarking on middle age.

The tragedy might signal some sort of mid-life crisis for Charles, but those reports of a nervous breakdown were cruelly premature – amounting, at root, to yet another index of how deeply he is misunderstood. The Prince spent the rest of what should have been his holiday, understandably, in glum retreat at Highgrove, returning briefly to Klosters to visit Mrs Palmer-Tomkinson in hospital (where, with both legs shattered, she would remain for several months). But back in Britain he was out and about within a week, characteristically using his office to lobby politicians on one of the causes close to his heart – this time, the environment. The UK, he declared, while presenting awards as Patron of the European Year of the Environment, "could do a lot more" to protect our natural heritage. There was even room for the usual defensive joke, when he mocked the pervasive prejudice which typecasts environmental campaigners as "bearded, be-sandaled, shaven-headed mystics who retreat every now and then to the Hebrides or the Kalahari Desert to examine their navels and commune with the natives." Prince Charles, to a relieved nation, seemed to be himself again.

Only two days before, herself back in the thick of things, the Princess of Wales had told anxious inquirers that her husband was "bearing up well." Over Easter there were reassuring public smiles all round as they and their sons joined the annual family holiday at Windsor. Only the following week, however, Charles perversely courted a new tidal wave of marriage rumours by setting off for another week's fishing in Scotland – without his wife and children, but not alone, for again he was escorted by his faithful friend "Kanga" (accompanied, though some papers chose to overlook the fact, by her husband).

Expected to believe merely that Charles insisted on his fishing, and that Diana found it boring, an affectionate nation simply could not understand why so soft-hearted a father would choose to spend yet another week of the school holidays away from his children. This was not the "normal" modern marriage portrayed by the publicity machine. This was a marriage over which icy differences had settled. Diners in London's trendy L'Escargot restaurant rushed to phone the gossip columns when they saw the Princess openly weeping at her corner table (where the Wales's friend Nicholas Soames MP, whose wife had been with them in Klosters, was lamenting his own newly broken marriage). "WHERE'S MY DADDY?" screamed the front page of the *Sunday Mirror* on behalf of young Prince William. The post-Klosters sympathy had lasted exactly one month.

The kindest explanation of this latest national embarrassment was that the Prince and Princess were still learning to live with their grief. The following week both were to be found playing a full part in the state visit of King Olav of Norway, a favourite "uncle" to the Prince. By the Thursday he was meeting community leaders for more inner-city talks, before travelling to Norfolk to visit beneficiaries of the Prince's Trust. The Princess's increasingly separate schedule, meanwhile, had her in St Albans and Bristol. On the Sunday she presided over the start of the London Marathon, which of course entailed another weekend apart from her husband.

And that, for the present, is where the matter rests. In the absence of any explanation from Buckingham Palace, or from the principals themselves, Charles's future subjects have now come to the reluctant conclusion that his marriage has reached a state of cool mutual indifference. The twelve-year age gap, as always, is taken as the prime index of the gulf between the couple, followed hard by their very different dispositions, their very different interests and enthusiasms, their very different choice of friends. Perhaps it is possible for a Prince and Princess of Wales to conduct their lives at a sophisticated distance. But it is not the marriage that most of their contemporaries and future subjects would choose for themselves, or indeed for the royalty most of them idolize.

Speculation will no doubt run rife until Charles inherits the throne, twenty or thirty years hence, and beyond. He has no protection against the prurient malice of the British tabloid press, or the insatiable appetite of its readers for royal gossip. In human terms, however, on the evidence of those who know them, it is possible to piece together a sympathetic jigsaw which, while seeking to understand, must also apportion some blame on both sides.

Charles knew when he married Diana that she was not going to win a Nobel Prize. He may have been sadly disappointed by her apparent intellectual vacuity, but she more than made up for it in street-wise smartness. To this day, she has not given an interview without her husband, to newspapers or television, on any subject. This would seem to be the Palace's own way of confirming Charles's disappoinment; the British people can only conclude that their dismay on hearing Diana speak for herself would be akin to that of hearing a silent movie star open her squeaky, disillusioning mouth. Better to preserve the icon intact, keeping its own elegant counsel, for as long as possible.

Those who travel with the Prince and Princess of Wales know her conversation to be somewhat "Sloane Ranger"-ish; her vocabulary is full of "Wow"s and "Yah"s, and her favourite telephone greeting to friends is apparently "Hi, this is Di-sco from KP." Diana is lost in overtly highbrow or soul-searching discussion, but she loves to gossip. Her chattiness at the traditional press receptions on overseas tours – abandoned after one indiscretion too many – was legendary. In Saudi Arabia she told journalists how she had enjoyed flirting with Arab sheikhs. In Australia she managed to dub the locals "male chauvinist pigs" without its being noised abroad. Gradually, however entertaining all this was, Diana-watchers realized that she had become drunk with her own cover-girl power.

In Australia in January 1988, when the couple's bicen-tennial tour reached Melbourne, a visit to a music college was one of the highlights of a very banal day. Confronted by his former Geeling cello teacher, in front of a master class of young students, the Prince knew with sinking heart that he would have to play the cello for the massed ranks of the photo corps. It was, he could quickly see, a set-up; but he obliged with good grace – giving the cam-eras, both still and moving, the apparent highlight of their day. Diana stood back watching, eyes on the move, unused to surrendering centre-stage to her husband.

Then, even as he was still in mid-photo-opportunity, the Princess pounced. Striding between the Prince and the cameras, Diana made for a grand piano in the far corner of the room, taking the eyes of the lensmen with her. She removed the cover, lifted the lid and broke haltingly into the opening bars of Rachmaninov's second piano concerto, still lodged in her mind from her schooldays. The cameras, of course, went berserk. Never before had the Princess of Wales played the piano in public. (An aide later confirmed this, adding that she occasionally played in the evenings "to entertain the Queen.") Once the elderly professor had pronounced her "very musical" and planted an unwelcome kiss on her left cheek, Diana's triumph was complete. Charles return to the cello was already photographic history, consigned to the cutting-room floor. He had watched the entire episode with this knowledge in his heart and a deep sadness in his eyes.

On the same trip the Prince one day donned an Australian "slouch hat" – just the thing to cheer the photographers, whose hearts sink when he wears the same grey suit wherever he goes. In that suit alone, he might as well be in Skegness as in Sydney; in a slouch hat he can only be in Australia, and to the enterprising freelance every picture is worth thousands, sometimes tens of thousand of pounds. One knowing photographer, however, kept his deep-focus lens trained on the Princess. He had photographed Diana for eight years, ever since the famous "see-through" dress shot at the Pimlico kindergarten, and he knew that even now, after being the world's Number One cover girl throughout the 1980s, the Princess's self-love knew no bounds. She had, in short, a cruel penchant for upstaging her husband.

Sure enough, the photographer saw Diana give him a sidelong glance to make sure that he was watching. Then, imperceptibly, she slid the hem of her skirt further up her knee – revealing, to this expert eye, "precisely an inch more thigh than we'd ever seen before." After another sidelong glance, to make sure that he had got the point, and the picture, the regal hemline descended again. Thus was confirmed the extraordinary truth that even Diana, Princess of Wales, over whom photographers have fought for nigh on a decade, will still do anything to get her picture in the papers.

Diana's limited understanding of her constitutional

role – she is still, after all, only in her twenties – has left her in love with the superstar rewards of being royal and bored with the tedious round of duties which are its price. She has a husband who no longer understands her – nor even, it seems, much likes her. In turn, to be fair, she is saddled with a marriage of opposites, to a man who cannot share her youthful *joie de vivre*, and who places an emphasis on his public life which is way beyond her. Most of the time, it is all too clear, she is bored with him. More importantly, she in turn is deeply saddened by his compulsion to be alone, abstracted, meditative, self-pitying – even to the point of spending weeks on end without his children. The single most striking index of the distance between them is that it is so out of character for Charles, once the most doting of fathers, to revert to royal type and abandon his sons for days at a time to their fleet of nannies. Diana – who, unlike him, has had a chance to live in the real world – is too devoted a mother ever to do that.

Such character analysis is regarded by the Prince as deeply intrusive, and so it may be. But the British people have a constitutional right, as much as an emotional need, to see him going about his duties with his Princess at his side – and to attempt to maintain some belief in the fairy-tale motif from which the Prince and his marriage derived so much mileage in its early years. Charles's continuing failure to gratify this affectionate whim on the part of his future subjects – in fact, his open defiance of it – has now come to reap its own rewards. Publicly, the couple undertook fifty public engagements between them in the months of May – July 1988, of which precisely four were together. Privately, his insistence on unnatural amounts of time – unnatural within *any* marriage – abandoning his wife and children for the company of others comes at a price, a price which has over the years cost other public figures their professional lives. It is a price he is apparently prepared to pay.

FIFTEEN

King Charles III

"I don't mind praying to the eternal Father,
but I must be the only man in the country
afflicted with an eternal mother!"

Bertie, Prince of Wales,
at Queen Victoria's diamond jubilee service

T HE YEAR is 2015. The new King Charles III, approaching his seventieth birthday, reigns over a proud but
tired old Britain, whose role on the world stage is not quite
what it once was. Queen Diana, well-preserved in her
mid-fifties, still brings her own unique sparkle to public
life. The monarchy is as popular as ever, thanks to
Charles's hard work during the old age of his late mother,
Queen Elizabeth II – who, like her mother before her, out-
did even Queen Victoria in regal longevity.

Both Parliament and people have warmed to the King's
first, bold initiative in doing away with the Civil List,
insisting that the monarchy subsist on the revenue from
the Crown estates. Only a stubborn school of devout loyalists dissent, arguing that the "privatization" of the monarchy demeans the head of state, robbing the Crown of
much of the dignity and independence which are its constitutional prerequisites. The King, of course, says nothing – but privately sees their point and wonders whether
he has again been badly advised.

As he enters his thirties William, Prince of Wales, has won his spurs in the armed forces and is now struggling to carve himself out a productive public role. After a few false starts, he has high hopes of his new chairmanship of the British Design Council, currently campaigning to ensure that his father's profile appears on the new "Euro-dollar" banknotes soon to be standardized throughout the EEC. William's more dashing brother Harry, the toast of the gossip columns, is busier breaking the hearts of many an English rose; he is frequently photographed at fashion-able London night-spots after finishing work backstage on the latest West End musical mounted by his Uncle Edward, the impresario. Their younger sisters, the first princesses in English history to win themselves places at Oxbridge, are every newspaper circulation manager's dream: the most eligible bachelor girls in the world. The recent series of glittering Buckingham Palace balls, hosted by their mother to launch them upon society, were the most lavish show-business occasions seen in Britain since the millenium.

A charming vision of life nearly three decades from now? Or merely an action replay of this generation a quarter of a century on? Thanks largely to Diana, the show-business dimension of British royalty seems set to expand, to the dismay of those loyal subjects who under-stand and value its constitutional functions. But the face of monarchy otherwise changes by very slow degrees, its traditions die hard. It will not be surprising if the brief, long-awaited reign of King Charles III is little more than an updated, slightly more risqué version of the soap opera we all enjoy today. There will scarcely be time, alas, for his reign to record a lasting imprint on history, which is why Charles has decided to earn his place with posterity as a Prince of Wales turned lobbyist.

But *should* Charles wait until his dotage, until the active prime of his manhood is past, to inherit the throne? The question was put to readers of a British national daily newspaper in May 1987, and the result made modern history. For the first time in living memory, more than a third of the British people – thirty-six per cent of respondents – said that they would like to see the monarch retire and hand on the role to her heir. Not even in 1936, when King Edward VIII's affair with Mrs Simpson had brought the monarchy to its knees, did the British people favour abdication; it was the political machine – and the constitution – which had forced Edward to go.

Ten years before, in the late 1970s, a similar poll saw barely a quarter of Britons prepared to countenance a handover "before too long." The figure dropped among the over sixty-fives, typical of whom was an elderly woman who cried: "We want the Queen and I'd hate to see her go." But Elizabeth II was only just into her fifties at the time and her heir was an increasingly desperate thirty-year-old bachelor, still living at home with his parents. The intervening decade had seen great changes, marked especially by the huge success of the Queen's silver jubilee in 1977 and the popularity of Prince Charles's marriage six years ago. As the Queen and her husband both themselves reached the status of old-age pensioners, Charles and Diana had also set their genealogical minds at rest by producing two healthy male heirs, which would seem to make abdication an easier prospect to consider.

The truth, ironically, is quite the reverse. Abdication has been a vexed question in Elizabeth II's mind for some years. But the older both she and Prince Charles have grown, the more they have realized, to their mutual dismay, just how impossible it would be. The Queen sees the logic of handing over to her son while he is still at the height of his powers, rather than forcing him to spend most of his life waiting in the wings for the role to which he was born. But the constitutional implications are unthinkable.

Abdication, they both believe, would spell the beginning of the end of the British monarchy as we know it. The question was first discussed in December 1965, when the Queen and Prince Philip held that secret dinner party at Buckingham Palace to discuss the Prince of Wales's future. In front of the Prime Minister, the Archbishop of Canterbury and other senior advisers, the Queen mentioned the unmentionable. What did the distinguished assembly feel about abdication? "It might be wise," she ventured, "to give way at a time when Charles could do better."

"You might be right," said her husband light-heartedly. "The doctors will keep you alive so long!"

The Queen may have been ready to discuss the topic when it was a "safe" one, merely hypothetical, because Charles was too young for it to be taken seriously. But today abdication is a subject you raise in royal circles at your peril. In the intervening years, Elizabeth II has changed. At the time of her silver jubilee, ten years ago, she was not averse to boasting that she had already been served by seven prime ministers; were it not for Mrs Thatcher's political longevity, that total might now be several more than eight. "Parliaments and ministers pass," said Gladstone of Elizabeth's great-great-grand-mother, Queen Victoria, "but she abides in lifelong duty, and she is to them as the oak in the forest is to the annual harvest in the field." Since 1977, those close to Queen Elizabeth II have discerned that she has a personal vision of advancing towards Victorian venerability. The older and more experienced a monarch she becomes, the greater the affection and respect she commands among her people, and the more she chooses to exert her consti-tutional right "to be consulted, to encourage and to warn." And so it will continue. However much she may wish as a private citizen to quit the public scene, she will grow stronger in her determination as a constitutional monarch that it can never be done.

The irony is that as her private self, a human being, there is nothing Elizabeth would rather do than leave London and lead the life of a country lady – which is what she really is – with her family, her horses and her dogs. But she believes, as does Prince Charles, that a handover of the throne would irreparably devalue it, reducing the British monarchy to the ranks of its junior European counterparts – the so-called "bicycle-kings," who believe, as the British royal family sneered of the Dutch after Queen Wilhelmina's abdication in 1948, that the Crown is a pensionable job like any other, to be tossed lightly aside at the age of sixty-five. Abdication would also create, as has happened in the Netherlands, an irresistible precedent. Prince Philip was once tempted by a newspaper proprietor's advice that he should give regular press conferences, then abandoned the idea for fear of committing his heirs to continuing the tradition. If the Queen were to hand over to Charles on her sixty-fifth birthday, in 1991, would be he obliged to hand over to Prince William three years short of his own silver jubilee?

The official biographer of Lord Mountbatten and King Edward VIII, Philip Ziegler, observed in his book *Crown and People* that the British "like their monarchs either old, wise and paternal, or young and hopeful." A sixty-year-old King Charles III, Ziegler argued, would be neither. The logical conclusion was for the Queen to hand the crown straight on to her grandson, Prince William: "The Golden Jubilee of 2002 might be a suitable occasion."

Ziegler was gracious enough to concede that this might be something of a waste of the Prince of Wales, requiring as it would his "premature disappearance . . . the need for which he might consider inadequately proven." Many more Britons, perhaps, would now agree with that sentiment than when it was first expressed a decade ago. The Prince's stature has grown enormously since his involvement with Business in the Community has tightened the focus on his kaleidoscopic public work. Gradually, over the next few years, it will seep into the public consciousness that Kurt Hahn, Carl Jung, the United World Colleges, organic farming, homoeopathic medicine, community architecture and the regeneration of Britain's post-industrial inner-city landscape are all parts of a giant jigsaw which piece together as a cohesive world view.

Between them they amount to a princely Bill of Human Rights, based on Charles's belief in the innate qualities of the individual, his right to live in conditions in which he can take pride, as part of a caring, prejudice-free community which functions smoothly and effectively. It is not merely a personal vision entirely befitting a future King. His work towards achieving it, both in Britain and around the Commonwealth, is a crusade which – despite its few wobbles – does pride to the history of the twenty-one English Princes of Wales.

If it took the Prince thirty-five of his forty years to unite all these strands himself, it will most likely take his future subjects another few years to grasp the substance of the world-view he has finally forged, and the clear purpose it gives to his public role. The popular press is unlikely to be of much help. But his next major hurdle, during the process of public enlightenment, is to dovetail that role with the prevailing political verities of the day, and with his own ambitions to take on clearly defined, higher-profile public positions. It may no longer be necessary to commiserate with the Prince about his long "wait in the wings," now that he himself has perceived the advantages of remaining Prince of Wales. But the less self-pity he feels, the more his self-esteem will demand outward and visible signs of his growing authority.

Charles, in short, is working towards a redefinition of the office of Prince of Wales. At its most potent, in the eighteenth century, the position cast its holder as unofficial head of the political opposition of the day, sustaining its eventual hopes of office, acting in constructive defiance of what has since become known as the Establishment. "Nothing is more natural," wrote Macaulay, "than that, in a monarchy where a constitutional Opposition exists, the heir-apparent to the throne should put himself at the head of that Opposition." But those were the days when the appointment of prime ministers and their Cabinet colleagues rested largely with the sovereign, subject to the developing whims of the electoral process. To the constitutional monarchy as we now know it, those days are long gone – though it is not insignificant that Charles's claim to a large public constituency coincides with a period in which British government has long been devoid of any effective political opposition.

It may still be the monarch's prerogative to sign legislation into law, but he or she has no say in the formulation of those laws. The British monarchy today, brave face though it may put on an often awkward relationship, is utterly at the behest of its governments and survives only on their sufferance. The will of the people, clearly, has a major role in that process. But the British constitution would oblige the Queen – should any of her parliaments, after a democratic vote, be rash enough to place it in front of her – to sign her own death warrant.

In the contemporary world, the sovereign's functions are almost entirely ritualistic. He or she is the living embodiment of the state, personifying its continuing existence, symbolizing its character and creeds, perhaps adapting to its gradually changing ways. The longer a monarch's reign, the greater the benefit of wisdom available to a prime minister – should he or she choose to apply for it, let alone to heed it. Titular head of the Church and the armed forces as well as of the state, the monarch's prime constitutional value to a modern democracy lies in the power the office denies others.

There is thus, in the modern world, a case for a dynamic and purposeful heir-apparent to take over some of those ritualistic functions on his parent's behalf. He in turn, as he has already hinted, would be pleased to hand on his various Trusts and charities to his sons, when he himself is "too old" to be an inspiration to their young beneficiaries. Elizabeth II is unlikely for many years yet to become a royal matriarch *in absentia*, still the nominal head of state, but leaving most of the public duties of that office to a son who could carry them out with the vigour and dash of a new generation. But there are interim possibilities.

On the morning of Friday, 25 March 1988, the Prime
Minister paid a call upon the Prince of Wales – at his
request – at Kensington Palace. Though few noticed either
the announcement or its significance, the audience was
(most unusually) listed in that day's Court Circular,
because it was more than just a chat about mutual anxieties; the discussion carried major constitutional implications, some of which would inevitably become public
sooner or later.

The meeting had been convened to pre-empt any further awkwardness between Prince and Prime Minister. At
times Charles had seemed to be on an almost wilful collision course with the Thatcher government; at others he
had seemed the very embodiment of Thatcher's Britain.
Better to reach an understanding, than feud from a distance.

There had for some time been rumours of bad blood
between Prince and Prime Minister. Until Mrs Thatcher
launched her own inner-city crusade, on the day of her
1987 election victory, Prince Charles's frequent remarks
about social decay and unemployment levels had seemed
to carry an implicit criticism of her government's policies.
There had been no great public controversy, as the Prince
had chosen his public words carefully (so carefully, in fact,
that the tabloids had made constitutional chumps of
themselves by suggesting that Charles might he given a
seat in the Cabinet, "to take responsibility for the inner
cities"). Only once had the Prime Minister seen fit to
intervene directly – over Charles's reported vision of one
day reigning over a "divided" Britain; had these been
Charles's own directly expressed views, rather than his
friend Rod Hackney's, the Prince would have been way
out of bounds.

Mrs Thatcher, nevertheless, had come under pressure
from her more extreme right-wing party colleagues to
curb the impudent young puppy's increasingly wayward
conduct. In the House of Commons itself Prince Charles
was described by Tony Marlow, Conservative MP for

Northampton North, as "unfit to be king." Charles, besides, was a child of the Macmillan era, an old-fashioned "One Nation" Tory who believed in the welfare state, and the basic principle that the state had a duty to aid and comfort the less fortunate. Mrs Thatcher had spent almost a decade unpicking that philosophy, making Britain into an every-man-for-himself society. Having fundamentally realigned many another major British institution, perhaps it was time the Thatcher revolution reappraised the monarchy as well?

There were two extreme alternatives. The Queen could be told that henceforth the monarchy's function was purely ceremonial – a tourist attraction which kept its mouth shut – and that her son was to be seen but not heard. Or the British monarchy could be reduced to the "puppet" status of the few minor monarchies which had survived the republican surges of the twentieth century, its role being overtly to endorse the policies of the government of the day. Perhaps the Queen or the Prince of Wales, for instance, would care to present the key to the millionth council house sold since that controversial Conservative reform was introduced?

These and other permutations – all amounting to fundamental revisions of the constitution – were in active discussion in lofty Conservative circles throughout late 1987 and early 1988. Had the Prime Minister chosen to issue any such dictat to Buckingham Palace, the Queen would have had no choice but to comply. The story of the British royal family's survival of a turbulent century as the world's pre-eminent monarchy is, after all, one of meek, if dignified, compliance with the changing whims of its passing governments.

But Mrs Thatcher, the proud daughter of the grocer-Mayor of Grantham, is herself a devout monarchist. One of the reasons she is less liked personally by the present royal family than some of her recent predecessors is her excessive obsequiousness in their presence; the Queen and to some extent Prince Charles, despite their private politi-

cal views, warmed more to the respectful homeliness of
Harold Wilson and James Callaghan, the last two Labour
prime ministers, than the stiff, ice-cold Conservatives
Edward Heath and Margaret Thatcher. It would take
more than a few passing frictions for even her to wish to
go down in history as the prime minister who emasculated
the monarchy, thus precipitating its eventual abolition.
Even the Labour Party recognized the dangers of med-
dling with the bond between royalty and people, and has
as yet refrained (apart from the Hackney débâcle) from
making political capital out of the Prince of Wales's public
concerns. So Mrs Thatcher went to Kensington Palace
that morning in significantly emollient mood.

Item One on the agenda, at their mutual wish, was the
feasibility of the Prince's performing the State Opening of
Parliament, in his mother's place, in the autumn of 1988.
It would be a symbolic attempt – in the words of the bald,
and constitutionally dubious, briefing which subsequently
emerged from Downing Street – "to give him more real
responsibility for state affairs." There were convenient
practical reasons: the Queen's overseas travel commit-
ments that autumn, and the unusually heavy legislative
programme, would make it appear more a pragmatic
development than a usurpation of the sovereign's functions. There were protocol problems, which would also
protect the monarch's necessary dignity. In her absence
such a ceremony would not, technically, be a *State* Opening; there would be no royal procession to the throne, and
the Prince could only preside in his capacity as a "Lord's
Commissioner" – an attendant lord, reading the Queen's
Speech from a bench within the Chamber. Still, it was a
start.

On the two previous occasions when the Queen had
been forced to miss a State Opening – in 1959 and 1963,
when pregnant with Prince Andrew and Prince Edward
respectively – the Queen's speech was read on her behalf
by the Lord Chancellor. Charles, the argument would go,
was too young at the time to step in and take her place.

Now, it would seem a fitting tribute to his new public *gravitas*. It would help solve his eternal problem in persuading the public that he had a role; his "symbolic presence" at this "one-off occasion" would be said by Downing Street to be just the beginning of his taking on "more official state duties." It would also, Mrs Thatcher coolly pointed out at the time, gratify those peers who were, shall we say, disappointed at how infrequently the Prince ever attended, let alone spoke in, the House of Lords. Perhaps this was a missed opportunity, especially now that the House of Lords is televised?

Delighted by the notion, Charles raised another delicate question. Might it be possible for him in the longer term, as he took over more of his mother's ritualistic state functions, to assume a title which overtly acknowledged his contribution and gave the public a clear impression of his standing – such as Prince Regent? Mrs Thatcher, as he expected, had to reply that this particular title was a constitutional impossibility. The matter had been raised before; she had recently taken the chance of the Prime Minister's annual weekend as the monarch's guest at Windsor to raise it again. The Queen was firmly opposed. The arguments were very much the same as those against abdication; the integrity of the monarchy was of more importance than the heir apparent's worldly vanity.

But the Prime Minister had an ace up her sleeve with which to surprise the crestfallen Prince. Now it is being made public, it will also surprise the British electorate, as it shows her assuming that she will still be in Downing Street almost a decade from now. If Prince Regent was out, she had hatched another plot for the Prince to ponder. Mrs Thatcher recalled Charles's frustrated ambition to become Governor-General of Australia. As a politician of the Malcolm Fraser school of thought, and with her new understanding of the Prince's problems, she sympathized that political niceties had eventually ruled it out. But there were no such obstacles to his becoming Governor of Hong Kong for the last year of its life as a British dominion – just as his beloved Uncle Dickie, Lord Mountbatten, had been the last Viceroy of India before its independence in 1948.

Hong Kong, under an agreement signed in 1984, is to be returned to Chinese sovereignty in 1997. The long and tortuous process of economic and physical disengagement is already well under way. By a year or so before the formal handover, all the political niceties will have been resolved by a succession of professional diplomats holding the title of Governor. The colony's last twelve months under British sway will be purely ceremonial – a chance for Charles to hold conspicuous, quasi-monarchial sway, while showing himself a man of his times in his "dealings" with a contemporary power of the scale and importance of the People's Republic of China.

The Prime Minister was dangling a political carrot which the Prince of Wales found sorely tempting. The Hong Kong skyline was scarcely to his architectural taste, nor its lifestyle especially close to his wife's fun-loving heart, but the symbolism – and the cunning link with Mountbatten – struck home. It was precisely the clear-cut, overt public office which he had coveted for so long. There were other, lesser possibilities in the meantime, like presiding over more investitures, garden parties – the ritual flummery of royalty which anyway went unpublicized. Hong Kong was a highly attractive prospect, but it seemed a long time away.

Thatcher held out the tantalizing prospect of other substantial advances in the meantime: representing the Queen, for instance, at the annual Commonwealth Prime Ministers' Conference. To Charles the remnants of what was his grandfather's empire, and will one day be his own global kingdom, are of paramount importance. He shares his mother's deep-seated belief that it is among the contemporary monarch's primary duties to preserve the Commonwealth and promote its interests. The only public disagreement between Elizabeth II and her eighth prime minister, as yet, was over the issue of economic sanctions against South Africa; the Queen had felt obliged, by judicious leaks, to take the bold constitutional step of making her opposition to government policy known. All too often, given Britain's diminishing role in contemporary geopolitics, the Commonwealth will take last place behind the United States, NATO, the EEC, even the Warsaw Pact in the British Government's calculation of self-interest. The monarch's stubborn resistance to this process was another reason urged upon the Prime Minister by her backbenchers to deprive the monarchy of its last, lingering fingerhold on political sway.

There was another, very specific recent example of such disharmony, as the Prime Minister was now at pains to point out to Prince Charles. In November 1987, at a conference of environment ministers from North Sea states, the Prince had chosen to mount his conservation charger and denounce the North Sea as "a rubbish dump." There was outrage at the Department of the Environment, who had been given no prior knowledge by the Prince of Wales's office of what he intended to say. A copy of the speech had been passed to a junior official at the DoE, rather than the Secretary of State's office, as would be normal. In previous and subsequent speeches on the same subject, moreover, the Prince appeared content to overlook up-to-date statistics and information with which the DoE had been at some paints to provide him. As luck would have it, the Secretary of State at the time was Nicholas Ridley, whose parliamentary private secretary happened to be Nicholas Soames MP, one of the Prince's closest friends for many years. Mr Soames (at whose wedding the Prince was best man) took it upon himself to smooth over the breach with the style to which courtiers are even more accustomed than politicians.

But the Prime Minister was not so easily placated. The prospect of "more official state duties," of Downing Street's announcement that this would be the first of many "consultative" meetings between the Prime Minister and the Prince of Wales, and indeed of Hong Kong would come at a price. "Ministers hope," said the subsequent briefing, "that greater involvement in the nation's affairs will curb the Prince's recent spate of outspoken attacks which have caused deep resentment in some government departments."

It was clear what the Prime Minister had implied to the Prince of Wales; and the mildness of his speeches immediately thereafter, notably what was expected to be a tirade to an inner-city conference at Lancaster House in early May, seemed to suggest that he had taken her point. Far from even implicitly attacking government policy, in front of the latest version of the same Anglo-American gathering which had launched BiC, the Prince even managed to praise one of Mrs Thatcher's Cabinet ministers by name. He was "very grateful," he said, "for the personal energy and enthusiasm which Mr Kenneth Clarke is putting into his whole operation from the government's side."

This was indeed a remarkable transformation. Ten days after the Prince's meeting with the Prime Minister at Kensington Palace, however, Mrs Thatcher's finger had been rather more publicly wagged at the Prince by one of her most senior lieutenants, the former Cabinet minister and Conservative Party chairman, Norman Tebbit. The Prince's concern over the inner cities, said Mr Tebbit on *Panorama*, the BBC's flagship current affairs programme, could prove "dangerous" for the monarchy if he were to take "too far." His anxieties about the unemployed, for instance, must derive from his own precarious hold on anything worth doing.

> I suppose the Prince of Wales feels extra sympathy towards those who've got no job because in a way he's got no job, and he's prohibited from having a job until he inherits the throne. . . . He's forty, yet he's not been able to take responsibility for anything, and I think that's really his problem.

The characteristically sinister tone in Mr Tebbit's voice carried menacing echoes of the Prince's recent conversation with the Prime Minister. "We're in for a period of

eight, ten, perhaps twenty years of Conservative government," Tebbit went on, "and therefore any criticism of the
world as it is sounds like a criticism of the government."
There could be "danger" for the Prince if he persisted. "If
he advocated a socialist solution, a Labour Party solution,
that would begin to get dangerous."

Well-known as a mouthpiece for Mrs Thatcher since he
left her Cabinet after the last election – to spend more
time with his wife, who was crippled by the IRA bombing
of the 1986 Conservative Party Conference – Tebbit's
words were taken by political commentators as if they had
come from the Prime Minister herself. It was idle to point
out that Tebbit could not have mounted such criticism of
the heir to the throne were he still in government – were
he not himself, in other words, politically unemployed.
Given another recent interview in which he had expressed
a "willingness" to succeed Mrs Thatcher as Prime Minister, were she ever to retire without having anointed a like-
minded successor, Tebbit was also, indeed, another would-
be heir to another throne. His remarks thus began to
sound uncomfortably like some form of moral blackmail.
If the Prince wanted the prizes dangled in front of him by
the Prime Minister, said her putative successor, he must
heed the gospel according to Thatcher.

But the nation's other universal mother – and the
Prince's own – was not going to see her sacred trust abused
in this way by mere politicians. The following evening, at
a Windsor Castle banquet in honour of King Olav of
Norway, Queen Elizabeth II attracted more attention to
herself than is her wont by calling for greater efforts to
keep the North Sea free of pollution. "It is in the interests
of both our nations," said the Queen, "to see that the
health and cleanliness of the North Sea are maintained,
and that its renewable resources are only exploited on a
sustainable basis." The monarch's remarks, though
apparently anodyne enough, were by her standards
unusually outspoken. The full significance of her refer-

ence to the North Sea, however, was lost on all but two of her glittering array of guests.

Among the Queen's audience that evening, by no coincidence, were both Prince and Prime Minister. Elizabeth II, with her own politician's skill for the telling gesture, was warning Mrs Thatcher in her turn that she too could go too far. Only three people in that great chamber at Windsor knew the connection between the Kensington Palace meeting, the Tebbit television interview and the Queen's welcome to one of her closest friends among fellow-monarchs. It was typical, however, that the Queen chose to couch her coded riposte to the Prime Minister in the form of a covert tribute to an heir who was now fulfilling all her hopes and aspirations.

In a week when Charles had been under fire from a possible future Prime Minister, in a year when he had suffered a series of bruising ordeals both private and public, in an age when a Prince of Wales can sometimes be forgiven for thinking that he cannot put a foot right, this was the sovereign's proud and affectionate way not only of keeping her Prime Minister in her place, but of making it clear – as publicly as possible – that this is a son in whom she is well pleased.

Appendix A

Chronology of Principal Events in Prince Charles's Life, 1948-88, including Foreign Visits

1948

14 November	Born at Buckingham Palace
15 December	Christened Buckingham Palace

1950

15 August	Birth of Princess Anne

1952

6 February	Becomes heir apparent and Duke of Cornwall on death of his grandfather, King George VI and accession of his mother as Queen Elizabeth II

1954

April-May	Visits Malta, Libya (Tobruk) and Gibraltar to greet his parents home from coronation tour of Commonwealth

1957

28 January	Joins Hill House School as day-boy
23 September	Joins Cheam preparatory school as boarder

1958
26 July   Created Prince of Wales and Knight of
                   the Garter

1960
19 February   Birth of Prince Andrew

1962
1 April   Leaves Cheam School
1 May   Joins Gordonstoun School

1964
10 March   Birth of Prince Edward
July   Passes five GCE 'O' levels

1965
26 November   Plays Macbeth in Gordonstoun school
                   play
20 December   Wins Duke of Edinburgh's Silver
                   Award

1966
2 February   Joins Timbertop, country annex of
                   Geelong Church of England Grammar
                   School, Melbourne, Australia, for two
                   terms
May   Visits Papua New Guinea and tours
                   Australia during school holidays
August   Visits Mexico en route from Australia
                   to Commonwealth Games in Jamaica
14 November   Eighteenth birthday. Made Counsellor
                   of State. Now eligible to succeed to
                   throne in own right

1967
January   Made head boy at Gordonstoun
July   Passes two GCE 'A' levels
October   Joins Trinity College, Cambridge to
                   read archaeology and anthropology,
                   later history

| 31 October | Attends first State Opening of Parliament |
| December | Visits Melbourne for funeral of Prime Minister, Harold Holt |

1968

March	Contributes article to *Varsity* magazine: archeological expedition to France and Jersey
9 June	Wins half-Blue for representing Cambridge at polo
14 June	Awarded a II, 1 in Part One of Cambridge Tripos
17 June	Invested as Knight of the Garter at Windsor
11 July	Attends first Buckingham Palace garden party
30 July	First flight (familiarization)
10 December	Chairs first meeting (Steering Committee for Wales, 'The Countryside in 1970' Conference, Cardiff). Also occasion of first public speech

1969

14 January	First solo flight
February	Takes part in Cambridge revue *Revulution*
2 March	First sound radio broadcast: interview with Jack de Manio (BBC Radio 4)
20 April	Arrives for one term at University College of Wales, Aberystwyth
11 June	Inauguration ceremony for Royal Regiment of Wales, of which he is Colonel-in-Chief; receives freedom of City of Cardiff
26 June	First television appearance: interview with Brian Connell and Cliff Michelmore

1 July	Investiture as Prince of Wales at Caernarvon Castle
2-5 July	Tour of Wales
October	Germany: funeral of Margravine of Baden
November	Malta: inaugurates new campus at Royal University

1970

February	Strasbourg: Council of Europe's European Conservation Conference
11 February	Takes seat in House of Lords
March	Obtains Grade A private pilot's licence
March-April	Tours Australia and New Zealand with Queen and Prince Philip
April	Tours Japan (Expo 70)
June	Graduates BA (Hons) from Cambridge
July	Visits Ottawa, then joined by Queen and Prince Philip for tour of Canada; with Princess Anne, guest of President Nixon in Washington
October	Fiji: independence celebrations; Gilbert and Ellice Islands; Bermuda: 350th anniversary of parliament; Barbados
November	Paris: Funeral of President de Gaulle

1971

February	Kenya: safari with Princess Anne; Germany: visits Royal Regiment of Wales at Osnabrück
March-August	Flight Lieutenant in RAF; trained at RAF College, Cranwell
September-October	Acting Sub-Lieutenant in Royal Navy; six-week course at Royal Naval College, Dartmouth

| November | Gibraltar: to join HMS *Norfolk*. Promoted Sub-Lieutenant |

1972

July	Serves aboard HMS *Norfolk*
May	Joins Queen and Duke of Edinburgh on state visit to France
July	Shore courses at HMS *Dryad*, Portsmouth; familiarization flying with RN and Queen's Flight
October	Berlin: military and civic engagements
November	Served with HMS *Glasserton*, coastal minesweeper

1973

January	Visits Royal Regiment of Wales in Germany
February	Leaves Portsmouth aboard HMS *Minerva*, aboard which he serves until September (Gains bridge watch-keeping and ocean navigation certificates; promoted Lieutenant)
June	St Kitts: opens newly restored Prince of Wales's bastion
July	The Bahamas: independence celebrations
October	Completes shore courses for divisional officer
14 November	Wedding of Princess Anne and Captain Mark Phillips

1974

| January-August | Serves aboard HMS *Jupiter* as communications officer |

January– February	New Zealand: joins Queen and Duke of Edinburgh for Commonwealth Games
September– December	Royal Naval Air Station, Yeovilton, for helicopter conversion course
September	New Zealand: funeral of Prime Minister, Norman Kirk
October	Australia: inaugurates Anglo-Australian telescope; visits Tasmania

1975

January	Returns to Yeovilton for advance flying training
February	Visits Delhi en route for Nepal: coronation of King Birendra
March–June	Serves aboard HMS *Hermes*, commando ship, with 845 Squadron ('Red Dragons'); visits Caribbean
April	Bahamas: guest of Lord and Lady Brabourne at Eleuthera; Canada: tours Northwest Territories
September– December	Lieutenant's course at Royal Naval College, Greenwich
September	Papua New Guinea: represents Queen at independence celebrations
November	Germany: visits Royal Regiment of Wales in Berlin

1976

February– December	Commands HMS *Bronington*, minehunter, based at Rosyth. (Promoted Commander in RN and Wing Commander in RAF on leaving Services in December)

| July | Canada: private visit to Olympic Games in Montreal |

1977
March	Kenya: safari holiday; Ghana: official visit; Ivory Coast: official visit.
July	Canada (Alberta): official visit; made Indian chieftain; opened Calgary Stampede
October	USA: official visit
November	Australia: official visit; Germany: visiting 1st Battalion, Welsh Guards

1978
March	Brazil, Venezuela: official visit
May	Australia: funeral of Sir Robert Menzies
July	Norway: King Olav's seventy-fifth birthday party
August	Kenya: funeral of Jomo Kenyatta
October	Yugoslavia: official visit
November	Brussels: official visit to NATO and SHAPE headquarters

1979
March	Hong Kong, Singapore, Western Australia and Canberra
April	Canada: including first visit to Lester B. Pearson College of the Pacific (one of the United World Colleges) in British Columbia as president, UWC
May	Berlin: visits 2nd Parachute Regiment
June	France: UWC fund-raising dinner at Tours-sur-Marne

1980
| January | Switzerland: lunch in Zurich to mark sixtieth anniversary of British-Swiss Chamber of Commerce |

March–April	Canada: Ottawa and British Columbia as President UWC
April	Zimbabwe: independence celebrations; Netherlands: accession ceremony of Queen Beatrix
July	France: visiting the French armed forces
November–December	India, Nepal

1981
March–April	New Zealand, Australia
April	Venezuela: as President, UWC
April–May	United States: to receive honorary fellowship from College of William and Mary at Williamsburg, Virginia; attends Oxford and Cambridge and White House dinners in Washington DC
29 July	Marries Lady Diana Spencer in St Paul's Cathedral
August	Egypt: funeral of President Sadat

1982
June	France: commemoration of fortieth anniversary of Allied Raid, Bruneval
21 June	Birth of first son, Prince William Arthur Philip Louis
October	United States: New Mexico, as President, UWC, to open the Armand Hammer United World College of the American West at Montezuma; Canada: visits Lester B. Pearson College of the Pacific, British Columbia

1983
March–April	Australia, New Zealand (first visit with the Princess of Wales and Prince William)

June	Canada (first visit with the Princess of Wales)

1984

February	Brunei: independence celebrations
March	Tanzania, Zambia, Zimbabwe and Botswana: tour as director of Commonwealth Development Corporation
30 May	'Monstrous carbuncle' speech to RIBA 150th anniversary dinner at Hampton Court Palace
June	France: Ranville, Normandy, for commemoration of role of 6th Airborne Division in Allied landings of 1944
July	West Germany: visits Royal Regiment of Wales and Gordon Highlanders
August	Monaco: attends UWC gala in Monte Carlo; Papua New Guinea: opens new Parliament House
September	Netherlands: as Colonel-in-Chief, The Parachute Regiment, attends service to mark fortieth anniversary of Battle of Arnhem
15 September	Birth of second son, Prince Henry (Harry) Charles Albert David
October	Italy: visits Trieste and United World College at Duino

1985

February	Norway: visits 1st Battalion, Parachute Regiment, as Colonel-in-Chief
March	West Germany: visits 1st Battalion, Welsh Guards
April-May	Italy (first visit with the Princess of Wales – later joined by Princes William and Henry)
June	West Germany: takes salute at Queen's Birthday Parade, West Berlin

September	Becomes President, Business in the Community
October-November	Australia: Victoria (150th anniversary celebrations) and Canberra, with the Princess of Wales
November	Fiji (first visit with the Princess of Wales)

1986
February	United States: Texas and California
April	Austria: Vienna, with the Princess of Wales
May	Canada: opens Expo 86, Vancouver; visits British Columbia (first visit with the Princess of Wales)
May	Japan (first visit with the Princess of Wales)
June	Marriage of Prince Andrew to Sarah Ferguson
September	United States: Harvard (350th anniversary celebrations) and Chicago
November	Oman, Qatar, Bahrain and Saudi Arabia (first visit with the Princess of Wales)
November	Cyprus: visits 3rd Battalion, the Parachute Regiment, as Colonel-in-Chief

1987
February	Portugal: official visit with the Princess of Wales; France: Toulouse, for launch of Airbus
March	Belgium: meets survivors of the Zeebrugge ferry disaster; visits NATO headquarters in Brussels
March-April	Swaziland, Malawi, Kenya: official visit as a director of the Commonwealth Development Corporation

April	Spain: official visit with the Princess of Wales
November	West Germany: visits Bonn, Cologne, Munich, Hamburg, Celle and Hanover with the Princess of Wales
1 December	'Luftwaffe' speech at Mansion House, London

1988
January-
February	Australia: bicentennial celebrations; visits New South Wales, Victoria, South and Australia and Northern Territory with the Princess of Wales
February	Thailand: Bangkok on the occasion of the Kind of Thailand's sixtieth birthday
March	United States: attends Remaking Cities Conference, Pittsburgh
26 July	Thirtieth anniversary of creation as Prince of Wales
29 July	Seventh wedding anniversary
1 August	West Germany: attends Schleswig-Holstein Music Festival
2 August	Denmark: attends *Hamlet* at Elsinore as patron of the Renaissance Theatre Trust
26-27 October	Netherlands: as patron of the William and Mary Tercentenary Trust
7-11 November	France: official visit with the Princess of Wales
14 November	Fortieth birthday

Appendix B

The Prince of Wales's Descent

I N AUGUST 1977, at the age of ninety-two, Mr Gerald Paget of Welwyn Garden City, Hertfordshire, published his first book: in two volumes costing £60, containing nearly 1,000 pages and weighing 13 lb., it is entitled *The Lineage and Ancestry of HRH Prince Charles, Prince of Wales*. Mr Paget's introduction opens with the rare and enviable sentence: "This book had its origin about seventy-five years ago. . . . "

It was in Queen Victoria's diamond jubilee year, 1897, that the schoolboy Paget first became interested in genealogy. G. W. Watson's work on the ancestry of King Edward VII, published in *The Genealogist* some ten years later, gave him the idea of tracing the pedigrees of various European monarchs. With the birth of Princess Elizabeth in 1926 he decided to explore her ancestry, hopefully as far as William the Conqueror; but he was still immersed in his project twenty-two years later, when Princess Elizabeth gave birth to Prince Charles. So Paget, then sixty-three, decided to start afresh and pursue the new Prince's ancestry, though the introduction of Prince Philip's lineage of course doubled his work-load. Had he struck to his original intent, to trace Prince Charles back to William the Conqueror, the theoretical number of ancestors would have risen to the astonishing figure of 1,073,741,824. He decided to call a halt in the fourteenth and fifteenth centuries, at the eighteenth generation. Even so, his monumental publication leaves only some 40,000 ancestors untraced out of a total of 262,142.

These two paragraphs are by way of tribute to Mr Paget's life work, without which this appendix could scarcely have been written. I must also acknowledge a debt to an excellent two-part review of his work, in *Books and Bookmen* (vol. 23, nos 7-8), by the genealogist Sir Iain Moncreiffe of that Ilk, Albany Herald. Sir Iain's voluminous knowledge of his subject was able to detect a few minor errors and add some intriguing new dimensions; he has also had a large hand in the compilation of this appendix. As he himself says: "HRH's breeding is the most important in the world ... he is heir to the world's greatest position that is determined solely by heredity."

Through cousin marriages many of the ancestors traced by Paget, more than a quarter of a million of them, are of course the same people. The total number of individuals is thus greatly reduced, which is as it should be. The Blood Royal is proportionately the purer.

In Prince Charles's veins runs the blood of emperors and kings, Russian boyars, Spanish grandees, noblemen of every European nation, bishops and judges, knights and squires, and tradesmen right down to a butcher, a toymaker and an innkeeper. Readers curious for more detail than this appendix can provide should turn to Mr Paget's work. His discoveries include the fact that Prince Charles is a cousin or nephew, in varying degrees, of all six wives of Henry VIII; that he has many descents from the Royal Houses of Scotland, France, Germany, Austria, Denmark, Sweden, Norway, Spain, Portugal, Russia and the Netherlands. Many of his ancestors died bloodily, in battle or by the axe, especially in the Wars of the Roses and the reigns of the Tudor sovereigns.

The most significant of Prince Charles's forebears fall into three categories. First there are those who were historic figures in the British Isles, the immediate realm. Secondly, there are similar figures, especially royalty, in the rest of Europe from which emigrants have gone out in such numbers to the Old Commonwealth. And thirdly, there is a leaven of solid British stock of all classes: just enough to keep HRH down to earth, but not enough to dilute his royal blood unduly, or to give him too many inconvenient near-relations among his family's subjects.

In England, he descends over and over again from the Anglo-Saxon, Norman, Plantagenet and Tudor kings, indeed from every English king who has left descendants (even including Henry IV), except Charles I and his sons. He descends from the non-royal Protectors of England, Edward Seymour, Duke of Somerset, and John Dudley, Duke of Northumberland (but not from Cromwell; curiously enough, HRH does not take sides genealogically in the Civil War). Other famous characters abound in his ancestry: Alfred the Great; Hereward the Outlaw (better known, incorrectly, as the Wake), hero of the Anglo-Saxon epic, together with the King Harold slain at Hastings *and* their foe William the Conqueror; Simon de Montfort, Earl of Leicester, the first parliamentarian; Harry "Hotspur", Lord Percy, hero of the Ballad of Chevy Chase; Warwick the Kingmaker; and the great Elizabethans Essex, the Queen's favourite, Sir Frances Walsingham and William Cecil, Lord Burghley.

Thanks to the lineage of Queen Elizabeth the Queen Mother (born Lady Elizabeth Bowes-Lyon, daughter of the 14th Earl of Strathmore), the blood of some of England's noblest houses runs in the Prince of Wales's veins: including de Vere, Earl of Oxford; Courtenay, Earl of Devon; Percy, Earl of Northumberland; Talbot, Earl of Shrewsbury; Stanley, Earl of Derby; Clifford, Earl of Cumberland; Cecil, Earl of Salisbury; Howard, Duke of Norfolk; Russell, Duke of Bedford, and Cavendish, Duke of Devonshire. Queen Anne's chief minister Robert Harley and the Prime Minister Portland were direct ancestors; Sir Philip Sidney and the "Iron Duke" of Wellington his ancestral uncles; Charles Darwin, and – through the relationship of the Hastings, Earls of Huntingdon, to the

Ardens – probably Shakespeare, were the Prince's ancestral fifth cousins.

In Wales, the present Prince of Wales descends from such renowned characters as Davy Gam and such historic families as Morgan of Tredegar, but above all from the great Owen Glendower (Owain Glyndwr), proclaimed "Prince of Wales by the Grace of God" during the last Welsh rising. Moreover, he descends many times over from Llewelyn the Great, Prince of Wales, and all Welsh kings and princes by way of Hywel Dda back to Cunedda and Old King Coel himself, who reigned in the fifth century, soon after the Romans left Britain.

In Scotland, the Prince derives his title of Great Steward of Scotland from his ancestors the Stewart kings. Through George VI and Prince Philip he descends *twenty-two times over* from Mary Queen of Scots, and he has more than 200 direct lines of descent from King Robert Bruce and thus from the ancient Celtic kings of the Picts and Scots. Through the Lyons of Glamis, most of the historic Scottish houses contributed to his lineage: the "Black Douglas" Earls of Douglas and the "Red Douglas" Earls of Angus; the "lightsome" Lindsay Earls of Crawford; the "handsome" Hay Earls of Erroll; the "gey" (which means ferocious, not gay in any sense) Gordon Earls of Huntly; the "proud" Graham Earls of Montrose. A rather surprising ancestor was Cardinal Beaton, the murdered archbishop of St Andrews.

On the Borders his forebears included the Homes of Wedderburn, the "bold" Scotts of Buccleuch and their foes in many a ballad, the Kerrs of Fernihurst. In the far North, through the 1st Sinclair Earl of Caithness, he comes from the old Norse jarls of Orkney. In central Scotland, the Prince springs from the Lords Drummond and the Murrays of Tullibardine, the Moncreiffes of that Ilk and Stirlings of Keir, and the Stewart Earls of Atholl. Elsewhere in the Highlands, through his descent from the Grants of Grant and the 10th Chief of Mackintosh, the

Prince has Hebridean blood of the mighty Clanranald – and in the West, too, he descends not only from the Mac-Dougall chiefs of Dunollie and the Campbell Earls of Argyll, but above all (as befits the present Lord of the Isles) at least two dozen times over from the paramount Macdonald chiefs who were the original Lords of the Isles.

In Ireland, Queen Elizabeth the Queen Mother has brought Prince Charles the most distinguished Irish ancestry, the blood of the Dal Cais and Eoganacht dynasties of Munster and that of the Ui Neill high kings. Among his ancestors were the O'Brien Earls and Kings of Thomond (including the high kings Brian "Boru" and Toirdhelbhach); the McCarthy Reagh chieftains of the line of King Cormac who built the famous chapel at Cashel; the O'Donnells of Tyrconnell; the MacDonnells of Antrim (including "Sorley Boy"); the wild Burkes of Clanricarde; the FitzGerald Earls of Kildare and Desmond, and the Knights of Glin; the Butler Earls of Ormonde; and, above all, Red Hugh O'Neill, Earl of Tyrone, the last native King of Ulster, who died in exile in Rome in 1618.

To turn to the continent of Europe: Prince Charles, through his father, is Danish, in the direct male line of the Royal House of Denmark, which still reigns in Norway. He descends father-to-son through Christian IX, King of Denmark (1863-1906), from Christian I, King of Denmark, Norway and Sweden (1488-81). Among his celebrated Viking ancestors were King Sven Forkbeard of Denmark and King Harold Haardrade of Norway, but he also springs from the ancient "Peace-Kings," whose vast grave-mounds can still be seen at Uppsala in Sweden. King Canute was his ancestral uncle. So too were Gustavus Adolphus and Charles XII of Sweden, for his Scandinavian ancestry is octopoid, taking in the Royal House of Vasa as well as such locally historic names as Oxenstierna and Sture, Sparre and Gyllenstierna, Banér and Konigsmark, Bonde and Bielke.

In Russia, he is descended through Czar Nicholas I from both Catherine the Great and Peter the Great. He also has innumerable descents from the Grand Princes of the House of Rurik, who originally founded "All The Russias," among them St Vladimir of Kiev, who Christianized the Russians; Yuri Dolgoruky, celebrated as the founder of Moscow; and St Michael of Chernigov, executed by the Tartars for refusing to kneel to a statue of Genghis Khan. In Poland, he descends from the original Piast dynasty and from the Jagiellons up to King Zygmunt I (d. 1548). His Lithuanian ancestry goes back to Gedimin, last pagan sovereign of Lithuania (1316-41). His Byzantine imperial blood flows from the Angeloi and Comnenoi emperors of the East, and through the House of Savoy from the later Emperors Michael VIII and Andronicus Palaeologue.

In Bohemia, the Prince descends from all the kings who have left descendants, from the original Czech house of Přemsyl (the family of Good St Wenceslas) down through the House of Luxembourg to Anne of Bohemia, wife of the Emperor Ferdinand I. So his ancestors include the "Blind King" slain at Crécy, the Emperor Charles IV who founded the University of Prague, and above all the popular Hussite elected King George of Podiebrad. Other historic Czech names in the Prince's ancestry are Lobkowicz and Sternberg, and Ulric "the lame lord" of Rosenberg. In Hungary, he similarly descends from all the kings (who left issue) of the original Royal House of Arpad; moreover, the famous King John Szapolyai was his ancestral uncle. Also, through his great-grandmother Queen Mary, the blood of many Magyar noble families, including several of the Bathory voivodes of Transylvania, flows in his veins. In Romania, by way of Queen Mary's ancestry, he descends from Vlad Dracul, Voivode of Wallachia (father of the original Dracula) and thus from the Bassarab dynasty who were very possibly derived from Genghis Khan himself.

In what was the Holy Roman Empire, he descends over and over again from Charlemagne and Frederick Barbarossa and all the great dynasties, Habsburg and Hohenstaufen, Guelph and Hohenzollern, Bavaria and Saxony, Hesse and Baden, Mecklenburg and Württemberg, Brunswick and Anhalt, the Electors Palatine and other Wittelsbachs, plus many of the historic houses such as Hohenlohe and Galen, Moltke and Sickingen, Schwarzenberg and Trauttmannsdorff. Otto the Great and Philip of Hesse were his direct forefathers. Frederick the Great and the Emperor Charles v were his ancestral uncles.

In Portugal, the Prince descends from the marriage of the son of King John I of Aviz, Alfonso, Duke of Braganza, to Beatrix, daughter of the Blessed Nuño Alvarez Pereira, the "Holy Constable." The equally celebrated infante Henry the Navigator was an ancestral uncle.

In Italy, his forefathers include the Dukes of Savoy, the Emperor Frederick II "Stupor Mundi" and the medieval Kings of Sicily, as also the Orsini of Rome (Pope Nicholas III was his ancestral uncle), the Visconti of Milan, della Scala of Verona, Doria of Genoa and Gonzaga of Mantua (besides the great *condottieri* Colleoni and Hawkwood); in Spain, they include Ferdinand and Isabella (who financed Columbus's discovery of America) and thus El Cid himself. In France: the Carolingian, Capetian and Valois kings up to Charles VII (the Dauphin of Joan of Arc fame), among them St Louis many times over, and such historic names as Montmorency and Rohan, Polignac and La Rochefoucauld and La Tour d'Auvergne. In the Netherlands: through his wife Charlotte of Bourbon, none other than William the Silent, Prince of Orange and founder of the Dutch Republic. In the Low Countries, too, Prince Charles bears a remarkable likeness to portraits of Charles the Bold, Duke of Burgundy, who was his direct forefather.

HRH's immemorial roots of course go back far, far beyond the generations covered by Mr Paget's monumental work. The Prince's Anglo-Saxon and Danish royal forefathers sprang from Dark Age kings who incarnated the storm-spirit Woden (after whom Wednesday is named), and among his pagan Celtic royal forefathers were King Niall of the Nine Hostages and the dynamic Iron Age sacral kings of Tara, the great sanctuary of ancient Ireland. Through the Lusignan crusader kings of Cyprus, titular kings of Jerusalem, Prince Charles descends a millennium further back from King Tiridates the Great, the first Christian monarch of all (under whom Armenia was converted in AD 314, before even Rome itself), and thus from the divine Parthian imperial House of Arsaces (247 BC), which reigned over Persia and Babylonia and was in its time the mightiest dynasty in the Ancient World.

Finally, down to earth. In 1779 Mr George Carpenter, of Redbourn in Hertfordshire (writes Sir Anthony Wagner, ex-Garter King of Arms, in his *English Genealogy* "had the plumber down from London to repair the roof of his house. With the plumber came his daughter, and both remained at Redbourn some time. Mary Elizabeth Walsh, the daughter, was then eighteen years of age, and Mr Carpenter upwards of sixty, yet notwithstanding the disparity of their ages and positions he married her. Their daughter married the 11th Earl of Strathmore' – the Queen Mother's great-great-grandfather. The Prince of Wales is thus eighth in descent from that plumber, John Walsh. There are many other plain English names in his ancestry; but it is through the plainest of them all, John Smith, that Prince Charles is one of the nearest living relations of George Washington, first President of the United States.

Appendix C

Bibliography

Books and articles consulted by the author, or which would provide the reader with more detail in specialist areas, include:

ARNOLD, Harry. *Charles and Diana* (London: New English Library, 1981).

ARNOLD-BROWN, Adam. *Unfolding Character: The Impact of Gordonstoun* (London: Routledge & Kegan Paul Ltd., 1962).

BAGEHOT, Walter. *The English Constitution* (Fair Lawn, NJ: Oxford University Press, 1933).

BARRY, Stephen. *Royal Service* (New York: Macmillan, 1983).

BEAVERBROOK, Lord William Maxwell Aitken. *The Abdication of King Edward VIII*, edited by A. J.P. Taylor (New York: Atheneum, 1966).

BOOTHROYD, Basil. *Prince Philip: An Informal Biography* (New York: McCall Books, 1971).

BRERETON, Henry Lloyd. *Gordonstoun: Ancient Estate and Modern School* (Edinburgh: W & R Chambers, 1968).

BURNET, Alastair. *In Person: The Prince and Princess of Wales* (New York: Summit Books, 1985).

CHANNON, Sir Henry. *"Chips": The Diaries of Sir Henry Channon*, edited by Robert Rhodes James (London: Weidenfeld & Nicolson, 1967).

COUNIHAN, Daniel. *Royal Progress* (London: Cassell, 1977).

CRAWFORD, Marion. *The Little Princesses* (New York: Harcourt, Brace and Co., 1950).

DALE, John. *The Prince and the Paranormal* (London: W.H. Allen, 1986).

DONALDSON, Frances. *Edward VIII*, paper ed. (New York: Ballantine, 1976).

DUNCAN, Andrew. *Queen's Year: The Reality of Monarchy* (Garden City, NY: Doubleday, 1970).

EDWARDS, Anne. *Matriarch: Queen Mary and the House of Windsor* (New York: William Morrow, 1984).

GILL, Crispin, ed. *The Duchy of Cornwall*, with a foreword by HRH The Prince of Wales (Devon, England: David & Charles, 1987).

GORE, John. *King George V: A Personal Memoir* (New York: Charles Scribner's Sons, [no date]).

HIBBERT, Christopher. *The Court of St. James: The Monarch at Work from Victoria to Elizabeth II* (New York: William Morrow, 1980).

HOLDEN, Anthony. *Prince Charles: A Biography* (New York: Atheneum, 1979).

————. *Their Royal Highnesses* (London: Weidenfeld & Nicolson, 1981).

————. *The British Royal Family: Great Front Pages*, paperback original (New York: The Vendome Press, 1984).

HOUGH, Richard. *Mountbatten* (New York: Random House, 1981).

JENNINGS, Ivor. *The British Constitution* (New York: Cambridge University Press, 1961).

JUDD, Denis. *Prince Philip, Duke of Edinburgh* (New York: Atheneum, 1981).

JUNOR, Penny. *Charles* (London: Sidgwick & Jackson, 1987).

KEAY, Douglas. *Royal Pursuit: The Media and the*

Monarchy in Conflict and Compromise (New York: Dodd, Mead & Co., 1984).

LACEY, Robert. *Majesty: Elizabeth II and the House of Windsor*, paperback (New York: Avon, 1978).

——. *Princess* (New York: Times Books, 1983).

LONGFORD, Elizabeth. *The Queen: The Life of Elizabeth II* (New York: Alfred A. Knopf, 1983).

LOWRY, Suzanne. *The Princess in the Mirror* (Topsfield, MA: Merrimack Publishers Circle, 1986).

MAGNUS, Sir Philip. *King Edward the VII* (New York: E.P. Dutton, 1964).

MARPLES, Morris. *Princes in the Making: A Study of Royal Education* (New York: Humanities Press Inc., 1965).

MARTIN, Kingsley. *The Crown and the Establishment* (Baltimore: Penguin Books, Inc., [no date]).

MARTIN, Ralph G. *Charles and Diana* (New York: Putnam Publishing Group, 1985).

MENKES, Suzy. *Royal Jewels* (London: Grafton Books, 1985).

MORRAH, Dermot. *To Be A King* (London: Hutchinson, 1968).

MORROW, Ann. *The Queen* (New York: William Morrow, 1983).

MORTIMER, Penelope. *Queen Elizabeth: A Life of the Queen Mother* (New York: St. Martin's Press, 1986).

MORTON, Andrew. *Inside Kensington Palace* (London: Michael O'Mara Books, 1987).

NICOLSON, Harold. *King George V: His Life and Reign* (Garden City, NY: Doubleday, 1953).

PAGET, Gerald. *The Lineage and Ancestry of HRH Prince Charles, Prince of Wales* (Baltimore, MD: Genealogical Publishing Co., 1977).

PALMER, Alan. *Princes of Wales* (London: Weidenfeld & Nicolson, 1979).

PEARSON, John. *The Selling of the Royal Family: The Mystique of the British Monarchy* (New York: Simon & Schuster, 1986).

PEEL, Edward. *Cheam School from 1965* (Gloucestershire, England: Thornhill Press, 1974).

POPE-HENNESSY, James. *Queen Mary 1867-1953* (New York: Alfred A. Knopf, 1960).

ROHRS, Hermann. *Kurt Hahn*, with a preface by the Duke of Edinburgh (London: Routledge & Kegan Paul Ltd., 1970).

ROSE, Kenneth. *King George V* (New York: Alfred A. Knopf, 1984).

ST JOHN-STEVAS, Norman. *Walter Bagehot* (published for the British Council and the National Book League by Longmans, Green, 1963).

SKIDELSKY, Robert. *Hahn of Gordonstoun* (London: Penguin Books Ltd., 1969).

STEWART, William L. *The Thirties and Gordonstoun* (London: Macmillan, 1968).

TALBOT, Godfrey. *The Country Life Book of Queen Elizabeth The Queen Mother* (London: Country Life Books, 1978).

THOMPSON, John. *Community Architecture: The Story of Lea View House* (London: RIBA Publications, 1985).

VAN DER POST, Laurens. *Jung: And the Story of Our Time* (New York: Pantheon, 1975).

———. *Yet Being Someone Other*, reprint (New York: William Morrow, 1983).

———. *A Walk with a White Bushman* (New York: William Morrow, 1987).

WADE, Judy. *Inside a Royal Marriage* (London: Eden Paperbacks, 1987).

WALES, HRH Charles, Prince of: Foreword to Brooke, John, *King George III* (New York: McGraw-Hill, 1972).

———. Review (unheadlined) of *Twice Brightly*, a novel by Harry Secombe, *Punch* magazine, November 6, 1974.

———. "Legend and Reality," a review of *Queen Vic-*

toria Was Amused, by Alan Hardy, *Books and Book-men*, November 1976.

————. Foreword to Gill, Crispin (ed.), *The Duchy of Cornwall* (Devon, England: David & Charles, 1987).

WARWICK, Christopher. *Princess Margaret* (New York: St. Martin's Press, 1983).

WATES, Nick and Charles Knevitt. *Community Architecture: How People Are Creating Their Own Environment* (London: Penguin Books Ltd., 1987).

WHEELER-BENNETT, Sir John. *King George VI* (New York: St. Martin's Press, 1958).

WHITAKER, James. *Settling Down*, paperback (Boston: Charles Rivers Books, 1982).

WILSON, Colin. *Lord of the Underworld: Jung and the Twentieth Century* (Northamptonshire, England: Aquarian Press Ltd., 1984).

WINDSOR, HRH The Duke of. *A Family Album* (London: Cassell, 1960).

————. *A King's Story: Memories of HRH The Duke of Windsor* (New York: G.P. Putnam's Sons, 1951).

ZIEGLER, Philip. *Crown and People* (New York: Alfred A. Knopf, 1978).

————. *Mountbatten* (New York: Alfred A. Knopf, 1985).

Illustrations

With his father at the funeral of Lord Mountbatten (© *Tim Graham*)

Relaxing in the garden of Highgrove (© *Tim Graham)*

Sketching water-colours in Japan (© *Tim Graham*)

Three Princes and a piano (© *Tim Graham*)

In contemplative mood, in the wild-flower garden at Highgrove (© *Heather Angel/British Wildlife Appeal*)

The crusading Prince inspects "intolerable" housing in East London (*Associated Press*)

A planning meeting with his private secretary, Sir John Riddell (© *Tim Graham*)

Learning about community architecture with John Thompson (*photo: Stephen Sharples, Hunt Thompson Associates*)

With Rod Hackney in Macclesfield (© *Charles Knevitt*)

Charles lives the life of a Duchy of Cornwall farmer (*Western Morning News*)

Fishing at Balmoral (*Times Newspapers*)

A disastrous flying visit to Wales (*Press Association*)

Seeking solace from "Kanga," Lady Tryon (*photo: Jim Bennett,* © *Alpha*)

The tabloids go on the rampage (*John Frost*)

Returning home from the tragedy in Klosters (*both photos* © *Tim Graham*)

Australia, January 1988 (*photo: Glenn Harvey, Camera Press*)

Diana takes to the piano to upstage Charles's return to the cello (*both photos* © *Mail Newspapers*)

At Balmoral with his fishing-rod and labrador (© *Anwar Hussein*)

Index

Note: The Queen, and the Prince and Princess of Wales are abbreviated to QE, C and D, respectively.